S0-AAE-727

DRESSAGE

A Study of the Finer Points of Riding

by

HENRY WYNMALEN, M.F.H.

Published by
Melvin Powers
WILSHIRE BOOK COMPANY
12015 Sherman Road
No. Hollywood, California 91605
Telephone: (213) 875-1711

To His Royal Highness
Prince Bernhard of the Netherlands

by his gracious permission

This book, which deals with the Art of Riding,
of which He is such a distinguished exponent and
so ardent a supporter, is respectfully dedicated
by his most devoted and obedient servant

HENRY WYNMALEN
London, August 1952

Printed by

HAL LEIGHTON PRINTING COMPANY
P.O. Box 3952
North Hollywood, California 91605
Telephone: (213) 983-1105

Printed in the United States of America
ISBN 0-87980-187-5

FOREWORD

by

Colonel V. D. S. Williams, O.B.E.
Former President of the British Horse Society

MANY are the occasions on which I have been asked to recommend a book on dressage written in English. I have always found a great difficulty in supplying an adequate answer to this question.

Numerous books have been written by both English and American authors which fulfil, to a greater or lesser degree, the wants of those whose requirements are limited to hunting, hacking or polo. A number of books on dressage proper have been written in French and German; one or two, notably those by Fillis and Müseler, have been translated into English; but they have lost much in the translating and, personally, I find them difficult to understand and consider some of their teaching as definitely dangerous in hands other than those of the expert who knows how to discriminate.

Mr. Wynmalen has provided the answer!

Here is a book, written in English, attractive to read, easy to understand, based on the classical teaching of the great masters of the past and on a life-time's experience of practical horsemanship according to modern requirements. This book takes the reader from the correct elementary training to the heights of classical equitation.

The author's description of the real meaning of dressage is brilliant and the book worth reading for that chapter alone. Through his intimate knowledge of foreign languages he is able to give us an exact translation of those foreign expressions which so aptly describe the different degrees of collection which have been so loosely explained in the past. He has brought the understanding of dressage to the door of everyone who cares to open it.

Inevitably, there always will be points on which experts hold differing opinions. Both Baucher and the Comte d'Aure achieved outstanding results with what appear to be, on paper, the most contradictory methods and Fillis spent much time in criticizing Baucher.

The author is well aware of this circumstance. In his own words "teaching cannot and should not be didactic"; "there is no room for must or always"; "it all depends". He gives clear and adequate reasons for his methods but is content to let practice and experience guide students towards the formulation of their own, as may best suit their particular mentality, temperament, and physique.

This is a great book, based on sound principles proved by practical experience. It should be read by every horseman and must be read by everyone who professes to be a student or instructor in the Art of Dressage.

CONTENTS

		PAGE
FOREWORD		7
INTRODUCTION		17

CHAPTER

I DRESSAGE 19

II HORSE AND MAN . . . 28

Voluntary and Involuntary Actions – Calmness – Suppleness of body and mind – Confidence – Gentleness – Confusion – Fear – Memory – Trainer's responsibility

III SIMPLE PRINCIPLES AND THEIR APPLICATION TO ELEMENTARY WORK . . 33

Impulsion – Aid of the voice – Aid of the whip – One man to one horse – One thing at a time – Claustrophobia – Need to perceive responsiveness immediately – The hand – Contact – Pulling – Hand: "relaxed", "unyielding", "active" – Teaching to lead – Bits – Boxing

IV REFLECTIONS ON LUNGEING . . 47

Gear – Objects – Balance – Contact – The walk The trot – The canter – Side-reins

V THE BIT 59

The mouth – The snaffle – The double bridle – Acceptance of the bit – Side-reins – A good mouth – The drop noseband – The long reins

9

CHAPTER

PAGE

VI BACKING 68

Confidence – The way to halt – Use of the hand – The way to move off – Use of the leg – Alertness – Nappiness – Forward urge – Steering dependent on movement – Steering from the quarters – Gear – Concerted action – The importance of going forward – Leg control – Rein control

VII THE SEAT 81

Where to sit – How to sit – Purpose of the stirrups – Unity of balance – Theory of the centre of gravity rebutted – Balance and grip – The German school – Bracing the back – Aids by association

VIII THE LURE OF THE OPEN SPACES . . 100

IX THE GAITS 106

X SOME IMPORTANT PRINCIPLES . . 108

Language between horse and rider . . 108

Straightness – Control of the quarters – The mouth 109

The "rassembler" – Collection – The "ramener" – The "mise en main" – Importance of the mouth to forward movement . . 111

Combined effects of legs and hands – Flexions – Acceptance of the bridle – Use and purpose of the double bridle 117

Control of the quarters 121

XI CONSIDERATIONS FROM THE SADDLE 124

Objects of schooling 124

Muscular development 125

CHAPTER   PAGE

Reward and punishment(?) 126

Use of the whip 127

Use of the spur 128

Use of the leg 130

The hands 131

Surrender of the hands (La descente de main) 135

Riding with one hand 137

XII THE TURN ON THE FOREHAND . . 138

(Preliminary form)

XIII CIRCULAR TRACKS 141

Lateral flexibility – Physical development – Rein-effects – The direct rein – The indirect rein – Seat and position of rider – Leg effects – Alteration of direction

Circular figures 149
  The circle – The volt – Riding through the corners – Other circular figures

XIV WORK ON TWO TRACKS . . . 153

Objects – Difficulties 153

The shoulder-in (épaule en dedans) . . 154
  Corners – Circles – The turn (pirouette) on the forehand (final form)

Quarters-in (la croupe en dedans) . . 160

Quarters-out (la croupe en dehors) . . 163

"Quarters-in" and "quarters-out" . . 164

Circular tracks 165

The turn (pirouette) on the haunches . . 168

The half-pass ("l'appuyer" or "tenir les hanches") 169

Effects of hands and legs . . . 174

CHAPTER
                                                    PAGE

The pirouettes (definition) . . . 175

Counter changes of hand on two tracks . 176

A powerful aid in difficulties – Shying . . 177

XV   THE WALK 179

A pace of four time – The free walk – The walk on a loose rein – The ordinary walk – The collected walk – The extended walk

The driving aids 183

Uses of the walk 184

XVI   THE REIN-BACK . . . 186

XVII   THE TROT 190

The gait, its advantages and its limitations . 190

The rising and the sitting trot . . 193

Development of the trot . . . 195

The collected walk . . . 200

The extended trot . . . 202

The mitteltrab 204

The trot on two tracks . . . 204

The passage and the piaffe . . 207

XVIII   THE CANTER 221

The gaits of canter and gallop . . 221

Aids for the canter . . . 223

Slowing the canter . . . 227

Starts at the canter . . . 231

Transitions from canter to walk . . 232

Transition from halt into canter . 234

Transition from canter into halt . 235

The simple change of leg . . 237

CHAPTER PAGE

The counterlead 237
The changes of leg in the air . . . 240
The canter on two tracks . . . 247
The pirouette 248
The extended canter 250

XIX DRESSAGE COMPETITIONS . . . 253

Appeal of dressage competitions . . . 253
Degrees of difficulty 254
Basic requirements 255
Purpose of competitions 256
Composition of tests 256
Arenas 257
System of marking 259
Preparing for a competition . . . 261
Taking part in a competition . . . 263
Judging 265
Practical hints for the novice rider and the
novice judge 272
Role of the judge 274

XX THE HORSE FOR DRESSAGE . . . 276

BOOKS OF REFERENCE . . . 282

INDEX 284

HIS ROYAL HIGHNESS PRINCE BERNHARD OF THE NETHERLANDS ON "NO NO NANETTE"

LIST OF ILLUSTRATIONS

*Where the illustrations are not facing the page given
they are inside the set beginning on that page*

H.R.H. Prince Bernhard of the Netherlands FRONTISPIECE

		PAGE
1	*The Author on "Bascar"*	64
2	*The Halt. The Author's "Ibrahim"*	65
3	*Commandant Lesage on "Taine"*	80
4	*Captain v. Oppeln-Bronikowski on "Gimpel"*	81
5	*Commandant Wattel, Cavalry School, Saumur*	81
6	*Captain Hans Moser on "Hummer"*	96
7	*Lt.-Col. A. R. Jousseaume on "Harpagon"*	96
8	*Captain G. A. Boltenstern on "Trumpf"*	96
9	*"Alert and cheery"*	97
10	*Shoulder-fore*	176
11	*Left shoulder-in, walk*	176
12	*Half-pass, walk*	176
13	*Right shoulder-in, trot. Spanish Riding School*	176
14	*Quarters-out, walk*	176
15	*Free walk on a long rein*	177
16	*Free walk on a loose rein*	184
17	*Ordinary walk*	184
18	*Collected walk*	184
19	*Collected walk. Commandant Wallon, "Taine"*	184
20	*The rein-back*	185
21	*The ordinary trot*	192
22	*The collected trot*	192
23	*The extended trot*	192
24	*The Mitteltrab. Herr Richard Waetjen*	192
25	*Natural passage of a racehorse. "Mont Tremblant"*	192
26	*The soft passage*	193

                                                              PAGE
27 *Passage.   Colonel Decarpentry. "Professeur"*   200
28 *Passage.   Commandant Wallon on "Taine".*   .   200
29 *Passage*   200
30 *Passage.   Capitaine Lavergne, Cavalry School Saumur*   201
31 *Lt.-Col. Podhaysky, The Spanish Riding School*   .   208
32 *Piaffe*   209
33 *Piaffe.   Capitaine Lavergne*   .   .   .   209
34 *Irregular passage.   The "Saut de Pie"*   .   .   224
35 *Collected canter*   225
36 *Counterlead*   256
37 *Change of leg to near-fore leading*   .   .   256
38 *Extended canter*   257
39 *Canter on two tracks (half-pass or "Appuyer")*   .   257
40 *The end.   Salute! "Bascar"*   .   .   .   272

My grateful thanks are due to Miles Bros., Eric Guy, "Sankt
Georg", H. Blanchard, *L'Année Hippique, Sport and General*,
R. Goodwin, W. Rouch, and B. Kerschner for photographs
reproduced in this book.

                                                   H.W.

DIAGRAMS IN THE TEXT

		PAGE
1	*Yearling bit and accessories* .	43
2	*Horse's skeleton* . . .	82
3	*Centre of gravity* . . .	91
4	*Riding through corner* . .	150
5	*Left shoulder-in* . . .	156
6	*Right shoulder-fore (Steinbrecht)* .	157
7	*Turn on the forehand* . .	158
8	*Shoulder-in on a circle* . .	159
9	*Quarters-in* . . .	161
10	*Quarters-out* . . .	164
11	*Quarters-out on the circle* . .	166
12	*Quarters-in on the circle* . .	167
13	*Turn on the haunches* . .	167
14	*Quarters-in round a corner* .	168
15	*The half-pass* . . .	172
16	*Turn on the centre* . .	176
17	*Counter-change of hand* . .	205
18	*Transition from canter to walk* .	233
19	*Large dressage arena* . .	258
20	*Small dressage arena* . .	259

INTRODUCTION

"Expliquer et laisser faire".

This book has been composed in daily consultation with my horses. Without their help, it could not have been written. It is they who are the real teachers. They have taught me the inner truth of the French maxim "Explain, and let us find the answer".

The sport—and art—of dressage riding is attracting ever-increasing numbers of new enthusiasts to its ranks.

It is for them in particular that the chapter on Dressage Competitions has been rewritten and a new chapter on "The Horse for Dressage" added.

CHAPTER I

DRESSAGE

T HE current use of the word "dressage" is, in England, of comparatively recent date. The word has been taken over verbally from the French, as a term connected with horsemanship. The fact that there just is no exact equivalent whereby to translate "dressage" into English probably goes a long way to explain the misunderstanding, and sometimes even the touch of mystery, whereto the use of this word has given rise.

But, though the term itself may be untranslatable, its correct meaning can be explained easily enough. The French word "dressage", which has its precise equivalent in many continental languages, as for instance "dressur" in German, is derived from the verb "dresser". In a general way this is used only in connection with animals: *on dresse un chien* (dog), *un cheval* (horse), *un elephant, un lion,* or for that matter most any kind of animal that is teachable. Thus the word means teaching, or schooling, an animal. It means a good deal more than the English word "training" which, used in connection with sport and with animals, generally refers more particularly to the creation of physical fitness; in dressage the emphasis is rather more on the mental approach to the animal's understanding.

The difference goes further than that, since the term dressage is really only used to indicate a more advanced stage of animal teaching, to teaching him rather more, or possibly a lot more, than one requires ordinarily from an animal.

Thus the ordinary house-training of a dog, teaching him to come when called and to comply with similar fundamental rules of doggy behaviour does not qualify as dressage, but the training of a gundog, or a sheep or police dog or that of a performing dog in the circus certainly does, for that is dressage!

Likewise, in the case of the horse, the term dressage is not used, in the country of its origin, in connection with the ordinary process of rendering a horse amenable to carrying a rider peaceably and reasonably effectively, and well enough for most people's ordinary requirements. That process, which may require anything up to about twelve months, is known in France by the term *débourrage*, which has a somewhat unpleasant sound in much the same way as the more or less equivalent English terms of "breaking" and "rough-riding".

It leads to a stage of plain usefulness beyond which very few horses ever progress, and this remark applies nearly as much to continental countries as it does to England.

Now dressage is the art of improving one's horse beyond the stage of plain usefulness, of making him more amenable, easier to control, pleasanter to ride, more graceful in his bearing and better to look upon.

Success in every art depends upon a measure of talent, enthusiasm, hard work, tenacity of purpose and finally upon a sound knowledge of the principles of such art. Sound knowledge is mentioned last because it is gained last, as the result of much experience; there just is no other way.

With dressage it is no different, and here also it is experience alone that can ultimately lead to knowledge. The road to experience is, I am afraid, a long one; in fact it is more than that, it is never-ending. In the hands of the true enthusiast, the artist at heart, even the most accomplished horse is always improving, just a little every day, or every week, to come just a shade nearer the absolute ideal, which, because it is unattainable, is never attained. But the pursuit of the ideal is a passionate quest in itself, full of reward in the constant discovery of newer and ever more subtle harmony between horse and rider.

It is only thus, by striving for that very harmony, that the full object of dressage can be approached, and expressed in that degree of "lightness" which distinguishes above all else the finely schooled horse. Above all else because true lightness includes all else, balance, grace and action.

Certainly, the attainment of these greatest heights lies well beyond the realms of ordinary, practical horsemanship, and the number of riders prepared and able to devote a lifetime in its pursuit will always be small.

Dressage in its higher forms in a speciality, a never-ending study of the finer and of the finest points of riding, it is the University, the true High School of riding. Its value for practical riding purposes is great and twofold. In the first place it is the living academy of scientific horsemanship, of the "équitation savante", wherein alone the root-principles of that art can be studied and perpetuated.

In the second place it provides, in so doing, the guidance whereof every horseman stands in need who wishes to raise his own horsemanship, and with it the performance of his horses, just that much above the standard of mediocrity as will make all the difference to his enjoyment and success. In fact, it does more than that. For, although dressage itself can only begin where ordinary breaking and riding leave off, it provides none the less invaluable principles whereby methods of handling and breaking horses can be improved immensely, to the untold benefit of all parties concerned.

And of course every horse, to be really effective for any purpose above the very minimum standard of plain utility, needs at least a modicum of dressage, and some require a good deal. The troop horse, the police horse, the officer's charger, the hack, the international show-jumper, the Olympic cross-country horse, must all be trained and schooled to standards considerably above the minimum. And, since all such special schooling is dressage of a kind, it may as well be dressage of the best kind.

The fact as to what is, and what is not, dressage of the best kind is not really open to discussion. Its principles are laid down in the laws, and in the application of these laws by competent judges, of the F.E.I. or, to give the institution its full name, the Fédération Équestre Internationale. It is the international body whereto all equestrian nations of any moment belong, and it is governed by the most competent horsemen which such nations can produce. Its prescriptions on matters of dressage are based upon the traditions and the practice of the world's leading and most famous equestrian institutes such as the French Cavalry School at Saumur and its Cadre Noir, the Imperial Riding School of Vienna, the German Cavalry School at Hanover, heirs to the proud traditions of former famous Imperial and Royal riding establishments in that country, the Cavalry Schools of Sweden and of Switzerland, both famous for the fine riders they have produced, and others of equal or almost equal renown.

Such authority is not open to question.

Its dicta have been laid down in a booklet, translated by the British Horse Society, the representative National Authority in England, called *Notes on Dressage*. It contains only brief notes on the manner wherein the schooled horse is expected to perform his work.

It contains no indication as to how these results can be obtained, which is only logical since instruction as such is not, and should not be, the responsibility of any governing body.

We live in a time when, under the influence of mechanization, cavalry has lost its usefulness, in a manner that appears final and without redress. As a direct result some of the famous schools of horsemanship have already closed their doors, others are due to follow suit and all appear to face a dubious future. The pity is that with them will disappear the fountainheads of living knowledge; for *l'équitation savante* is above all else a living art; its traditions and its principles cannot be fixed in stone nor its technique preserved in paintings; nor even can its precepts be fixed in books of learning. By its very nature the art can only live in the lives and loves and works of horsemen and horses of flesh and blood, who can but try to carry on noble traditions during their own short allotted span.

But though the history of cavalry may draw to its close and the most famous riding institutes be threatened with extinction, the noble sport of riding is still with us, and thriving. In fact it appears to be doing so almost more than ever before. Shows and competitions, national and international, are crowding upon each other; the number of competitors and the severity alike of competitions are increasing constantly. To be successful a high standard of riding is more than ever necessary. To ensure this, it is essential that the traditional higher school of riding be kept in being.

Riding as a sport is a wonderful pastime, a marvellous exercise and a school without par for the formation of character, determination and grit.

Riding as an art is more than that; it is part and parcel of our western culture, and as such should be treasured and preserved.

As an art it is extraordinarily difficult to teach, on account of its complexity. It involves the problem of creating harmony, both physically and mentally, between two living beings so utterly different in these respects as man and horse. The interplay between them is constant and ever varying, and is made up of multitudes of little actions and reactions that may be separate and inseparable all at once.

In truth the art cannot really be taught, either by a teacher or by a book, however good either of them may be. The only thing the teacher, or the book, can hope to achieve is to point the way along which the student may travel to the goal of ultimate understanding. Thus, teaching, to be effective, must be understood. Likewise, to be understood, it must be effective; it will be so effective if the student can be made to "feel"; actually to "experience" some improvement, however slight, as a result of the advice given him.

It follows quite logically, or so it seems to me, that such teaching cannot and ought not to be didactic; it cannot be a matter of laying down a set of rules, regulations and prescriptions; it can only be an attempt to pass on to the student bit by bit and as may seem to fit the case, some of the wisdom which the master himself has gained as the result of his own hard work and years of experience.

The teacher, who is on the spot, has the advantage of being able to see his students work and thus to select for them the particular piece of advice most likely to benefit them there and then.

That is something which a writer cannot do; he can only attempt to offer a source of information whereto the student can turn in his moments of perplexity, and he can only hope that his students will do so with intelligence and discretion and with the knowledge that, in riding, one principle must be mastered thoroughly before the next one is attempted; in riding it is thoroughness that is quick and speed that is slow. The one point wherein the writer scores over the teacher is that he is accessible at all times and to an unlimited audience.

And so it is the object of this study to place my experience and the views, reflections and conclusions based on them, at the disposal of my readers in the hope that it may help them in forming their own. In so doing we base ourselves, as to form, entirely and solely on the authoritative requirements of the F.E.I. That means in accordance with that body's regulations or laws; these, in sympathy with any other kind of self-respecting law, are somewhat obscure, and their true meaning can really be assessed properly only from the interpretation put upon them by the decisions of competent judges. Where occasion arises I will endeavour to clarify the position in that light.

The fact remains that, as to forms of execution, we are tied down within certain limits formulated by indisputable authority; as to form we are, in a sense, presented with dogma.

This is no longer so, at least not in my opinion, when it comes to the precise method of preparing individual horses and individual riders for the attainment of that form. The fact that they are individuals, that no two riders nor any two horses are ever alike excludes, *eo ipso*, any dogmatic approach in that respect. Though we undoubtedly must and do have a school based upon common theories and ideals, their interpretation must be left, ultimately, to the individual rider and his individual horse.

Individual exponents of merit cannot help but stamp their schooling and their riding with their personality; in art it must be so, since without it there would be no art. It is a fact about which we may well rejoice even though it does add to the complexity of the student's problem. It is also, unfortunately, a fact whereof equestrian authors have rather frequently lost sight; they are sometimes led to construct their personal experiences into a dogmatic basis of dictation to, or maybe argument with, others.

The famous controversy which raged around the middle of the nineteenth century in France, between the rival schools of Baucher and the Comte d'Aure, is rather a good example. According to Baucher the hand must always act before the leg, with d'Aure standing just as firmly by the principle that legs must always act before the hands. In my opinion there is no room, in advanced riding, for either of the words "must" or "always"; I prefer to think, what I feel to be the truth, that "it all depends". In the delicate movements of the higher forms of riding we are constantly endeavouring to maintain an equilibrium of balance and rhythmic action; the slightest disturbance of either is bound to affect the degree of perfection of our presentation adversely. In these movements the rider and his horse assume much the same delicacy of movement as the tight-rope dancer on his cord; disturbance of the equilibrium is always threatening and can be prevented only by constant slight action, or maybe inaction, of either hand, or leg, or both, or seat, or balance of body or any or all of the many little means of control whereof the skilled rider disposes. But, as in the case of the tight-rope dancer, these little actions are, and can only be brought into play by subconscious instinct, born of experience.

The great value of "theory" in the Art of Riding does and can only lie in the guidance that may be derived from it; if elevated into dogma it becomes a straight-jacket wherein the art itself will finally be strangled.

The theory of modern dressage, and much of its practice, find their roots in the schools of the eighteenth and seventeenth centuries which reached their zenith in the *École de Versailles* and found their most famous exponent in de la Guérinière, immortal author of *École de Cavalerie*.

Although this school ceased to exist as a result of the French Revolution, its traditions were kept alive throughout the nineteenth century, and up to our time, by other schools in Germany, in Vienna, in France and other countries, and by a number of famous écuyers of varying nationality.

We have a number of authoritative books of the period so that the sources of study of this, the classical method, are not lacking. To mention but a few there are, apart from de la Guérinière himself, Du Paty de Clam, Baucher, d'Aure, Hundersdorf, Raabe, Le Noble du Teil, Steinbrecht, Rul, Faverot de Kerbrech, L'Hotte, Barroil, Fillis. Through all of them runs a thread linking back to the pure classicism of a Guérinière.

This must not be taken to mean that there have been no innovations during all this time; there certainly have. Baucher introduced the repeated changes of leg at the canter, not practised by the ancients, and a host of other new and very difficult exercises of great appeal to the circus. So did Fillis. The Comte d'Aure began to show a marked interest in outdoor forms of riding, as a sport and art combined.

But, taking everything as a whole, these books reveal the classical school for what, in essence, it was: a school for training the horse for the main purpose of giving indoor displays of refined, elegant and advanced classical riding. That tradition has been maintained to this day in unadulterated form by the Spanish Riding School of Vienna. And a great school it was, and in Vienna still is; to it we owe and from it we can still learn the foundations whereon the principles of modern dressage rest.

All the same, in order not to be led astray, we ought to recognize that there are certain very important differences.

In the first place, there are the horses. The old school used, and Vienna still uses, horses with much knee action, as we would consider somewhat of harness type to-day. Horses apparently mostly of fairly small size with much carriage in front and frequently low in the quarters; very suitable therefore for the pronounced sitting position beloved by the ancients in their favoured "airs" of *piaffe* and *terre à terre*. The *piaffe* and the *passage* were taught thoroughly and with very great care before any schools at the canter were attempted. The presentations were mainly based on the execution of intricate *manège* figures, with much emphasis on the *volts*, which were squares or rectangles, the corners being always taken on two tracks.

In fact work on two tracks at the passage and at the canter, shoulder-in and pirouettes, formed the highlights of these presentations, whereat the horse was always shown with head and neck bent so as to be looking at the public, which was known as *le beau pli*.

The whole of this work was done *dans le rassembler*, in the highest degree of collection. Changes of leg at the canter are not mentioned in the old school and could hardly have formed part of it; the change of leg demands a position of the horse more horizontal than the old school favoured; for the same reason extended paces were not thought of.

In elegance of execution, seat and precision of movement that school still stands as a model, hard to equal and impossible to surpass.

But it is no longer the school of to-day. To-day we ride horses, thoroughbred or of thoroughbred type, bigger, faster, more powerful and with an entirely different type of action, low and long striding. To-day our interest is no longer concentrated on indoor presentations; we no longer make horses specially for that purpose. Our main interest to-day is that of outdoor riding, for sport; for a long time that has been the only interest, to such an extent that the principles of the Art of Riding have been almost completely lost in the process.

And that is where, in my opinion, the modern school of dressage is giving rise to a renaissance of the art in a form more closely akin to the requirements of the day. Our modern school lays as much emphasis on freely extended paces as it does on the most highly collected movements of the classical school. It requires moreover, in its competitions, continuous transitions from collected to extended paces and vice-versa, which introduces very great and very real difficulties wherewith the ancients were not troubled. It includes further the repeated changes of leg at short intervals and at every stride, which are of great difficulty, and it demands finally that our horses shall be able to perform this exacting programme in the open.

Quite rightly so, and most fortunately!

But it cannot be achieved by a horse exclusively *manège* trained. It demands the free-going, high-couraged horse that has first been thoroughly trained and schooled in the freedom of God's open country, and preferably one that has been well and truly hunted.

It is with such horses that I like to continue that dressage which " is the art of improving one's horse beyond the stage of plain usefulness" and that is, in brief outline, the system that I recommend and whereon the construction of this study is based.

CHAPTER II

HORSE AND MAN

---

*Voluntary and Involuntary Actions – Calmness – Suppleness
of body and mind – Confidence – Gentleness – Confusion –
Fear – Memory – Trainer's responsibility*

T H E accomplished Dressage Horse has to be a perfect athlete, supple and strong in every muscle, nerve and sinew.

However gifted by nature with all essential qualities, no horse or man can become an accomplished athlete without a great deal of special training.

In the case of man one is fully justified in using the word " training ", because the development of physical fitness, of suppleness and ability of muscle, are clearly the aims. There is no mental problem of any consequence. The human athlete himself knows the object of his training; it is his own ambition to excel and to shine, and the role of his coach or trainer is confined to helping him with guidance and advice; moreover it can all be done in perfectly clear language, with no mystery in it to either party.

How infinitely more difficult is the case of the horse! Here, we have a highly strung, nervous and sensitive animal, who has to be trained in a manner whereof he cannot know the purpose, and who has to be spoken to in a language which is, to begin with, completely unintelligible to him. Moreover it happens all too often that the particular human being who is to do the training, is himself a stranger in the use of the horse's language.

For the horse, most definitely, has a language of his own; all animals of the higher order possess a language, or rather a method of communication. It is simple and is based on the expression of feelings and intentions by attitude and behaviour. Dogs possess this aptitude in a marked degree, which makes it comparatively easy to understand them, for us as well as for animals of other species.

It is perfectly certain that animals of different species can understand each other quite well and can and do communicate amongst each other satisfactorily, provided only that fear has no part in the proceedings; that there exists, in other words, a degree of confidence. It is most important to realize these facts. They imply that we shall not be understood by the horse unless we possess ourselves, or acquire, the aptitude of talking to him by attitude and behaviour; and even then we shall never succeed fully unless we do so in that calm and quietly determined manner whereby confidence is inspired.

Confidence is absolutely essential because without it the horse just cannot make a sufficient surrender of himself, mentally and physically, to learn and to absorb our teaching. Mental and physical processes are so intimately connected, that they cannot be separated.

Everyone understands that it is an essential object of our training to obtain control of the horse's voluntary actions. But it is less well understood that it is impossible to succeed in doing so with any degree of complete success, unless we gain control of his involuntary actions also. And that is much the more difficult task of the two.

Involuntary actions, or rather reactions, are called forth by the working of the horse's nervous system independently of his own free will. It follows that, since the horse cannot himself control such reactions, the trainer cannot do so either, at any rate not directly. But the trainer can realize that these reactions arise, involuntarily, under the influence of outside stimulants, such as fear and nervous excitement; it is an important, perhaps the most important element in the trainer's art not to create any such disturbing influences himself.

No one can avoid occasional upsets in a highly strung, high-couraged horse, under the impact of extraneous influences, such as unusual surroundings, noise, strange objects or the behaviour of other animals. But the talented rider shall be able to insure that no upsets or excitement are caused by his own conduct on the horse. And that is, incidentally, the interpretation placed by leading judges on the requirement that the dressage horse shall be calm; the merit of the horse's calmness is in the confident and willing acceptance of his rider's requirements; there is no merit in calmness due to virtual "extinction" of the horse's liveliness and brilliance.

In dressage we hope to arrive ultimately at complete suppleness of the horse's body, that is of every muscle, joint and tendon, and we shall never be fully successful unless we achieve complete mental suppleness as well. Nerve and muscle are inextricably bound up together and any nervous tension, however slight, sets up a corresponding stiffening of muscular condition.

Every human being knows from his own experience how his body will tighten up under the influence of fear or premonition, in the dentist's chair for instance; even though he knows full well that this reaction is unreasonable and in fact somewhat cowardly! Yet how difficult, not to say impossible, it is even for *homo sapiens* to control his own involuntary reactions in such cases.

It is exactly so with the horse; he also stiffens up under the influence of fear, premonition and nervous tension; under such conditions he cannot relax, and without relaxation our search for suppleness becomes a hopeless quest.

This, truly, is the fundamental difficulty to be overcome by every successful trainer with every horse, and there is only one way wherein that can be done, by gaining the animal's complete confidence and trust. If we ask little, the achievement is comparatively simple. But if we ask much, and in advanced dressage we are bound to go on asking more and more as time goes on, it requires great tact to maintain this trust and confidence by never asking more than a very little progress at a time.

It is essential to understand the general nature of a horse's mentality and in particular to study and observe the nervous make-up of each particular horse with whom we have to deal. It is equally essential to keep on observing one's own ability of being in sympathetic communication with each individual horse; they all differ and in many respects we ourselves have to learn along with every animal we school.

The horse is by nature very gentle. Gentleness is indeed his most endearing and his most valuable trait. Then let us do nothing to despoil it. For the horse is also, by nature, easily subject to fear, to fright and to confusion; in fact confusion is perhaps the trainer's greatest difficulty since he can so very easily bring it about himself. Whenever the horse is asked a question which he does not fully understand, and its execution is insisted upon nevertheless, confusion is the inevitable result.

The horse is exceedingly sensitive to the use of active strength, deliberately used against him; he fears it, and through fear may easily be driven into the use of all his strength in an attempt to escape. Since that strength is very great and, especially when dominated by fear, very much greater than our own, and difficult to control, it is unwise to provoke it; it is also entirely unnecessary.

The horse possesses a marvellous memory; he never forgets anything that he has learned. It is a most valuable asset, since without it we could hardly succeed. But it is also a very great danger, since it is extraordinarily difficult to eradicate faults and bad habits, once these have been acquired.

Acquired faults are invariably the result of training, just as much as acquired qualities. It is, unfortunately, very much easier to teach the horse faults than to teach him qualities. To teach the horse qualities, to improve him, we have to proceed slowly, gradually, with extreme care, little by little and without causing confusion or excitement at any stage. This constructive work is very difficult and requires tact, experience, knowledge and much understanding. To teach the horse faults we need merely be unobservant. The horse is quite expressive, to the observant eye, of his appreciation of any of his trainer's actions. If these actions cause him discomfort, instead of comfort as they should do, the horse will signal his disapproval by seeking counteraction, whereby to minimize the effects. Such counteractions may be slight to start with, and then easy enough to counter, but they tend to assume more gravity as time goes on.

However, the main thing to remember is, that it is the trainer who makes the horse; it is he and he alone who is responsible for good and bad results alike. If bad results show up he should look in the first place to himself, and not to the horse, for improvement. He will have to think and ponder and try, by very careful and ever slight experiment to find which way the road to improvement lies; the indications are but of the slightest; the road is not signposted in a manner clear and easy for everyone to read, it can be found only by sensing.

For safe guidance we can only try to get back to the root

cause of a difficulty, try to remember when the first signs of it appeared, and attempt to reason just where we have been at fault. Having done that we may then be able to effect our own and, with it, the horse's cure.

There is no other way, and there is no specific or magic cure for any of the many difficulties that do beset the horseman's path. And even the very best advice that may be given us is of no real value unless we have the ability to carry it out.

With each difficulty overcome successfully we leave one milestone behind us on the road to success, on that long road to which there is no end. For even the greatest experts continue to have their difficulties; they have them daily and with every horse; only their difficulties are so much smaller, because they notice them so much more quickly, or at once; and they have their long and wide experience to guide them.

CHAPTER III

SIMPLE PRINCIPLES
AND THEIR APPLICATION TO
ELEMENTARY WORK

Impulsion – Aid of the voice – Aid of the whip – One man to one horse – One thing at a time – Claustrophobia – Need to perceive responsiveness immediately – The hand – Contact – Pulling – Hand: "relaxed", "unyielding", "active – Teaching to lead – Bits – Boxing

I T is often thought that the dressage—or the high-school rider—employs some complicated and mysterious system of his own, which no ordinary horseman could hope to understand and which would be useless for ordinary riding purposes at any rate.

That, of course, is not so.

The principles involved are extremely simple in themselves and apply just as much to the most elementary as to the most difficult work; there is not, basically, any difference of method between handling a new born foal and riding a Grand Prix Horse; it is merely a matter of degree. It is only the correct application of simple principles that becomes more complicated as the difficulty of the work increases.

Every horse must start from the bottom; so much is obvious to everyone. It is a great pity that so few horsemen appreciate that no one will ever go really far in the Art of Riding unless he has acquired an understanding of the basic elements involved. This can only be done by taking one's horses through all stages of breaking, making and schooling oneself.

Let us therefore take a horse through the various stages of his work, almost from the beginning, assuming that we are dealing with a colt which has been halter-broken and is quiet to handle. In that way we may then discuss the finer points of riding as they arise from the beginning, and follow the general development of their application.

Our first job is to teach our colt to lead well. Our equipment consists of nothing more than a head collar, a leading rein about eight feet long and a polo whip or a twig about four feet long.

Immediately we undertake this work we are faced with a number of basic principles of horsemanship in their most elementary form.

The first principle is "impulsion": the horse is to go forward freely whenever we require him to. That is so obviously the basis of any horse's usefulness to man, that it needs no elaboration.

It also happens to be the horse's own natural inclination, so that there is little or no difficulty in getting him to do so; whatever little difficulty there is consists in teaching him to do it in accordance with our will and under our control.

The young horse, who has been well and kindly handled, will always follow his human leader easily enough; he does that more or less of his own volition and by using his own intelligence; he knows perfectly well that he is being taken out to a field or brought into a warm stable, both of which are agreeable associations.

But now, to lead well, we require just a little more. As an important element of the principle of impulsion we wish the horse to go "in front of us", we do not want him to drag behind. The leader's place is beside the horse's shoulder, with the horse leading the way boldly.

To that end we may have to create a little more impulsion. We have two aids at our disposal.

The first aid is the voice. It is a most important aid in all our work with horses. They are exceedingly sensitive to the human voice and understand and act on it surprisingly quickly and well, provided it be used with a system. The horse's hearing is both sensitive and acute, so we should always speak softly and calmly, no matter whether we are just teaching, approving or reproving; loudness never does any good and denotes a lack of horsemanship. A simple vocabulary should be adopted and adhered to and the same words or phrases used always in the same context. Though it is true that the horse acts largely on intonation, it is none the less certain that he is capable, in time, of acquiring a fairly extensive vocabulary and of coming to understand the meaning of certain words and phrases quite perfectly. I talk a good deal to my horses and those with whom I have worked and associated intimately enough for a number of years understand remarkably well. It is of the very greatest help in pacifying or in encouraging a highly strung or nervous horse. It creates undoubtedly a bond of understanding, of confidence and of friendship. Some readers, I know, will doubt the last of these feelings. The horse is not like a dog, very expressive of his feelings; quite likely too they are not felt so warmly or so deeply. But they are there none the less. Proof is forthcoming constantly in the degree of generosity wherewith the horse will serve the man with whom he is in sympathy, rather than the man whom he fears.

The making of other noises with the mouth, such as clicking the tongue, cannot be considered as using the voice; though we can hardly make out a case against the use of such noises on any question of principle, it must be conceded that they lack style; they are rather more easily associated with the carter than with the horseman.

The second aid to help create impulsion is the whip.

The whip, used as an aid, is a prolongation of the arm and hand, which enables us to touch, and so to control, the horse in places which the hand cannot reach; it is, in effect, the rider's "third hand", according to the expression used originally, I believe, by Rarey.

It provides the trainer with a very long arm; standing quietly by the horse's head or shoulder, he is able to touch the animal's quarter's without difficulty; the good trainer will work by himself, in accordance with the principle "one man to one horse", and he will certainly not allow any assistant or other person to occupy any position behind the animal, than which nothing is more certain to distract the horse's attention; consequently if the horse be touched he knows at once that the action emanates from the very same man who stands so quietly by his head.

It makes a deep impression on him; he feels himself controlled at both ends by one human being; he will never forget that basic element of all equitation.

It will do even more than that, provided only that the whip is used correctly, sensibly and quietly as an aid and not, and never, as an instrument of punishment. In conformity with everything else, no matter what it is that has to do with the horse's training, the value of the use of the whip "as an aid" depends entirely on the horse's unequivocal confidence.

Thus in the case under discussion we require our youngster to take a step forward; we lift our hand, carrying the whip, quietly and methodically, and so that the horse can see our action, and tap him gently on top or rather just beyond the top of his quarters; we tap him just once, gently; in fact so gently that in all probability he will take no notice or action whatever; which, showing confidence, is an excellent beginning.

One thing at a time is the fundamental principle of all methodical horse-training; to be able to explain one thing at the time to the horse, to give the horse time to understand it, and to be able to see that he has understood it is the very essence of the trainer's art.

Therefore we make certain first that the horse has understood that he need not fear the whip, that his confidence in us remains unshaken. We now proceed with the next step, one step forward on his part this time. We retain our position by the horse's head, quietly as before, the horse standing freely and without constraint from hand or leading rein. The latter condition is very important; nothing upsets a horse more, and arouses his suspicion more certainly, than being held tight; in that respect the horse almost suffers from a touch of claustrophobia; it is worth remembering, and understanding, this trait of his character which can cause a lot of trouble between horse and man.

However, we now lift our whip again; since we are still "explaining" to the horse we do so quietly and deliberately; again we touch him on the quarters gently, once; if need be, after a second or so, we touch him again, possibly just a shade more distinctly; perhaps we may have to repeat three or four times, always with a little interval so as to give the horse time to understand. He will presently move forward, just a step or so, which is all that is required; and of course we shall not fail to show our satisfaction, clearly but quietly. After a few seconds rest we repeat, perhaps once, perhaps twice, and that lesson has been learned. We can now walk on and use the aid of the whip, always methodically, whenever we need a little more impulsion, maintaining the horse's shoulder about level with our own.

The lighter we can apply the aid the better; such simple

lessons are absorbed quickly by the horse; presently it will be sufficient to just point the whip; there is no need to touch when pointing suffices.

The important principle from the trainer's point of view is to cease the aid immediately the horse responds. It is a basic principle in all equitation that the degree of the trainer's perceptiveness of the horse's slightest response is a fair measure of his talent.

As the result of this work, well done, the horse assimilates the wisdom that it is "safe to come up to the whip" and that "safety lies near his trainer".

These then are our two aids to impulsion in this elementary work: the voice and the whip. For the sake of clarity they have been described as separate entities. But the intelligent reader will have understood that they are not used as such, but in conjunction with each other. Thus, when the whip is lifted to be brought into action, the trainer's voice and indeed his whole attitude tells the animal that he has nothing to fear; and the talented trainer will not of course, bring the whip into action unless he is satisfied that the horse has understood, and shown that he has understood, that there is nothing to fear. Then, when the whip is brought into action, the trainer will use at the same time his chosen word of command for the movement required. Voice and gesture will help each other; they will be understood by the horse first jointly and gradually also severally.

The trainer's object is the establishment of a clear language between the horse and himself and to perfect this more and more as time goes on.

It will be clear again that the aids to impulsion, the voice and the whip, could not be used without bringing into operation, at the same time, aids appropriate to control that impulsion. These are once more the voice and the hand which holds the leading rein.

The use of the voice has already been explained.

The use of the hand is by far the most important element in equitation; the hand holds the extremely fine and delicate key wherewith alone the intricate lock that opens the door to the final revelation of horsemanship can be worked.

The importance of its correct use is equally great in the most simple as in the most difficult work. In fact it may well be more important in this very simple early stage wherein the horse receives his first impressions which he will never forget.

In schooling the horse we take him through a great many stages; each stage is intended to contribute something towards "making" him into our ideal mount; but success depends entirely on our ability to do the "making". Making demands constant, reasoned, patient, careful and able attention at every stage, however elementary it may seem to be. Spoiling the horse can be achieved much easier, very quickly and quite thoroughly at any stage.

Logically of course, there are no elementary stages, as far as the horse is concerned, since he has to learn something new all the time.

However, to revert to the use of the hand.

The hand's primary object is to maintain contact with the horse's head, in the present case by means of a leading rein attached to a head collar, later on by means of reins attached to a bridle. The definition is given in this form only because I know from experience that it helps in leading up to understanding. Actually I do not consider it correct. In my opinion the definition should read:

The hand's primary object is to allow the horse to maintain contact with the hand by means of the rein! This implies that the function of the hand is, in the first place, passive: it allows the horse. It is only active in the second place in that it regulates the length of those reins and decides upon the amount of contact which the horse shall be allowed to make.

The hand's secondary object is to guide the horse; this will be dealt with more appropriately in our chapters on riding.

The hand's final object is to stop the horse. This the skilled hand does quite simply by no longer following the horse, by first retarding and finally arresting its own, the hand's, forward movement; the horse, who is in contact with the hand through the rein, will do the same.

I rather welcome the opportunity to explain these principles as they arise in the simple case of the man on foot teaching his colt to lead. Here we clearly have two separate entities, a man and a horse, both on their own feet, but linked together by a leading rein. In reality, I warn my readers, no different from the man sitting on the horse and connected to him by a rein; but certainly very much easier to understand.

However, let us proceed with our colt. We walk beside his shoulder. We hold the leading rein in one hand. As long as we and the colt walk at the same speed there is no tension on the rein, there cannot be since neither of us pulls; there need be no tension since the weight of the rein itself is sufficient to maintain contact or feel between the horse's head and our hand. As long as the horse maintains the same speed as we do he, quite obviously, cannot pull; we, equally, have no reason to pull; we are well satisfied to hold our hand still, allowing the horse to maintain the same light contact by the weight of the rein through maintaining the same pace.

The horse is desired to walk with a nice, free and long stride, quite naturally. This pace is quiet and unhurried but somewhat faster than the ordinary human walk. The trainer will therefore have to assume a somewhat long-striding walk himself; he should adapt himself to the horse's best pace and endeavour to make the horse maintain that pace; but the horse should not be hurried; hurry causes loss of rhythm and may quite easily disturb purity of gait.

If the horse drops behind we use the aids, already described, to encourage impulsion; the hand does not come into active operation and no attempt is ever made to pull the horse forward. Trying to pull a horse forward is one of the gravest sins a horseman can commit; it is also, curiously, one of those most commonly met with. The horse resents it by instinct and by instinct will resist it; the harder he is pulled forward, the harder he will pull back and, inevitably, he pulls the harder. Thus, if we use an aid to make him go forward and pull at him simultaneously he will follow his instinct and not the aid; he will go back. Whilst we can teach the horse a great deal we can never alter his nature; the able trainer works in sympathy with the horse's instincts, never against them.

So, whilst we urge the horse forward, the hand which holds the rein does nothing else but maintain light contact through the weight of the rein.

Tension on the rein will only occur if the horse attempts to go faster than is intended, if in other words he attempts to move faster than the trainer going by his side. The effect on the trainer's hand is that of a forward pull exerted by the horse; this the trainer will resist completely passively by not accelerating his own stride and by not yielding his hand at all to the horse's forward pull. In other words he will leave all the pulling to the horse without doing any pulling at all himself. If the trainer is really able to do so he will find that the horse will stop pulling almost immediately; the horse does not go on pulling unless he be pulled at!

If the trainer be able to do so?

It sounds a great deal easier than it actually is. This question "you pull—I pull" is the horse's instinct, as nearly everyone knows; but it is also our own instinct, which a thing very few people indeed have come to realize; accordingly very many people pull without being in the least conscious of it.

The human hand is the prolongation of the arm; it is in effect the grip at the end of a very long lever by means of which very considerable strength can be exerted, even by people who are not particularly muscular. In the normal course of events, using one's limbs in the ordinary way of life, one just does not realize the amount of power developed. But it is very important, in dealing with the horse, to arrive at a clear mental picture of the action of one's hands, and of their power.

We may distinguish three main types of function of arms and hands.

The first, and normal function is to be "relaxed". Arm and hand are carried naturally, without any tension or stiffness in muscles or joints. In that condition we perform all the ordinary little daily tasks of life, which require so little strength or effort that muscular activity is not really noticeable. That, incidentally, is also the manner wherein to conduct the ordinary little daily task of controlling our horses, whether from on foot or from the saddle.

The second, and not normal function is to be "unyielding". It is not normal, because it is against our instinct; but we are creatures of reason and we can therefore learn it. In horsemanship it is essential that we should, because the horse can never be so taught. For the hand to be unyielding we have to tighten the joints, wrist, elbow and shoulder so that the limb becomes difficult to move. It can be done without using our biceps, in fact it can be done in that manner only, for the moment we use our biceps we become active and start pulling ourselves even though we may not realize it.

The third, and normal function is to be "active", "to pull".

It comes into operation by instinct and most of the people most of the time do not realize it at all; they merely imagine that the horse is pulling and that herculean strength is needed to stop him from doing so; they fail to realize that both parties are pulling and that both parties act in accordance with exactly the same instinct.

If we hold out our hand in the normal way, relaxed, and something or somebody, or a horse, starts pulling at it, our immediate subconscious natural reaction is to span our biceps and to pull back, meeting force with force. The instinct is strong and our arms are strong; the reaction is produced without any conscious action of the brain; it is very difficult to relate subconsciousness to consciousness. The ability to ride with a passive and unyielding hand, when needed, is one of the great basic difficulties in riding.

Now to revert to the young horse we are leading.

If the horse increases his speed to something faster than our own walk, he will, by getting ahead of us, take up the slack in the rein, which will thus be brought into tension by himself. And, provided we keep our hand passive, the horse will immediately ease the tension; it is his nature not to pull at any fixed object, for who has ever seen a horse pull at a pillar rein?

Generally, in this work the horse will but seldom exert any tension on the rein; he is a most observant animal and will realize very quickly that he is meant to move, or to stand still, in unity with his trainer. So, normally speaking, the work is simple and light.

But there are exceptions. Young, unbroken, high-couraged horses can be scatty, take fright or be just a little too high-spirited. In such circumstances they may suddenly plunge forward, or sideways, and exert such a sudden jerk on the hand that it is quite beyond our power to maintain, not only the position of our hand, but that of our whole body. We are obliged to lessen the impact of the sudden excessive strain by paying out a few feet of leading rein, which is eight or nine feet long, for that very purpose; probably we shall also be dragged half a dozen strides or so from our intended position. All the while we offer the maximum passive resistance whereof we are capable, letting the horse do all the pulling. In that way, and in that way only, the release of strain will be automatic and immediate the moment the horse moderates or ceases his pulling; and that is the whole secret.

In connection with this particular type of occurrence, when a led horse becomes troublesome, the trainer should make full use of the best strategy at his disposal. Even though he walks beside the animal he may well find himself, in case of a sudden lunge forward, as nearly straight behind him as matters. That is a hopeless position to be in; firstly there is no human being who has the slightest hope of offering effective resistance, with nothing more than a head collar and leading rein, to a horse pulling away straight in front of him; secondly there are safer places than just behind the heels of a scatty young horse. So the experienced man moves at as acute an angle as he can to the left or near side of the horse's direct line of progress; even a fairly slight angle is usually effective. The angular resistance to the horse's head causes him to bend it to the left and, inevitably, to swing his quarters to the right. In another stride or two he will swing right round and face one, when the battle is as good as won. He may still continue pulling backwards for a stride or two, but no horse likes moving backwards and every horse, in that for him awkward situation, will stop immediately we manage to slacken the rein. The horse is never slow in learning this particular lesson and a recurrence is very rare indeed.

Speaking generally, this work of teaching the horse to lead well is simple enough and more often than not proceeds without any difficulty at all. As soon as the horse walks well, halts well, stands still, moves on when required and is generally well-behaved and manageable, we can teach him to trot in hand, to go from walk into trot, from trot into walk and from trot into halt. It can all be done in a matter of ten days or so with daily lessons of no more than ten to fifteen minutes. And with plenty of opportunity at that to teach the horse to stand well, to show himself well, to step back a stride or two, and to do a bit of a turn on the forehand. These latter two movements are essential in order to be able to position the horse nicely and easily. Since we have taught him to accept the aid of the whip with equanimity, it is only a matter of a little patience and tact to make him step back with a few light taps on his breast and to make him move his quarters sideways in answer to a light tap against his flanks.

It will be noticed that the whole of this work has been done without a bit in the horse's mouth. This is most important. Many a finished riding horse has had a perfect mouth spoiled by being led from his bridle. Very many more young horses have had their mouths ruined in exactly the same way before they have even had a saddle on!

But there are cases where some sort of bit is unavoidable.

We may wish to show a youngster in public. Yearlings can quite well be taken anywhere in a yearling head collar and lead-

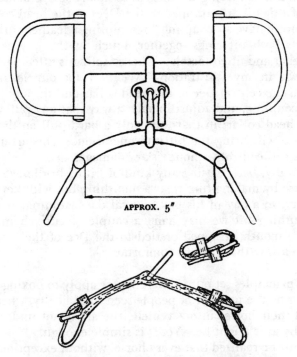

APPROX. 5"

DIAGRAM 1. YEARLING BIT AND ACCESSORIES

ing rein. But things may be a little different with the more powerful two year olds and particularly so with great big three year olds, possibly highly fed to bring them into show condition. In the excitement often caused by strange surroundings they may well be somewhat more difficult to control than at home. In such conditions some sort of bit may be needed; besides some of the big shows will not admit them into the ring without one, which is not unreasonable from their point of view.

The usual answer, most frequently seen, is a double bridle, complete with curb-chain and all. Now a double bridle is the most unsuitable outfit for any horse with an unmade mouth; its misuse is liable to ruin the mouth and, resultant thereon, the animal's action and balance.

I use a yearling bit of a special design, whereof I publish a working drawing; any reputable bit-maker can produce it; I have a few of varying width so as to fit any size of mouth. The rings of this bit are strapped to the Dees of the head collar. In addition we have a " coupling" resembling a leather curb, which connects both bit rings together, much in the way as a curb, but higher and fitted loosely. This coupling is fitted with a ring, as shown in my illustration. We now fix our leading rein through the central Dee of the head collar and through the ring of the coupling, and adjust in such a way that any pull acts first on the head collar; in that way, only a hard pull on the part of the horse will bring the bit into operation. This arrangement ensures full control without risk of damage.

Naturally, before using any kind of bit or bridle, we prepare the horse by making him wear a mouthing bit, with keys, for an hour or two a day in his box, several days running; if we have no mouthing bit we may hang a couple of curb-chains in the animal's mouth, strapped or tied to the Dee of the head collar in such a way that they fit comfortably.

The principles set out in this chapter apply to boxing a horse. Judging by the number of people seen in difficulty, when trying to load their horses into a vehicle, the art is not understood as generally as it might be. Yet it is simple enough.

It must be realized that every horse, without exception, begins the operation with an instinctive reluctance which is perfectly natural. A horsebox ramp is not his natural type of going; it is not solid earth and he views it with some suspicion. At the other end of the ramp he sees a small enclosed place, possibly so much darker inside than the surroundings that he cannot even see in properly. So it is wise to place the box in such a way that the sun shines into the box and not in the animal's eyes. Finally he is faced by a very low roof, too low in his opinion to get under without knocking his head. Horses hate low roofs, so his final aversion is probably the most powerful of all. Anyway, whatever his reasons, he has no confidence in the contraption.

So, as always, creation of confidence is our first care.

It can be done with any horse that has never seen a box, in a matter of from five to twenty minutes. And what are five, or twenty, or even thirty minutes in the total time needed to turn out a well-trained horse? A mere nothing. So we can afford to be patient. We can afford in particular to satisfy the horse of our patience, than which nothing is more conducive to gaining his confidence. Naturally we act alone; we need no help; we certainly do not want other people standing about to distract the horse's attention from us; most decidedly we do not want anyone behind him.

We have the box standing in a convenient place. We lead the animal up to it in the usual way, the way wherein he has been trained, walking freely beside and somewhat in front of us on a loose leading rein. Naturally, on approaching the ramp, he will stop; so do we; he may well decide he doesn't like the look of the thing and reckon it is safer to move back a couple of steps. So we let him, being particularly careful not to let him feel, at any time, even the slightest tension on the rein. Any such tension will only put ideas into his head that we are trying to force him much too near something dangerous; in his opinion potential danger he can jump away from is one thing, and may be bearable, but potential danger when held tight is quite another and definitely unbearable. So, with proper respect for his method of reasoning, we move back to his side, talk to him pleasantly, pat him and offer him a piece of apple or some other delicacy he is fond of. It all helps in establishing the right atmosphere. Quite soon he will stand peaceably in front of the ramp. Another bit of apple and time to look around. All the time on a loose rein. Presently we shall encourage him to move up the ramp. One foot at a time is enough. In fact it is more than enough. Horses are quite intelligent really, in their own way, in tackling such problems. From the very moment the horse has been presented in front of that box he knows quite well that he is meant to go in there; but, since fear withholds him, he "thinks" he is not going to take such an unwarrantable risk and accordingly, and quite logically, decides that he will not step into the unknown. Gradually, influenced by our own obvious patience and calm, by agreeable pieces of apple and by the discovery that the suspicious-looking thing is at any rate not doing anything actively hostile, he begins to think again. The measure of a trainer's talent is in his ability to spot the slightest indication of the horse's thoughts coming round in the desired direction at once. It may be no more than the twitch of a muscle to indicate that the animal is now beginning to consider the idea of moving forward as coming within the realm of possibility.

From that moment on, the fundamental difficulty has been overcome. The horse must be recompensed immediately and convincingly and given a little rest; the more his mental tension relaxes the better.

We can now begin again; proceeding step by step and always quietly; we need not hesitate to use the aid of the whip, since the horse knows it, provided we are satisfied with one step at a time and particularly on condition that we keep a loose rein all the time. If the horse decides to step back off the ramp, or even back out of the trailer we shall never offer any resistance with the rein. It will now all be over in a matter of minutes anyway.

The horse may then be given a little feed in the box, be led in and out a few times and the exercise repeated daily for four or five days. We shall then have a horse easy and reliable to box for the rest of his life.

If we have to deal with a broken horse who is difficult or impossible to box, because injudicious handling has made him thoroughly averse of the operation, our procedure is much on the same lines. Only we must, if he does not already know it, first teach him to come up to the whip with confidence; if the trainer knows his job this can be achieved in a very few minutes. Also we should act alone; the horse can understand one man fairly quickly and give him his confidence; he cannot understand half a dozen at a time.

CHAPTER IV

REFLECTIONS ON LUNGEING

*Gear – Objects – Balance – Contact – The Walk – The Trot
– The Canter – Jumping – Side-reins*

EVERY step in the horse's training should be a step of
progress on the road to ultimate success. The horse himself
cannot make it so; he can only know the present and not the
future. It is the trainer's art to bring him along, always carefully and step by step, from the known to the unknown, so that
the unknown of to-day may become the known of to-morrow.

The horse can only learn that which is being taught him, can
only step in the direction wherein he is being taken. It is the
trainer's task to see that his direction be the right one that will
lead to the ultimate goal. Of that he must have a very clear
picture in his mind. His mind's eye must see not only the little
progress that can be made from day to day, but the big progress
which he hopes to achieve in one, or two or three years' time.

So let us, with this in mind, examine the points arising on the
next step in our horse's education: lungeing. In leading that
discussion I shall beg permission to use the personal pronoun
so as to make it quite clear that the opinions that follow are mine,
based on my own experience and convictions and not on any
dogma.

The ultimate goal that I have in mind is the production of a
happy horse that shall in due course under my saddle be as free
and brilliant as nature can make him; I hope for a horse unconcerned about my presence because unhindered by it and therefore generous and unstinting in his obedience.

Accordingly I select for my horse steps that will confirm his
own very best natural balance; I endeavour to encourage him

47

to use his own most pure and rhythmic gaits; I avoid anything even remotely liable to interfere with that purpose and I concentrate the while on keeping his confidence as the easiest and surest way to his obedience.

Obedience is the least of my troubles; the horse, allowed and helped to understand, and understood, gives that more easily than anything.

For my lungeing then I rely, in the main, on maximum freedom of the horse and on minimum interference by me. I take into consideration also that being lunged is the next step forward for the horse from being led. Therefore I do not change the character of my gear; my only step forward is that, instead of leading the horse on a comparatively short rein whilst walking close up beside him, I now lead him on a rather longer rein and get gradually farther away from him until he walks round me on a circle; in the beginning I keep on walking myself on a small circle; I must expect the horse, from his previous experience, to stop when I stop, so I must help him and give him time to realize that he is now expected to go on walking when, presently, I shall be standing still, or almost so.

The gear I use is simple and of the type wherein the horse already has confidence: head collar, lungeing rein and lungeing whip.

For the first few days I am well satisfied if the horse will walk freely and quietly round me, halt, walk on, and come up to me in answer to a few simple gestures and words of command. I make him walk to both hands from the very first day. At first, the horse will be a little awkward going righthanded, only because he is not used to being handled from that side; we have to be rather nearer to him, to start with, and explaining it may well take five or ten minutes and it is more than likely that he will attempt to turn round once or twice; it is nothing; as long as we remain quiet and calm the horse will do the same.

It is wonderful how much a few weeks of this work in hand, or from the ground, can do and will do in establishing the necessary bond of understanding between man and horse. The horse learns to accept human ascendancy more and more as a natural phenomenon, he becomes used to it. Gradually he forms habits of obedience to signs that he has understood; it becomes second nature to him. In essence, the whole of our training is based on creating this habit of obedience and of making use of it, once it has been established, for our specific purposes.

It is most important to realize this. It is sometimes advanced that certain actions or aids, used by the rider, compel the horse by some physical or mechanical law to obey them, that he cannot do otherwise. That is most certainly not so; if it were, riding could be reduced to the simplicity of driving a motor-car.

In a general way the effect of whatever aids we use is only relatively compelling in that they induce the horse to obey by habit to that which he has learned. I do not know of any aid that is absolutely compelling in the way that it must be obeyed through physical necessity, even by a horse which has made up its mind to fight its rider with all its power. The most that we can say is that, as a result of methods of advanced training, we shall come to dispose, in time, of a few aids which come very near to compulsion, physical as well as mental. What these are we shall see later.

During this period of lungeing, then, the horse has time to become better acquainted with his trainer, to observe him and to learn his ways. But the trainer too, may observe a great deal concerning his horse, his paces, the degree of his balance, the state of his mind and his temperament.

That, then, may well be ranked as the first objective.

Next come balance and lightness. These are, as we have seen already, the very ultimate objectives of our training. They should never be lost sight of, from the beginning until the very last! That the horse obeys by force of created habit is, in my opinion, axiomatic, and not open to contradiction. It is an important, quite possibly the most important, basic element of horse-training. Accepting that to be true, it is just as easy, and more logical, to create the habit of obedience to the lightest possible aids as to stronger ones.

That is one reason why I believe, and trust, in the primary use of nothing but a head collar and lungeing rein, to be handled as delicately and lightly as possible.

But there is another reason and a very sound one. Ultimately, we look for the highest possible degree of lightness and balance. Now what exactly can that mean? Assuredly one thing and one thing only, namely, the best state of balance and lightness whereof the horse is by nature capable!

Let us make no mistake about it, we can never presume to improve upon nature and we can never, under any circumstances, create in the horse any qualities wherewith he has not by nature been blessed. We can, most certainly, by skilful training and exercise, develop, supple and strengthen these qualities so as to secure their maximum effect. And gradually, provided we do possess the necessary skill, we should succeed in raising the maximum effect than can be derived from the horse's natural attributes. Meanwhile it must be clear that the best form, the best paces, the best balance, the best carriage that we may hope to attain during any stage of the horse's training are those that approach most closely to his best natural form.

Now the horse's best natural form is the one he shows in nature, when free and completely unimpeded he proudly moves, under the stimulant of some excitement, round his meadow. Trotting or cantering, head up, ears pricked, neck curved, tail up; trotting with a cadence, shoulders and front legs swinging gracefully and to time, toes pointing and barely touching the carpet, hind legs also full of swing with marked hock action, treading far under the body to deliver impulsion forward and upward, into the well marked moment of suspension, or jump, of the trot stride; cantering equally gracefully and, be it noted, going in both gaits in a very high state of natural collection.

What a picture to aim at reproducing, some time or another, under our saddle and at our will, any time, by simple command; but how difficult it is, and how long it takes!

And why so long, and why so difficult? Because by placing the bonds of servitude upon him, we deprive him of that very freedom that is the source of his beauty. Because the bonds of servitude, however skilfully applied, hinder him and because only time and great skill will finally make him forget those bonds enough to display once more, but now under saddle, the full beauty of that very freedom.

Is it not then clear that we ought, at all time, to reduce the hinder imposed by the inevitable use of some form of bond of servitude to the very minimum compatible with safe control in skilled hands? And that is a further reason for using none but a head collar and a lungeing rein.

In the initial stages of the work itself then, I keep two main objectives in view: the horse's best natural paces and the lightness of control.

The horse's best natural walk is a moderately extended gait, wherein he takes fairly long and roomy strides; his position is horizontal with a long neck and low head carriage; the freedom of head and neck, with their clearly visible balancing swing, are essential to the freedom of the gait itself. The walk is a calm and peaceful gait, whereat the horse moves forward with the minimum of exertion. The ability to walk well is a fundamental quality for any riding horse.

In our service we require the horse to be energetic in all his work; energetic therefore also at the calm and peaceful walk; there is no contradiction between calmness and energy; on the contrary; energy displayed calmly is efficient and long-lasting, whilst energy displayed excitedly is inefficient and burns itself up.

We are therefore to require our horse to walk energetically and with a purpose, but not to hurry! Hurry destroys at one and the same time the calmness and the pure, comparatively slow, four-time rhythm of the true walk.

With this in view I ask, on the lunge, no more than a quiet, nicely sustained walk without laziness or slacking.

Rein-control, at the walk, is automatically so light and easy that it calls for little comment. Contact is maintained by the weight of the rein in such a manner that there is a distinct catenary from the horse's head to the trainer's hand. I avoid the word "loop", which might be taken to mean a rein hanging quite loose; that is most certainly not the idea; firstly because that would imply complete, or almost complete loss of contact, and secondly because a loose-hanging lungeing rein is a potential source of danger; the horse, or the trainer, or even both, may get a leg entangled in such a rein, which leads to indescribable complications.

All authorities agree that the cultivation of a good trot is basic to the development of balance, and that as such it is the key to all advanced training. That is no doubt so because the trot's rhythm is simple, naturally regular, and naturally familiar to our own conception; it is a pace of two-time, much akin to the human walk or trot. It is also a pace whereat the horse goes very easily and wherein head and neck are kept still and are carried high. In the trot the horse shortens himself to some extent and assumes a position of natural collection; trotting with some energy, the horse goes well off his hocks.

On the lunge then I encourage the horse, gently and with tact, to trot with nice energy and, above all, with nice rhythm. I look for a graceful, balanced, lively and expressive stride, but avoid all excessive speed and hurry. Hurry, again, would destroy the so essential rhythm, and speed, at this stage, will destroy everything I have in view. The essence of a good trot is rhythm; ultimately, though the schooled horse shall be able to vary his pace at the trot within a very wide range, from quite slow to quite fast, the rhythm itself shall remain the same; slow, the horse shall move with brilliance, delivering a comparatively long stride slowly; fast, the horse shall move sedately, delivering the longest stride whereof he is capable without hurry.

Contact at the trot will of necessity be rather more positive than at the walk, though I insist that it shall be maintained lightly, by the weight of the rein; the catenary of the rein will be a little less than at a walk.

I insist on this lightness of contact for four reasons.

Firstly, I desire my horse to deliver the best natural trot, in the best natural attitude whereof he is capable; under my control, certainly, but, still more certainly, without any hindrance on my part; a light hold on the lungeing rein is amply sufficient for all the control I need and it does not hinder the horse in any way.

Secondly, I desire him to acquire the habit of obeying to light controls.

Thirdly, I lay great stress on allowing the horse, from the very beginning, to curve himself easily and naturally in accordance with the circle whereon he is going. I use the words " to allow " on purpose, because there is no need " to teach " him that which he will do all by himself, so long as he is not being hindered. To this I attach very great importance. It is the horse's nature, as we have already discussed, to pull when being pulled at. If we use strong contact in this work the horse will tend to get away from the circumference of the circle; he will try to hold head and neck towards the outside; he will stiffen and straighten his body in sympathy; he will no longer curve himself on the circle; in fact he will no longer move on a true circle at all, but be moving on a number of short straight lines at a tangent to the circle. In doing all this we must, inevitably, by creating stiffness, destroy just that degree of relaxation and unconcern without which balance and rhythm are unobtainable.

Finally, I desire my horses to work happily, gaily, with plea-sure and with zest. If we manage, throughout our training to preserve both the gentleness and the gaiety of our horse we shall not, in the end, go very far amiss. Horses really are sensi-tive to atmosphere. If we enjoy working with them and do so in a cheery frame of mind, in the spirit of learning and doing something together, they will respond generously. Under such conditions it is just as easy to keep them up to their work and energetic, as it is to control them lightly. Lightness both ways, in impulsion and in control of impulsion must, surely, be aimed at.

In order to preserve the happy disposition of a pupil his work should be made light and pleasant to him. Whilst it will become necessary to give a young horse sufficient work to keep him in a reasonable frame of mind, and not too much above himself, he should yet never be tired, or worked too long, or sweated unnecessarily. I do like to see a little gaiety and per-haps a little buck or a jump or two; they can be controlled so easily with a little tact and a word or two. I never punish a horse for showing, in the only way he can, that he is going to enjoy his work and that he will settle down to it presently with all the more zest.

In fact, I hardly ever punish a horse; at any rate, why should I? It is clear, or should be, that I, the trainer, am directly respon-sible for the horse's behaviour, good or bad; so what good can I do by punishing the innocent party? It is hardly justice, it isn't sense, and it isn't necessary. Naturally there are cases of somewhat extravagant exuberance and also, on some occasions, of distinct naughtiness, but I have always found them rare. However, when they do occur, I may have to issue an immediate and peremptory call to order; I use my whip, and my voice, distinctly and decidedly yet with but little weight. My horses are so thoroughly confident of the whip, and so com-pletely unafraid of its use, that a somewhat sharp application, on account of its very rareness, makes a deep impression on them.

The use of the velvet glove is better understood by the horse than that of the iron glove; it is also, in the long run, more effec-tive since it will not sour him; incidentally it is a good deal pleasanter, and more elegant, to use.

Naturally these considerations apply to the canter on the lunge quite as much as they do to the trot. I prefer to postpone any attempt at cantering until the horse goes really well, and gives me complete satisfaction at the trot.

The horse, in freedom, uses the canter much as an alternative gait to the trot, perhaps when he intends to go just a little faster, but not a lot faster, for the canter is essentially a collected pace, wherein the horse goes off his hocks with head and neck carried high. To go fast, the horse will gallop, which is a horizontal pace, with head and neck stretched and low. He can strike off at a canter, in freedom, just as easily from a walk as from a trot.

But, when striking off from a walk, he collects himself first, lifts his head and places his leading hind-leg somewhat further under. Obviously, on the lunge, we shall have difficulty in obtaining this effect because we cannot, on the lunge, obtain the essential moment of collection.

On the lunge, we can only obtain the canter from the trot; I said *from* the trot, not *through* the trot; this makes a great deal of difference! To strike off from the trot means that the horse, whilst going at a nicely balanced, quiet pace shall strike off, on receipt of our command and without accelerating, at an equally balanced canter with the correct leg leading.

It is not an easy effect to obtain without a deal of judgment, tact, and knowledge of the gaits. Assuming that we are trotting the horse around on the left rein, anti-clockwise. To lead off at the canter on the near-fore leading we are to catch the one right moment when the horse is balanced perfectly, is well curved on the circle, with the head looking inwards, when the moment of suspension commences with the left diagonal, near-fore and off-hind, coming into the lead. That is the precise moment to attempt the strike off at the canter, which may and can only take place from the off-hind leg at the instant this touches down.

Naturally, it is just as likely that we may not succeed at the first attempt, since the horse does not yet know, and cannot be expected to understand, just what we want him to do. If we fail we have to wait a little, make sure the horse is settled and try again just when the ideal conditions re-present themselves. We may have to try several times but, if our judgment is sound, we shall succeed presently.

It is not easy, and usually it does not proceed that way.

What happens usually is that the horse is driven faster and

faster, until he loses all balance and is hanging well and truly to the outside of the circle and finally, through sheer despair, begins some sort of a sprawling canter, invariably on the wrong lead; he could hardly do otherwise.

That is of course valueless and a big step in the wrong direction. If we cannot obtain the canter in the correct way described, we had better not canter at all, or else try the much easier way of obtaining the canter over a small obstacle.

Yes, jumping!

As a matter of course, I teach all my horses to move over obstacles from the very first day I lunge them. Very small ones to start with, naturally, nothing more than a pole on the ground. I begin by inviting the horse, quietly, kindly, and without ever a suggestion of compulsion or threat, to follow me over it at a walk or from a stand. In a couple of weeks my horse will walk over, trot over and jump over all sorts of small obstacles perfectly quietly, obediently and without any excitement. He will halt, from a walk or trot, at my bidding, in front of the obstacle, then go over it when I want him to or else he will go over the obstacle and, again at my bidding, stop quietly and stand perfectly still.

Thus, in the first place, I create absolute confidence first; always the basis of everything, it is the basis also of that very courage without which no riding horse is worth his salt; courage to go forward without hesitation into, over or through any place, however formidable and forbidding looking, where his rider bids him go.

Soon the horse will take quite reasonable little obstacles from a trot.

It is then eminently simple to obtain the canter; just a little extra encouragement and he will assume automatically what is, in effect, his only natural gait for jumping.

And it is equally simple to make him land, and continue the canter, with the inside leg leading; we have but to wait until the horse is in the air, above the obstacle, and then, carefully and gently, effect a slight pull on the rein, just enough to bring his head just a shade towards the inside; he will invariably land to continue cantering with the inside front leg leading.

Here we have, incidentally, a piece of knowledge almost invaluable in the art of jumping and one which appears, curiously enough, to be little realized.

In jumping over a twisty course of fences, show jumping, in cross-country competitions, or even hunting, it is important to ride the approach with the appropriate leg leading. It is also important to continue, after the jump, leading with the particular leg most appropriate to the next sharp turn or to the next obstacle, as the case may be.

That may be the same leading leg as before, or it may have to be the other leg.

Everyone knows that the horses are able and often apt to change their leading leg during the jump; it is very easy for the horse to do so; on account of the length of time of the period of suspension it is very much easier for him to do so during a jump than during the so much shorter moment of suspension of an ordinary canter or gallop stride.

He uses this ability, quite naturally, to suit his feel of balance whilst in the air and preparing to land; he does not use it, as some think, unaccountably or as a matter of habit, but only according to balance.

So the truly sensitive rider, of sufficient experience and skill to be able to continue riding his horse during the jump, can quite well determine the leading leg of his horse's next stride after landing by selecting the appropriate balance whilst in the air.

He has merely to feel either the left or the right rein a shade stronger, so as to obtain the slightest bend to that side, and the horse will gallop on accordingly. Obviously to be able to do so is a feat of refined horsemanship that cannot be put into effect very well excepting during a normal, smooth and balanced jump.

Reverting to the canter, what I look for is an easy, rhythmic and balanced gait, not at all fast and done equally well to both sides. I am particularly anxious to avoid all excitement and attempts at rushing. In the beginning I just practise starting from the trot, half a dozen or so canter strides and back into the trot again. In that way I will obtain a very light canter, obedience and calmness. The latter is absolutely essential.

Thus, I continue this work, walk, trot, canter and a little jumping, until my horse does it all very well, freely, with balance, with pleasure, with a quiet and confident eye, liking and not fearing it.

And all of it, as I have explained, with nothing but a head

collar and a lungeing rein so that the horse shall have the maximum of freedom to find his own form and balance. I am anxious in particular, and careful, that he shall have the full and free use of his head and neck; their weight and their position play a preponderant part in determining the horse's balance; if we tie them down, we tie the horse's balance with it, possibly into forms that are undesirable and most certainly into forms that hinder the horse; anything to hinder the horse sets up stiffness and stiffness is inimical to relaxation and therefore to the very balance we seek.

This system of lungeing the horse by means of a head collar, or cavesson, and a long rein only, leaving him the maximum amount of freedom possible, is not practised by me alone. Far from it. It is widely used on the continent, and in France almost exclusively so, for the purpose of training and schooling jumpers. It is recognized that the jumper *must* have the full, free and untrammelled use of his head and neck since he cannot, without that, achieve the delicate and ever varying balance for that exacting work. It is recognized and understood, by the informed trainer of jumpers, that he cannot assist but only hinder his horse by tying him up in side-reins.

In my opinion exactly the same consideration applies, even if less obviously so, to the whole of this preliminary work with the unbroken young horse.

However, lungeing the horse is finally also the approach to backing and breaking. To that end he must be introduced gradually to the various essential articles of tack. I do that gradually and do not begin until I am satisfied that the initial objects of my lungeing as such have been obtained.

First I introduce a roller; a day or two later a bit, worn by itself and without any reins; I follow this with reins, fixed to the bit rings and tied in a knot over the horse's wither.

Presently I fix the other end of these reins, side-reins, to two rings provided on the roller; these rings are fairly high up, to either side of the withers and about six inches below their level; about level therefore with the horse's mouth when the head is carried in the normal trot position.

I now fix the reins in such a way that there shall be no tension in the rein, and consequently no direct contact between bit and roller as long as the horse carries his head in the normal position; but in such a way that there is some indirect contact through the weight of the rein and not with the reins dangling in a long loop.

I continue to lunge off the head collar. When the horse goes in his normal attitude he will not feel any pressure from the bit; it is not my intention that he should. But he will, when carrying the head momentarily a little high or stretching it too far forward, meet the resistance of his bridle. He will, at first, try to free himself from this unexpected pressure on his mouth by snatching at it. We have to be a little careful, quieten him and not drive him too much. He will very soon stop hurting himself and learn to keep his head in the normal position, when the presence of the bridle will not worry him. Actually it will not really teach him anything else, except the habit of wearing a bit and reins and some very little experience of contact. That is all I intend it should do.

Next I replace the roller by a saddle, initially without stirrups and presently with stirrups dangling. Done sensibly none of this will cause any difficulty, and our horse will now soon be ready for backing.

The use of side-reins for the purpose of teaching the young horse to go into its bridle is advocated, perhaps more conventionally, by some schools. It involves the use of the bit, which raises considerations of such importance that we had better devote our next chapter to them. We will therein find the opportunity to consider the effects of side-reins and also the method of driving in long reins.

CHAPTER V

THE BIT

---

*The mouth – The snaffle – The double bridle – Acceptance
of the bit – Side-reins – A good mouth – The drop noseband
– The long reins*

THE correct use of the bit is at the beginning and at the end
of everything in equitation. It is the most important and
the most deciding single element. Before we begin to discuss
its use, it will be worth while to review briefly the purely technical aspects involved.

The horse's mouth is formed by an upper and a lower jaw.
Both jaws are shaped like a channel, or a basin; these basins or
channels are longitudinal in form, being of greater length than
width; the circumference of each channel is formed by the
jawbones; the channels themselves are concave cavities; the bottom of the lower jaw basin is formed by a group of muscles
whereto the tongue is attached; the top of the upper jaw basin
is formed by the palate; the tongue lies in the basin or channel
of the lower jaw and there is a certain amount of room between
the tongue, when at rest, and the palate; the tongue can move
about in the cavity of the mouth to a certain extent whilst the
mouth remains closed.

The jawbones are covered with a thin layer of flesh and skin,
the gums.

The horse's teeth are arranged in a somewhat peculiar fashion;
the incisors are placed in the front of the mouth; horses, and
occasional mares, have a pair of tusks close behind the incisors;
then follows a toothless part of the jaw before the molars commence; these toothless parts are called the bars; the bars therefore are the toothless parts of the gums. Those bars are gums,

consisting of a thin layer of flesh and skin, stretched over the jawbone; consequently they are exceedingly sensitive and fairly easily subject to injury.

The bit is fitted so as to lie across the bars and of course across the tongue.

There are, naturally, individual differences in size and shape of mouth between individual horses. Some have deeper or shallower mouths than others, and the thickness of the tongue may also vary.

If the horse possesses a deep jaw combined with a thin tongue, we may be able to place a straight mouthpiece across the bars, without causing pressure on the tongue. But, as a general rule, a straight mouthpiece is liable to cause discomfort by exerting too much pressure on the tongue.

Normally therefore we use a form of bit that will bear mainly on the bars, leaving sufficient freedom to the tongue.

The ordinary jointed snaffle is such a bit. It is suitable for the large majority of horses. But there are exceptions. The snaffle has a nutcracking, pinching type of action, which sometimes causes discomfort to thick-tongued horses; they will show distress by trying to get their tongue over the bit, if there is sufficient room under the palate, or else by sticking the tongue out sideways; such actions very quickly turn into habits and prompt attention is indicated. In such cases it is advisable to use a one-piece snaffle with a half-moon mouthpiece; they are soft in action and leave room for the tongue. Trouble is frequently caused by the use of snaffles that are too wide for the horse's mouth; it causes the joint to butt against the palate, which is uncomfortable and painful; to try and avoid it the horse will keep on opening its mouth wide.

However, in a general way the snaffle, whether of the usual jointed or of the one-piece half-moon-shaped variety, is the only bit suitable for all early riding purposes.

The purpose of the double bridle is to add further refinement to the making of the horse's mouth after a sound foundation has been laid with the snaffle alone.

The double bridle consists of a thin broken snaffle, already described, and a curb-bit. The curb-bit consists of the mouthpiece, the cheeks and the curb-chain. The mouthpiece is made in one piece, either half-moon in shape or else straight but with a port in the middle; the purpose of the half-moon shape and of the port is to afford room for the tongue, so that the pressure of the bit shall come on the bars of the mouth, and not on the tongue. The best shape for the port is rather wide and shallow and not narrow and high; a high port will touch and hurt the palate when the bit is brought into action, which is most undesirable. The cheeks are so arranged that the length of the lower arm, below the bit, is usually about twice as long as that of the shorter arm, above the bit. There are rings at the top of the upper arm of each cheek, to take the headpiece of the bridle; these rings also carry the curb-hooks, whereto the curb-chain is fastened. Since the curb-chain must lie easily and comfortably in the chin-groove, it will be obvious that the upper part of the cheeks must not be too long; if it is, the curb-chain will tend to rub upwards and to cause a sore. Thick curb-chains are considerably softer and more comfortable than thin ones. The curb-chain fixes the position of the bit in the horse's mouth, so that the lower part of the cheek, whereto the reins are fixed, acts as a lever. The longer the lower arm of the cheek is in proportion to the upper arm, the more powerful will be its action as a lever. However, great power is neither necessary nor recommended.

Apart from the action of the curb-bit and curb-chain described, it will be understood also that bit and chain combined exert a pinching action on the lower jaw. It is usual to fit a lip-strap to the curb-chain in order to prevent the horse from playing with the cheeks of the bit and eventually getting hold of them with his teeth, which would put the bit out of action.

It is recognized by all modern authorities that the best results are obtained through the use of mild bits; severe bits, with long cheeks, twisted snaffles, high ports, roughed mouthpieces and the like have no place in dressage. The only method of bitting admitted is a plain snaffle for the inexperienced horse and an ordinary double bridle for the more experienced animal.

Consequently the need to discuss any of the many existing varieties of fancy bits does not arise in this study. The bulk of them are out of place, anyway, in the saddle-room of the self-respecting horseman. The saying that "there is a key to every horse's mouth" is apt to be misleading. If it means anything at all, it can only signify that skilled horsemanship holds "the" key, and the only one there is, to every horse's mouth; unless it means to infer that bits and bridle must be fitted accurately and with great care in strict accordance with the size and peculiarities of each individual mouth. With that there can be no dispute; it is of the utmost importance and all too often overlooked.

From the horse's point of view the fact remains that, however careful we may have been in fitting his mouth with what we call a bit, he finds himself landed with a piece of iron in his mouth. The presence of an extraneous object in one's mouth is in itself unpleasant; if that object is being pulled at and starts pressing on one's gums it becomes irritating; it is difficult to keep one's mind off such a disturbance; it has a tendency to get one's nerves on edge and thereby to interfere with one's normal calm behaviour; in fact it may well begin actually to hurt and, as we all know, a pain in the mouth can be absolutely maddening.

The presence of a bit in the horse's mouth, and its action, is the first basic conflict between the interests of horse and man. From the point of view of man, it is the one absolute essential to the horse's usefulness to him; from the horse's point of view, it is the one particular bond of servitude most likely to cause resentment and, as a result thereof, more or less severe restraint on his ability to serve generously and gallantly.

We seek, in the higher forms of riding, for an expression of form, attitude and paces by the horse under saddle that are fully as good as the horse in freedom is able to show in his best moments. Such results can never be approached, leave alone achieved, unless and until the horse has accepted our presence and our actions in the saddle so unreservedly as to be morally and physically completely unconcerned about them. And that applies in particular to our action with the bridle. The horse's mouth is, like the human mouth, an exceedingly sensitive organ in exceedingly close proximity to the nerve centre. The slightest disturbance in the mouth at once sets up contractions that are reflected elsewhere in the horse's body, whereby both his physical and psychological freedom are affected adversely.

The complexity of the rider's problem lies in the fact that, whilst intent on avoiding disturbances in the horse's mouth, he must yet achieve the horse's unreserved acceptance of his bridle and his loyal surrender to its effects. It is a basic condition of all control in riding that the horse shall be ready at all times to go into his bridle; that he shall do so willingly, smilingly, and with pleasure is fundamental to any form of academic riding.

Such results cannot be achieved in a day, or a week, or a month, or a year, or for that matter in any predetermined period of time. In horse training progress must always follow the one methodical path that leads via confidence to acceptance, from acceptance to understanding and finally from there to achievement.

Habit plays a preponderant part in horse training. The art of good training resolves itself to a large extent in the art of creating good habits and, incidentally, in avoiding bad ones. The good habits are those wherein we may confirm the horse in his obedience to our wishes; it is a long and somewhat difficult process. Bad habits are those wherein the horse confirms himself in order to avoid obedience; that is frequently a short and easy process, whereto the horse resorts automatically if the rider forfeits his confidence by expecting acceptance of something which the horse has as yet not understood. In this respect the horse can be very cunning and it requires a deal of observance on the rider's part to notice any tendency to such avoidances at once; such difficulties are always of his own making and the cure therefore always in his own hands; if attended to promptly the difficulty should be but slight; but, once allowed to become confirmed, such bad habits may well offer almost insuperable difficulty.

These remarks are here made because they apply in particular to the task of making a good mouth, which is at the heart of every riding problem from the very beginning to the very end. It begins to occur as soon as we place a bit in the horse's mouth. Its fulfilment can be achieved only in course of much time as the result of the most complex of all riding problems wherein brain, feel, confidence, balance, seat, hands and legs all play their part. They are all elements of one symphony which depends for its harmony on the mellowness and on the intimacy of their co-operation. If one of the elements fails, the symphony fails; they are therein bound up together so inextricably that they cannot be separated and treated as individual entities.

We cannot, in a study of this type, write a chapter on how to make a horse's mouth and do justice to the subject. We can only hope to unfold the entire symphony gradually as we see the harmony between horse and rider develop.

But I can say this, and that with absolute conviction: there is no short cut, no mechanical means, no contraption, no method or invention of any kind whatever, whereby a horse's mouth can be made well and properly otherwise than by the skill and tact of his trainer.

That is why I have refrained, in the previous chapter, from advocating the use of side-reins otherwise than to familiarize the horse with the presence of a bit in his mouth, with the light contact that results from the weight of the reins, and with the limitation imposed upon him should he try to object against this very slightest of bit-actions by any discordant movement of head and neck. Using the side-reins in this way we take, it is true, only a very small step forward; but it is a small step which does a little good and which can do no conceivable harm and which is, as such, exactly in accordance with our principles. Moreover we do, by this method, leave the horse full freedom to move with completely natural carriage, that is to say head carried low with neck stretched forward vertically at the walk and with higher head carriage, nose in front of the vertical, at the trot.

I refrain, definitely, at this stage of the education of the unbroken horse, from any attempt at driving him into his bridle through the use of more tightly adjusted reins with a view to achieving a more positive acceptance of the bit.

Others think differently. The Spanish Riding School, of Vienna, make use of side-reins for this purpose and the system is fairly generally used and recommended in Germany. One has no wish to quarrel with alternative methods used by acknowledged masters; there are a number of roads that lead to Rome and there may not always be a lot to choose between them. But one may be allowed to point out that the system does present certain inconveniences, particularly if done a little less expertly and without a very clear insight into the precise bit-action allowable from time to time and without punctilious attention to the length of rein adjustments that are almost constantly required.

The explanation of the method, as I understand it, is that the length of rein is so chosen that the horse, sent forward energetically, must meet his bridle, must keep contact with it, must, in other words, effect some pull on these fixed reins and will, in so doing, begin to make a mouth and to form the habit of accepting the bit's pressure on it.

One would like to observe that unmade mouths do not, as a rule accept bridle pressure with any great enthusiasm. Their natural reaction is to try and avoid it, which can be done in many

THE AUTHOR ON "BASCAR"—WHO DID SO MUCH TO HELP HIM WRITE THIS BOOK

THE HALT. THE AUTHOR'S "IBRAHIM"

ways. If the length of rein allows it, the horse may bring his head up too high, go with an ewe-neck and concave loins, which is bad. If the length of the rein is such that he cannot get his head up, he may lower his neck, stretch it downward and go over his bridle, that is to say overbend with low headcarriage, flexing from the third or fourth vertebra behind the poll.

Now this work, to have any effect at all, must be done at a trot. The headcarriage described is certainly not the natural one at the trot and is equally certainly not the one ultimately desired. Its effect is to make the horse go with a convex back, increasing the distance between front and hind legs, leaving the latter somewhat behind, as it were, "stretching" the horse. Which appears, incidentally, to be the very aim of the German School; they call it "showing the horse the way to the ground" and they repeat work with a similar effect from the saddle.

One has certainly no fault to find with the principle that the horse shall be able to "lengthen" himself; it is absolutely imperative that he shall be able to do so freely and be encouraged and confirmed in the habit, so that he may never acquire the dreadful fault of "collecting himself against his rider" with the inevitable result of dribbling and jogging, instead of walking. But why choose for this work the trot pace, which is quite naturally a somewhat collected gait, and risk getting him overbent for ever? Why not the walk, whereat these effects can be obtained so easily and in complete harmony with the horse's nature?

The horse that overbends with sufficient confidence to go into his bridle will of necessity "lean on the bit" with a downward pressure on the rider's hands, than which I know no more unpleasant sensation in riding, nor one more directly opposed to the principle of "lightness".

Apart from trying to avoid the intended acceptance of his bridle by assuming undesirable attitudes, the horse may easily be taught to take evasive action with the mouth itself. He may get his tongue over the bit or else simply stick it out sideways. Or he may, more likely, open his mouth wide. Now a wide open mouth is not a good mouth. A good mouth merely "whispers" (la bouche murmure), the lower jaw relaxes just sufficiently to allow the slight up and downward movement of the tongue whereby the bit is lifted and dropped back again with but the slightest tinkle of steel.

The cure usually recommended to prevent a horse from opening its mouth is to fit a drop-noseband. It is a "preventative" certainly, but it is not a "cure"; preventing is not teaching. I see but little merit in the use of the drop-noseband as an aid to training apart from the fact that some of the pressure exerted by the reins may be transferred by it from the mouth to the nose.

Whilst the use of somewhat tightly adjusted side-reins on a horse in movement controlled by an expert may have arguments in its favour, the use of side-reins on a horse standing still in his stable, without impulsion, cannot be too strongly condemned; it is against all principles of riding.

It will be understood that the subject of side-reins has here been considered only with regard to the initial breaking of young unspoilt horses; the same considerations do not necessarily apply to the re-making of older, badly broken or spoilt horses; this book does not propose to deal with that somewhat ungrateful subject.

The use of long-reins, wherein young horses are driven from the ground, enjoys considerable favour in England. It appears a method whereof many of the older type of stablemen are fond, possibly as a relic from the time of carriage horses. Sometimes the reins run from the snaffle through rings fixed on the surcingle to the trainer's hands; at other times we may see the use of a saddle instead of a surcingle, with the reins running through the stirrup irons. Neither method is very satisfactory, as the friction on the reins is liable to be too great, whereby the feel on the horse's mouth may largely be lost. If long-reins are to be used at all, I would rather see them run directly from the snaffle to the trainer's hands, the inner rein direct and the outer rein round the horse's quarters, hanging more or less at the height of his hocks. I am a great believer in doing all work from the ground single-handed and without the assistance of any other person; but this cannot apply to teaching a horse to go in long-reins for the first time or two; if things go wrong at first, which they are very liable to do, the resulting tangle may be so considerable that the presence of a helper, to go to the horse's head, is absolutely essential.

Long-reining done by a careful man, who knows his job, will not do much harm; it may even do a certain amount of good in the way that anything done quietly and sensibly with the young horse has an educational value.

But from the point of view of scientific training, it has little merit and it is not without serious disadvantages. It is difficult, and at times impossible, for a man on his feet always to maintain sufficient delicacy of contact with the horse's mouth. And the idea of driving a horse in long-reins over obstacles, with a man trying to run behind him and hoping to maintain a soft and even contact with his mouth, can only be qualified as an equestrian monstrosity.

Long-reining as a method of breaking young horses is little used outside England, with the notable exception of the Spanish Riding School. But the system there used is of a different type and has different aims altogether; the remarkably docile Lippizaner horses are driven in very short long-reins, the trainer walking immediately behind the animal's quarters; the trainer is invariably a High School Expert and the driving in long-reins is part of the great deal of "work from the ground" done at this institution as preparation to, and part of, their particular system of High School training.

CHAPTER VI

BACKING

Confidence – The way to halt – Use of the hand – The way to move off – Use of the leg – Alertness – Nappiness – Forward urge – Steering dependent on movement – Steering from the quarters – Gear – Concerted action – The importance of going forward – Leg control – Rein control

HAVING thus considered the principal technicalities that arise initially from the fitting of a bit we may now take up the thread again from the conclusion of Chapter IV, where we left the horse proficient, quiet and contented in his work on the lunge, thoroughly used to, and familiar with the articles of his tack.

A horse by now confirmed in his confidence of our treatment.

A horse now quite ready to be backed and ridden. I have carried out this operation single-handed and without assistance with many horses, without any trouble. But, taking everything by and by, it is no doubt wiser and more efficient to call on the services of an assistant to do the riding whilst the trainer remains in control on the ground. The horse is by now used to obeying his man on the ground, whose visible presence helps to maintain his confidence better than if the same person suddenly disappears out of sight on his back. Also there always are certain possibilities of difficulties and upsets, which it is desirable to avoid in order not to cause any fright to the young horse, whose confidence should not be disturbed if it can be avoided.

The assistant should be a sensible, quiet person, thoroughly familiar with young horses, completely conversant with the trainer's methods and confident of them; rider and trainer should speak the same language, so as to be in sympathy with each other and with the horse; it is essential that the assistant, preferably a light weight, be a good rider, capable of remaining in the saddle without help from the reins and, initially, also without help from the lower leg; he, or she, must be able to sit still and be completely balanced.

We begin with the trainer standing by the horse's head, holding the leading rein quite loosely, so that the horse does not feel himself in the least restricted; trainer and assistant set about the whole business as if it were, which indeed it is, the most natural business in the world, with absolutely nothing to worry about. The horse is certain to take his cue from that, and to move neither an ear nor an eyelid. A foot in the stirrup, a little weight on the stirrup, presently standing up in the stirrup, and down again, repeated perhaps three or four times, is sufficient for the first day. The next day, or possibly the day after that, the assistant can take his seat in the saddle, sit there for a little while, get off and get on several times, always quietly and without hurry; always with the horse standing free of any perceptible restraint. It is a most important beginning to have the horse completely unconcerned, and therefore quiet, at being mounted and dismounted whilst standing still; it is a basic training which he will never forget.

Quiet to mount, and accepting the presence of a person on his back with equanimity, the horse may now be led, carefully at first, to move just a few steps; three or four steps, a halt, and another few steps is sufficient for the first lesson.

The next day or so we may repeat and then begin to lead the horse round; we keep close to him at first, holding the leading rein rather short, but always loosely; the latter is really most important; nothing shakes the horse's confidence more than being held tight, and nothing promotes his confidence in us more surely than to be shown our confidence in him. With animals however, we cannot simulate confidence; their power of perception is as nature made it, simple, unambiguous, and very acute. Gradually we lengthen the rein, get further away from him, and presently stand in our usual place in the centre for lungeing. We just go on lungeing quite calmly, since nothing much has been altered, apart from the fact that the colt now carries some quiet and well-meaning person, obviously a friend, on his back.

There is in that, by itself, nothing much to upset the horse;

certainly not the actual weight. The horse is a very strong animal, going on four legs, well able to carry some ten or twelve stones to begin with, without much effort; it is not so much the weight itself that is liable to cause problems later on, as the manner wherein that weight behaves itself. Now, initially, our rider has no other mission than to just sit still, be quiet and completely passive, excepting that he may use his voice, quietly and in normal conversational tones, if occasion arises, to address either the trainer or the horse. But, initially, the entire control remains with the man at the other end of the lunge, who will make the horse walk to both hands, stop him, make the rider get on and off a few times, and similar simple work. But always at a walk and never, in the beginning, for more than a few minutes at a time. Young horses, like young children, tire quickly of unaccustomed work and, in so doing, may well show some perfectly legitimate temper. The trainer's eye is there to see that things do not drift that far and that work is stopped on a note of general satisfaction and contentment. Much more good is done in five minutes of happy work than in thirty minutes ending in misunderstandings.

When, in a few days time, this simple work has proceeded satisfactorily, the rider may be asked gradually to take over control. Frequent halts should be the beginning, obtained by a very light hold on the reins, aided by the voice if necessary. The use of the reins should be delicate, only just enough to cause the horse to slow up and to stop in a matter of a few strides. The halt to be followed by standing still perfectly quietly for twenty or thirty seconds on a loose rein.

The manner wherein a horse is brought to a halt is very important, no matter whether we are demanding the answer from a fully-trained high-school horse or from a raw colt for the first time in his life. The action required ought to be understood by every rider, which is far from being the case. The principle has been explained in Chapter III, page 38, dealing with the horse led from on foot.

In that case we have seen, and easily understood, that the hand need do no more than retard its progress. In this case, from the saddle, the hand's action should be exactly the same. But, as we now sit in the saddle on the horse, we can obviously not alter the speed whereat our body is being carried forward by the horse. That is true, but there is, or at any rate there should be, considerable independence between our hands and that part of our body which is sitting in the saddle. Whilst we cannot prevent the seated part of our body going forward with the horse, we can see to it that our hands, forward of the body, slow up their movement and finally stop it altogether. In other words we let the horse carry our body closer to our hands and we do not retract the hands towards the body. It is a fine distinction but an important one.

As a result of this action the horse will notice that he himself is causing tension on the rein, because he is going faster than his rider's hands; exactly as when being led; and exactly so, and for the same reason, he will stop. The idea of pulling will not occur to him, because he is not being pulled at.

There is a further important consideration to bear in mind when halting a horse. Whilst going forward the horse moves his limbs in a definite sequence of movements. To complete a stride, or several strides, the horse must be able to complete the entire sequence of the movements of individual limbs which go to make up such a stride or strides. Now a good halt means a square halt, implying that the horse be allowed to round off his stride naturally and fluently and be not interrupted in the middle of it. This then implies a further refinement in the use of hands and bridle.

When the hand takes its retarding action, as described, the horse, meeting the rein's increasing tension on his bridle, will follow suit and will stop when the hand stops. But quite probably in the middle of a stride, not square, simply because the horse will not pull in order to be able to complete his stride. Therefore the hand should not stop, at any rate not completely, until the horse has stopped square, which he will do automatically provided he be given the chance. The action accordingly resolves itself into: (a) retardation of the hand; (b) retardation of the horse; (c) the horse halts; (d) the hand halts. The delicacy of the hand's action comes into operation after (b) and before (c); as soon as the horse has slowed up sufficiently to indicate that he is about to halt, the fingers will let the faint final impulsion slip through unhindered, so that the horse may round off his stride.

Incidentally, the use of the hand, in the manner here described, implies that the horse moves into and up to his bridle, so bringing his body and quarters nearer his head, instead of having his head pulled backwards towards his body. And this, as we shall be able to discuss presently, is one of the most essential of the finer points of riding.

Also, as we shall see later, the method is always effective on the fully-trained horse, brought into the *rassembler*, or collection of the highest degree, wherein the horse can be truly enclosed by the combined effect of leg and hand. Naturally it cannot, any more than anything else, be expected to answer with equal certainty, under all circumstances, when in difficulties with an untrained or half-trained animal. If it did, it would be magic; results in horse-training are obtained by long and patient work carried out on carefully considered lines, and not by magic. Consequently, occasions may well occur when we cannot help ourselves except by exerting some strength, and maybe effecting some pull, but we shall avoid it as much as possible.

We now revert to our young horse. After each halt, and short rest, the horse has to be put into motion again. At first the trainer will help with the customary command, but accompanied each time by a gentle pressure of the rider's leg; very soon this pressure of the leg alone with be sufficient. But this pressure, whilst sufficiently distinctive to be noticeable to the horse, ought to be really very gentle, for three reasons. Firstly, the horse is naturally so finely observant that a gentle touch is quite sufficient anyway. Secondly, we introduce the horse to a new sensation and a new experience, and we can only rely on his peaceful acceptance, and surrender, so long as we do not surprise and frighten him. Thirdly, it is our ultimate aim to produce a horse trained to react to the very finest and lightest touches of heel and hand, so why not start him on the right lines from the very beginning?

This leg aid will be assimilated very quickly, so that it can now be used for the purpose of teaching the horse to go always freely in front of the leg. The requirement that the horse shall always, at all times, go freely forward at a touch of the leg is so fundamental to all good horsemanship, that without its achievement good horsemanship just cannot exist. This achievement, though really quite easy and simple in itself, is all too often missed, either partly or completely, by the lack of attention and awareness on the part of the rider. It is a point that must at all times be uppermost in the mind of any rider, who undertakes the responsibility of "making" a young horse.

The horse learns, in the first instance, by being taught; but he only absorbs his learning by force of habit, whereby his obedience to certain signs ultimately becomes like second nature to him. In the ordinary course of riding we do not make a habit of pulling up constantly, or even frequently, and moving on again with a pressure of the leg; in fact we probably do so only a few times during a ride. It is not therefore in that way that the habit of "forward obedience" to the leg is formed.

That habit is, and can only be formed, by the much more frequent use of the leg for the purpose of keeping the horse at all times up to his work and reasonably energetic in it.

On the young horse we do most of our work at a walk; a pleasant walk, quiet and unhurried, but yet alert and with sufficient energy to maintain a nice, free, swinging stride. At any rate that is what we should do, but where all too many riders fail. At a walk many riders go to sleep or, at any rate, allow their horse to go to sleep. Young horses do so all too easily and naturally. If the rider of such a young horse is not attentive all the time, and does not perceive the tendency to slackness immediately when it occurs, or rather just before it is going to occur, he misses thousands of opportunities of cultivating the horse's implicit response to the slightest leg pressure. And, in all probability, in so doing, or rather neglecting to do what is his duty, he sows the seed of disobedience and quite possibly of nappiness. An inattentive rider can render the best intentioned young horse nappy very easily and extraordinarily quickly. For what happens? The young horse moves away gaily and brightly, and bright and gay he will go along, no doubt for a few minutes. Soon he may notice that his burden sits there nicely passive, without any apparent interest other than being carried as a burden; so why carry "it" with any more energy than the minimum required, the more so as young horses imagine rather soon that they are getting tired. The first result is that the horse begins to slack, the second that he assumes the habit of slacking, and the third that he soon fails to see why he should at odd and unforeseen moments be suddenly expected to do other than slack; in other words the seed of rebellion, sown there by the inattentive rider himself, begins to take root.

From there to nappiness is but a step and besides, a perfectly logical one. For again, what happens? The horse slops peacefully along, peacefully and sleepily carrying his quasi-inanimate burden and, as sleepy horses do, becomes semi-unaware of his surroundings. But sleepy young horses are capable of waking up with a start when the appearance of some strange object, of imaginary danger, suddenly dawns on their conscience. Then things begin to happen quickly, much too quickly, as a rule, to be dealt with effectively, which means prevented, by the inactive rider. Naturally the horse, not trained by habit to remain in front of the leg, stops, swings round and does any or all of the various things needed to convince him that "the thing" on his back has no real control and does not really need to be obeyed: the nappy horse has been started on his career!

No, the rider who pretends at "making" the young horse, needs to be cheerful, alert, attentive and at one with his charge during every minute, and every second, and every stride, of every ride. He needs to do but little, in fact surprisingly little, but what little he has to do, he should do well. His seat should be alert, well into the saddle, legs close to the horse's side, just "feeling" him, all the time, ready to exert a little pressure, with both legs or maybe with one leg, ready to feel the rein, ready to talk to his horse, to converse with him whenever needed, or just a little earlier than needed. He should watch his horse, his ears, his eyes, his every gesture. A rider so alert, keeps his horse alert; a rider so cheery, keeps his horse cheery. Alert and cheery horses do not go asleep, observe more keenly, see things quicker and less by surprise. They are, moreover, in constant communication, understanding, confidence and sympathy with their rider and soon learn the impulse to go forward readily, whatever happens!

The ability to maintain contact with the leg, constantly, softly, feelingly and with understanding, the ability to use pressure of the leg discreetly, appropriately, at the right moment, with the right degree of finely graduated strength is one of the two main basic talents required in riding; the other one is the use of the hand, whereabout more anon.

The aspects of the "forward urge", discussed above, are largely psychological.

There is another aspect, no less important, though but seldom referred to, which is physical. It is physically impossible to control, in the sense of steering it, any body not in movement through an impulsion of its own; a bicycle, a motor-car, or a plane cannot be guided unless in movement. The point is perhaps best illustrated by referring to a ship. As every sailor, or yachtsman, or anyone who has had anything to do with boats knows, a ship is uncontrollable unless it has sufficient way on. With the horse, it is no different; unless we are able to maintain him in forward movement at our will, we cannot control him.

As a matter of fact the analogy between horse and ship goes a good deal further than the comparison already made. The ship is steered by a rudder, from the stern; in order to steer to port we put the helm over to starboard, so causing the stern to swing round to the right and the bow to the left, the ship turning more or less on its centre. In a ship, the effect of the wind, or of the engines, is always that of a force of propulsion acting abaft the beam; the impulsion comes from behind.

Again we are in exactly the same condition with the horse; the impulsion derives from the hindquarters, and the horse steers from the hindquarters; left to his own devices, to turn to the left the horse brings his hindquarters to the right, turning, just as a ship, on his centre. We are so used to steer our bicycles and motor-cars from the front wheel or wheels, that we are inclined to imagine that a horse must follow his forehand, and is bound to turn left or right, in order to follow his head, turned in accordance with left or right rein pressure. Nothing is further from the truth; the horse is just as capable as we are of going straight on with his head turned to one side; the opening rein-effect, to turn left or right, is an acquired obedience, which the horse has learned, but there is nothing physically compelling about it! Rein-control by itself can never be reliable, unless based upon leg control. Ultimately, as we shall see, it is only by the combined effect of leg and rein that we may be able to arrive at an effortless mastery which is so nearly absolute that it becomes almost impossible for the horse to evade it.

These then are the imperative reasons for the care we should take, from the very beginning and forever after, in educating our young horse and in maintaining him in the habit of going freely forward in answer to the slightest pressure of our leg. Carried out consistently, cheerfully and with tact, it can all be achieved smoothly and easily.

In this way then the rider, who gradually takes over control from the trainer holding the lunge, concentrates in the first place on keeping his pupil walking nicely and alertly. As soon as a reasonable amount of leg control has been obtained, which does not take more than two or three lessons, provided the rider understands this work, we can begin to teach the horse the direct or opening rein-aids, to turn right or left. In the proper sequence, therefore, leg-aids and impulsion first, rein-aids and steering second. In these early stages, on a completely green youngster, we can do no more than use one rein at a time; we turn the horse's head to the left, or right, not so much by shortening the left or right rein as by carrying hand and rein well to the left, or right, of the horse's neck, according to the direction wherein we require him to go. He will be very awkward at first, not knowing what we want, and there is, as we have seen already, nothing physically compelling in the fact that we turn his head sideways. However, provided we are sensible and satisfied with the very slightest responses at first, the horse will again be ready and able to learn very quickly.

We are then so far that the horse has accepted his rider, moves off and walks on freely on a pressure of the leg, stops on feeling the retarding action of the hand, and turns left and right easily and gently in answer to the action of the direct rein. The horse is, in fact, quite ready to be ridden loose. However, ridden loose, there are always chances that the horse may jump forward at a faster pace than a walk, when the feel of the rider on his back will change, which may surprise him. I therefore like to give the horse a few trotting lessons, quite short ones, whilst still on the lunge.

After that, I have him ridden loose, in the enclosure which I use as a school; for the first day or two I still stand in the centre; the horse is used to my presence there, which inspires him with confidence; besides, there may be occasions when a word or a gesture from me may help either him or his rider. However, I let my rider take the horse gradually farther away from me, and after a couple of days or so my presence is no longer needed.

The routine is then always the same. More often than not we do our breaking during the winter, when it is not practicable to do so from grass. So these young horses are started and, although they do not receive much corn, they are given plenty of clover hay and do but little work; so they are quite full of themselves when they come out. Quite frankly I like them like that, since they will do their work with more ambition and zest, and will learn quicker. But we take the precaution to lunge them, with their tack on, for ten or fifteen minutes, so that they may blow off some of their superfluous steam, before being mounted.

After that they are ridden, with the very strictest of orders never, on any account, and however well they may appear to shape, to take them at anything more than a walk for the first fortnight or so. I am only interested in well-bred, very high-couraged horses, thoroughbreds or Anglo-Arabs for preference. It is only the high-couraged, high-spirited horse that will really repay, in the end, for the trouble and care devoted to his education. But care and trouble there must be, with judgment and without hurry.

At the walk everything goes quietly and peacefully; reactions need not be too quick, and the horse has time to let his lessons sink in, without any trace of nervousness. There is no risk of any loss of confidence; on the contrary, his confidence increases day by day as he goes along. There is no risk of nervous damage to his mouth: than which nothing is more difficult to put right afterwards; on the contrary, by slight variations of pace, halts now and again, careful circles and similar effects of one rein, he will soon begin to play with the bit and to show signs of beginning to make a mouth. Lastly, and not least, he will begin by learning a good, free and unrestrained walk, with plenty of freedom for head and neck; the idea of jogging will henceforth never dawn on him. And, after all, a good walk is the very basis of all later correct development; incidentally a really good walk is one of the most difficult things in riding, which it is almost impossible to achieve upon a bad original foundation. Consequently any time spent on that, is time well spent.

The gear we use is always the same. An ordinary saddle with a string girth; this variety is less liable to slip than a leather one and therefore better suited to a young horse which has not yet made his shape. My rider carries a whip, always, and uses it when required, as an aid; my horses accept its use with complete confidence. Spurs, of course, are never worn on the young horse. We use an ordinary snaffle bridle, with an ordinary noseband, and with two reins; the upper rein passes direct from the horse's mouth to the rider's hand, and the lower rein passes through the rings of a running martingale. I never send any horse with an unmade or unconfirmed mouth out without a running martingale; the martingale is adjusted to such length that it does not come into operation during ordinary riding at all, that is as long as the horse does not actually throw his head right up to a horizontal or near horizontal position. The martingale is mainly there as a safety device. A young horse, properly ridden, will not, normally, attempt to do so. But things are not always normal; a youngster with an unmade mouth might suddenly take fright, might throw his head up and bolt away from the cause of his fright; with an unmade mouth the rider is, under such conditions, practically powerless to regain control in time, unless he has this martingale; its presence may save both rider and horse from quite unnecessary danger.

It goes without saying that it is not the purpose of the martingale to force the horse's head down in the ordinary course of riding in order to make him assume the semblance of a bridled or collected position; to do so is merely a proof of ignorance. I can see no objection whatever to the use of a running martingale, adjusted as described in the preceding paragraph, on any horse brought out hunting in a snaffle; it is probably a very wise precaution, showing that the rider knows what he is about. But the presence of a running martingale on a horse ridden in a double bridle merely shows that the rider does not know what he is about; either he does not know what a double bridle is for, namely for a horse with a made mouth, or else he does not know how to use such a bridle: if, in addition, we see him fit his martingale to the bit-reins, then and in that case we need have no doubt but that he knows neither; the only thing we can do is to sympathize with the unfortunate horse.

After a couple of weeks of this work, we begin work at the trot. It presents no problems provided we adhere to the principle of quiet and gradual progress. At first we trot only short distances, thirty or forty yards or so, coming back to a walk each time; again, to do so, we use no strength and we do not pull; we merely retard the progress of the hand so that the horse, meeting the slightly increased tension of the rein, be able to neutralize its effect by slowing up; which is exactly what we require.

It is a basic principle, in introducing the horse to any of the faster paces, always to avoid excitement and always to ensure that we can slow him up, or halt him, without effort. In train-

ing a horse, we are in reality trying to form a partnership, where-
in the horse shall supply the motive power and the rider the
directing power or brain. But the horse is possessed of a brain
himself, and this cannot be short-circuited. We cannot, by
any physical means whatever, effect any direct influence or con-
trol over the horse's anatomy; if we could, the horse would be
a mechanical contrivance and not an independent living being.
We are to realize that the messages emanating from the direct-
ing power of our brain must and can only be transmitted into
the desired action by the horse, through the intermediary of
the horse's brain. The horse and the rider must learn to think
alike, in order to be able to act alike.

This can be realized only gradually, and in stages, even though
the horse is usually the more willing, and the more adaptable of
the two partners; so, it is not the horse only who has to learn
this assimilation of the working of two brains, but the rider must
learn with him, must indeed be anxious to do so all the time
and with each individual horse. In making a young horse, it is
never a question of a young horse who knows nothing and of a
rider who knows everything! The real problem is always that
of attuning the animal's and the human brain into concerted
action.

With a little tact and commonsense on our part, the horse
will soon be trotting round calmly and confidently; confidence
and calmness are, as always, the mainstays of successful schooling. But calmness is not to be confused with slackness; again,
just as in the walk, it is essential to cultivate calm energy, legs
always softly against the horse's sides, always ready to effect just
that little squeeze which makes all the `difference between a
rhythmic gait and a slogging pace.

Energy of gait is to be found in rhythm, not in speed. Any
rider can induce the horse to increase speed; in that there is
no merit. What is required is the ability to obtain, when needed,
increase of energy without perceptible increase in speed, and to
do so without perceptible restraint on the reins. It is a matter
of tact and constant observation.

The importance of going forward, of teaching the horse always, incessantly, but tactfully and with great care, the habit of
going freely in front of the rider's leg has been studied with
emphasis in this chapter. And rightly so, because it is the first
basic principle of control. It is moreover the one basic principle

which can, indeed which must be taught the horse from the very beginning, and it is also the one basic principle which can so be taught him without any risk of spoiling the horse.

The emphasis so laid must not be taken to mean that the second basic principle of control, the acceptance of the bridle, is less important. Indeed it is not. *Control depends upon these two elements equally, in fact it lies between them. But acceptance of the bridle is much the more difficult of the two to achieve, and the risk of spoiling, instead of making, a good mouth is great. The young horse is not ready for the experiment; safety and ultimate success are achieved better, and more surely, by nursing the young mouth. Contact there must be, but it can be of the lightest and the reins can be handled with the utmost care, and indeed with tenderness.* Everything should be done, in these early stages, to avoid discomfort to the horse's mouth; attempts at making the mouth are better deferred until the time comes when such can be done without risk.

There is a time for everything in horse schooling and it is of the essence of the trainer's talent that he shall be able to bide that time.

MMANDANT LESAGE, CADRE NOIR, SAUMUR, FRANCE, ON "TAINE", OLYMPIC GOLD MEDAL, 1932

[*Photo: Sankt Georg*
CAPTAIN V. OPPELN-BRONIKOWSKI (GERMANY) ON "GIMPEL".
OLYMPIC GOLD MEDAL, TEAM 1936

COMMANDANT WATTEL. CAVALRY SCHOOL, SAUMUR

CHAPTER VII

THE SEAT

Where to sit – How to sit – Purpose of the stirrups – Unity of balance – Theory of the centre of gravity rebutted – Balance and grip – The German school – Bracing the back – Aids by association

In the partnership of riding, the horse is the rider's vehicle; he has to carry the rider's weight and to provide the partnership's motive power. It is therefore elementary that we should, in anything to do with riding, consider the horse's comfort first. He can only develop his maximum efficiency under the most advantageous conditions; it is thus essential to reduce the hindrance caused by our weight in the saddle to the minimum.

It is clear from the horse's build that his ability to carry weight lies in the forehand, and that the strongest part of his back lies just behind the withers, in the lowest part of his back.

This statement can best be checked by an examination of the horse's skeleton. It will be seen therefrom that the horse's back is constructed in the manner of a girder, which is supported at one end by the forehand, shoulders and front legs, and at the other end by the quarters, croup and hind legs. This girder is made up of the spinal column and of the ribs attached to it, which give it depth. The resistance of a girder against bending stresses, the ability to carry weight, is determined by its depth. It will be observed, in the case of the horse, that this girder, formed by spinal column and ribs, is very deep, and therefore very strong, immediately behind the withers; that the depth of the ribs, and with it the strength of the girder, diminishes gradually towards the rear until, when the loins are reached, no ribs, no depth and, comparatively speaking, no resistance to bending stresses or ability to carry weight, remain. At this point the horse's frame has to rely on the strength of the spine alone, which makes it quite clear why the loins are the weakest part of the horse's back. The picture of the horse's skeleton, in the manner wherein it is here illustrated, shows convincingly also that the quarters are designed purely for the purpose of providing motive power and not for the purpose of carrying weight.

Accordingly it is in that lowest part of the horse's back, just behind the withers, and as close up to them as we can get, near to the pommel of the saddle and away from the cantle, that we should sit. On this point leading authorities are all agreed.

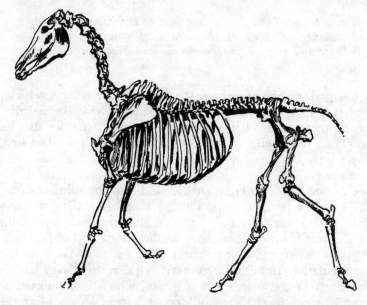

DIAGRAM 2.   HORSE'S SKELETON

It is achieved by a "deep" seat, right "into the horse" and "in" the saddle, and not "on top of the horse" and "on" the saddle.

This deep seat is characterized by a supple, erect position of the rider's body above the saddle, with somewhat hollow loins; by the seat itself on the points of the seat bones, instead of on the fleshy part of the buttocks; by the natural angle wherein the thigh, from hip to knee, finds its resting place against the flaps of the saddle: by the vertical position of the stirrup leathers, parallel with the girth; by the natural way wherein the lower leg, from the knee downwards, lies closely to the horse's flanks; by the pointed knee, which is the foremost point of the entire leg; by the position of the foot, resting the toe, or the ball of the foot, comfortably in the stirrup; by the fairly long leathers.

In this manner the rider sinks deep into the saddle under the influence of his own weight, and the influence of the force of gravity tends to drive that weight straight down, through thigh and lower leg, towards the stirrup, where his toe finds a resting place, and beyond the stirrup, where his heel, quite naturally, supple and without constraint, comes to rest in a position lower than the toe. Since the lower leg rests closely near the horse's flanks, the heel is closer to the horse than the toe, which is in the stirrup; the heel is down and inwards, the toe up and somewhat outwards.

But the position here described, and clarified with photographs of a number of horsemen of world repute, must and can only be found effectively through complete relaxation of the rider's entire body. The rider has to achieve total suppleness. As long as he fails to do so he will, no doubt unconsciously, resist the best manner wherein nature has intended that he shall sit on a horse. Resistance, even though unconscious, entails some stiffness, and stiffness in the rider, however slight, is bound to entail an answering stiffness and resistance in the horse.

In the dressage of our horses we aim finally at their complete suppleness and relaxation; in that we can never be fully successful unless we are truly relaxed and supple ourselves!

To attain this is a great deal more difficult than may at first sight appear. To begin with, there are ingrained habits; we are just as susceptible as our horses to assume bad habits rather than good ones, and our own bad habits are just as difficult to cure as theirs; and mostly for the same reason, the blissful ignorance that our habits are bad! Then there are preconceived ideas, which may be even worse than habits, in that they appear to supply a legitimate background for them. And finally, there are the stirrups, which are the greatest single agents in creating bad seats and preconceived ideas.

The purpose of stirrups is little understood. They are really there for one reason only: the human instinct of having to rest one's feet on something solid. Humanity simply hates to have its feet dangling in the air for any length of time. We sit with our feet on the ground or on the crossbar of a high chair; or on the lower rail of a gate; or on anything else handy; or on the stirrups!

Now, admittedly, in the good seat we also like to have our stirrups, for the very same legitimate reason of having a place to rest our feet on. For that purpose we require them just a couple of inches higher than the level whereto our feet would descend by themselves if we did allow our body to sink, by the force of gravity, into the deepest place of our saddle, and if we did allow our legs to sink, by the same force and unimpeded by "grip", into their natural position by the sides of the horse.

These facts are well enough known at the very few really thorough riding schools still in existence in the world of to-day, where pupils are made to ride without stirrups for months, or for just as long as is necessary to make them find that natural relaxed position.

That is not the way most of us, including your servant, the author, have set about learning their riding, at any rate not for a sufficient length of time. We have all been in too much of a hurry, too much intent on learning to stick on (meaning "on top") and enjoy ourselves. To that effect we have sought, and found, the support of our stirrups to keep us "on" the horse, and we learned to "grip" in order to strengthen our so-called "balanced" seat and, in so doing, what have we found? Invariably that we are liable to lose our stirrups at times. And what have we done to cure it? Deepen our seat, let our legs come down further towards our stirrups? Far from it; in ninety-nine cases out of a hunded we have pulled our stirrups up a couple of holes. In other words we have pushed our seat away from the pommel and towards the cantle; away that is from the place where the horse is strongest and nearer to the place where he is weakest; and in so doing we have affected his comfort, his ease of movement and his efficiency adversely.

The precise length of the stirrup leathers may need to vary to some extent in accordance with the particular type of riding wherein we are engaged for the time being. Actual schooling and dressage work, which must be done on a smooth and level site, requires maximum delicacy and efficiency in the use of the leg and needs long leathers.

In riding across country, on rough going, hunting and jumping, it will usually be necessary to shorten the stirrups a couple of holes; the result of such adjustment should bring the knees further forward against the flaps of the saddle and a little higher; but the position of the seat itself, on the points of the seat bones in the centre of the saddle and of the rider's body above the saddle, should not be affected.

It is to be remembered that the position nearest to the horse's withers is also the very place where the effect of his action is least noticeable; the very place therefore where it is easiest, or rather the only place where it is really possible to be quite undisturbed by the horse's action, to become one with that action, and so to avoid disturbing him through the effect of our own disturbance.

This lack of unity with the horse, of a degree of lack of mutual comfort, is the defect that strikes one first, and most forcibly, in the position most generally adopted by the majority of riders "on top" of their horses. But it does not follow in the least that such riders are themselves aware of such deficiency; far from it. They have adopted their actual position, whatever it may be, by habit; by habit they feel quite comfortable and by habit too they feel, and are in fact, quite secure. The importance, or rather the merit of being secure on the horse, of having a firm seat, is apt to be very much overrated. Actually there is in that no merit worthwhile mentioning; anyone with a reasonable disposition for sporting activity, and of a reasonably suitable physique, can learn that fairly quickly; that is merely a matter of habit and, as soon as that habit has become confirmed, it is actually quite difficult to fall off a horse.

The types of seat here referred to, which may be seen in many varieties, rely, for their security, according to the book, "on balance and on grip". Grip, that is, with the knees and thighs, which, supported by a shortish stirrup leather, maintain the rider's seat towards the back of the saddle, where he ought not to be, and prevent him from sliding into the front of the saddle, where he should sit. Grip and position combined prevent him effectively from relaxing completely into the horse's action; the rider cannot sit down to a trot with any comfort, that is for any length of time, without bumping, effort or fatigue; frequently he cannot even do so at a canter. These are certain signs of an inadequate seat and every reader, surely, knows how common a phenomenon they are.

Now, if our ambitions lie in the direction of obtaining the best results from our horses through careful riding and schooling, we must realize that schooling at its best cannot be achieved without riding at its best. That we must therefore begin by getting our seat right. There is not, in that, anything inherently difficult, excepting that a conscientious effort, an amount of perseverance and will-power, are always needed to overcome ingrained habits. In this matter of our seat we have to begin—and to this rule I know of few exceptions—by lengthening our stirrups, several holes as a rule. We have then to attempt, by natural relaxation, to sink deeper into the saddle and to let our legs sink lower by the side of our horse until our feet descend sufficiently and naturally to the lower level of our stirrups, to find there, in the end, a more natural, more comfortable and more secure support than they have ever done before.

The initial difficulties are mainly two. To begin with, we are bound to attempt, by habit, to retain our seat, our thighs and our knees, in their usual place; only, having lost the habitual support of the stirrups in the habitual place, we feel uncomfortable and, indeed, insecure; the natural tendency is " to grip"; until we stop gripping, we shall not make much progress. The stiffness caused by this gripping is usually accentuated by the tendency to arch the back, which is fatal, because it has the effect of fixing our seat towards the cantle of the saddle. Actually these actions of gripping with the knees and of arching the back are actions of subconscious resistance, quite natural in themselves, against the natural forces of gravity and momentum which tend to drive our body downward into the saddle and forward against the horse's withers. We have to learn, instead of resisting these forces, to abandon ourselves to them; the moment we do that we shall find ourselves glued to our horse and unified with his action, thanks to natural gravity and forward momentum, and without any need of personal effort.

Once having found this natural, relaxed position on the horse, we shall come to discover many things tending to add an amount of pleasure and interest to our riding that have been quite undreamt of before.

To commence with ourselves, we shall discover, first of all, that it is really quite easy to sit down to the action of a trotting or cantering horse without any tendency to leave the saddle, without bumping, without fatigue and without effort. We shall discover such a degree of softness, of mellowness and of round-ness in that action, as will make us wonder how we could ever have failed to enjoy that feeling before.

We have become "one" with our horse. If the effect of that on us is startling, the effect on the horse is more startling still. For he too, has now found a rider "one" with him, a rider who no longer disturbs the rhythm of his gait. He will answer in-stantly by assuming a roomier, longer striding, more balanced, free and easy gait; the weight, the disturbance, the hindrance have been lifted from his quarters; his motive power is free to work at the peak of its efficiency.

The effect of the forward position of the weight is by itself a determining factor in the efficient use of the horse's motive power. Hence the effectiveness of the jockey's position on the racehorse; the stirrup leathers are attached right at the front of the saddle; just behind and almost right underneath the pommel; the saddle itself is fitted well forward; the jockey, rac-ing, has really no seat at all, he just stands in the stirrups; hence his weight is carried by the stirrups exactly on the best place of the horse's back, immediately behind the withers; also, in that place, the jockey is least affected by the horse's action and he can keep quite still; consequently the efficiency of the horse's quarters is unimpeded; he can develop his longest stride and his greatest speed.

If these are the first, most striking advantages of this good seat, there are other consequent advantages, the importance whereof is hardly less great. The ease of the seat makes the rider truly independent of any need to find support from the reins; the harmony of the seat with the horse's action enables him to use the hands free from any disturbance by involuntary movements of the body, since there will be no such movements; the stillness of the seat enables him to achieve independence of action be-tween hands and body, and independence between one hand and another; the mastery thus gained over the use of his hands makes true lightness of control possible and avoids the tendency to exert that backward action of the reins that is always certain to destroy the horse's best action; the depth of the seat ensures a long line of contact between the rider's lower legs and the horse's flanks, in the one position where these legs can be most effective and least disturbing: just behind the girth; the security of the seat by natural forces, without need to grip, enables the rider to relax his lower legs, so that he can use them delicately, lightly, and independently of each other, for the purpose of giving aids; the position of the feet, behind the point of the knee, on, or just behind the girth, ensures that the feet can never counteract the effect of the forward impulse; that effect is always received and taken up by the seat and its most forward contact, the knee; accordingly the resultant remains always forward, towards the horse's shoulder and in the direction of his own movement; there is no thrust thrown backwards, in the wrong direction, as must result inevitably from any foot position forward of the knee.

It is always difficult to mend one's ways. So, it is obvious that the rider too, intent on mending his seat, will meet with initial difficulties. Some of these are apt to appear disconcerting. He may be told to sit more erect, and with hollow loins, in order to find supple balance and relaxation; in actual fact he will begin by finding what seems to him a distinct loss of balance and a distinct feel of stiffness. And some stiffness there undoubtedly will be, due, not to assuming an erect position with open shoulders above hollow loins, but due to counteracting the previously existing habitual, and therefore not realized, stiffness of a curved back and high knees. Some perseverance is needed to overcome these quite unavoidable difficulties; they are not, at any rate, as great as one is inclined to imagine at first; it is always best to attack them radically by discarding the stirrups for a time; one should practise "sitting down" at the trot for just as long as is necessary to learn that art so thoroughly that one can do it with real, complete and absolute comfort for hours on end, in fact without noticing any effort.

The reader will appreciate that the description of the seat given in the preceding pages is not to be taken in any formalistic sense. By that I mean that the efficiency and the quality of a rider's seat cannot be judged by his position and appearance alone. These are but outward values, of importance only because they do contain the key to the true inner value, the performance of the horse.

The quality of the rider's seat shall be apparent in the freedom, grace and swing of the horse's movements. Freedom and grace imply that the horse shall feel no hinder from the rider's presence, because rider and horse have merged into a unity of balance. Swing implies that the horse's entire muscular system takes an active, supple and fluent part in his movement. A horse may move, and many do so move, by the use of the legs alone; in such cases the back is merely a rigid girder, connecting forehand and quarters, whereon the rider may sit in comparative discomfort. A horse can move, and well-trained and ridden should so move, that the muscles of the back behind the saddle play and bend in unison with those of the legs; in such cases the back is an intimate and pliable link between forehand and quarters, whereon the rider may now sit in perfect comfort and with such delicate contact that he can feel the horse's every muscle and sinew move as clearly and as easily as if they were his own.

In fact, in a sense, these muscles then become his own so that, by feeling and acting with them and in unison, the rider can now control, stimulate, temper and attune their activity, and the measure of their play and swing, in conformity with his wishes. Unity has been reached. Unity, in the sense that the rider no longer offers any resistance to the horse's balance in movement. Unity, in that the rider's balance remains identified with that of the horse. Unity also, in that the rider is able to identify the horse's balance with his own. Unity in that there is now only one balance left, that of the complex " horse-rider ", wherein the rider controls the completely assimilated actions of both.

Horse and rider have found the inner secret of the art of riding in the integration of their respective unities of balance into one, into *the* unity of balance.

Unity of balance, a new term, it seems to me, in the language of equitation, for I have no recollection of having ever met it before. A new term it may be but not, assuredly, a new idea, a new conception or a new feel? For, something so predominantly of the essence of all good riding must have been sensed, and must have been felt, by all good horsemen, I think, without exception. And is not " feel ", when all is said and done, the final achievement and the final argument in this Art of Riding?

How then to explain that we appear here to have a definition not hitherto found in the yet so vast literature on riding? Is it perhaps because matters of feel are inherently difficult to describe, or are there other reasons? Personally, I think there are. Humanity has lived for more than a century in an ever intensifying machine age; humanity has begun to see almost everything, including the horse, in a machine way, and has been wont to try and explain everything, including the horse, by mechanical laws. But the horse is no machine, or not, at any rate, a man-made machine whose functioning can be calculated and explained by man-understood mechanical definitions.

Even if the horse be a machine, then he is, like man himself and all creation, a God-made machine, so intricately conceived and so miraculously attuned that the complexity of its workings, which are those of life itself, are beyond measurement by mere mechanical standards. None the less, it has been a fashion with numerous equestrian writers to try and do so, principally by introducing into their theories of horsemanship the theory of "the centre of gravity". On that subject arguments, highly technical in appearance, have been produced with such gusto, that some of them have gone to the length of whole books. And, as is so often the case of handbooks on riding, later authors have been apt to borrow, and to propagate further a theory which, with its nice impressive diagrams, rather tends to lend an atmosphere of solid scientific authority.

Actually, if we care to give the matter thought, we shall find that this theory of the centre of gravity, as usually applied to horsemanship, is such an absurd over-simplification of the problems involved that it possesses no scientific value whatever and is really quite meaningless. In clarification of the argument I reproduce the typical diagram, to be found in countless riding books, whereon the horse's presumed centre of gravity is neatly marked with a cross, with a vertical arrow downwards to show how the force of gravity is assumed to act on this particular one point.

Now, to begin with, the simple treatment of statics and dynamics apply only to very special rigid bodies; even then, these laws are only convenient when applied to rigid bodies at rest. The moment we have to deal with movement, even of rigid bodies, we have to take into consideration dynamical forces far more complicated than mere gravity, leading to considerable complexity even in fairly simple cases.

Whilst there would be nothing wrong, in principle, in attempting to apply mechanical laws to horse-riding problems, such attempts would have no scientific value unless the whole of the new and complicated factors arising had been taken into account.

It would be possible, for example, to make a very crude mechanical approximation to the problem horse-rider if we

DIAGRAM 3.   CENTRE OF GRAVITY

were to assume that each had all his weight concentrated at one point; but even so we should have to realize that we would, in effect, have two such points, with some kind of an elastic and non-rigid connection; the dynamical laws for such a difficult case of coupled motion would lead to very intricate considerations indeed.

And even that would only begin to probe the difficulties of describing the motion, or rather motions, of the complex horse-rider in scientifically reliable terms of mechanical dynamics. We must consider that even a steady onward motion of the horse is in reality made up of a complicated series of thrusts and bounds, of different limbs and parts of his body, upward, forward, downward, this way and that, involving rapidly varying accelerations and decelerations; and we know of course that each and all of these require a specific force.

Assuming, for the sake of argument, that a sophisticated physicist could, if he felt inclined to make the attempt, describe and calculate this rapidly varying system of forces in scientific terms, his results could still be no other than a jumble of completely unintelligible nonsense as far as the ordinary reader were concerned.

At any rate, the most that any physicist could do would be to say how the problem could be approached if the horse and rider were material points or were, at worst, rigid distributions of matter.

But, since horse and rider are in fact both living matter, non-rigid and altering their shape under the influence of and in response to the forces acting upon them, we can state quite safely that the problem is so involved as to be quite beyond the physicist.

The situation is analogous to that in other arts. The physics and chemistry of colours are interesting to the painter, yet they get him nowhere when it comes to creating a masterpiece. Similarly, the composer can profit preciously little from any knowledge of the physics of sound.

Yet, in all these things the brain can "feel" its way with a marvellous accuracy and good sense, which is the envy of the more ponderous scientific computer.

So let us, in our discussions of horsemanship, be content to limit the argument to those things which we can see and hear, observe and feel through the sensitivity of our brain and let us try to find the appropriate words whereby to convey to others those things which, through much thought and long experience, have gradually crystallized into sufficient mental clarity to be capable of being rendered in the written or spoken word.

And let us not confuse the issue, quite difficult enough already, by the use, or rather by the abuse, of quasi-mechanical or dynamical theories which do not possess, and cannot possess, the slightest scientific or any other value. And, having said that, I trust my readers will appreciate that our brief excursion into the realm of physics had no other intention than to demonstrate the absurdity of their attempted use in connection with the horse.

Indeed in connection with the horse! The horse, who is life and in whom body and impelling forces are bound up inextricably as long as life lasts. The horse, whose movement is part and parcel of his whole being, whose movement is his force and whose force is his movement. The horse, who moves on legs, and whose legs move him, by a God-made system unequalled and undoubtedly never to be equalled by mere human ingenuity. The horse, who moves with four legs, but never on four legs; who is supported now by three, then by two, next by one leg, in ever-varying combination; and each time a leg supports him it drives him on at the same time; and finally the horse proceeds, at all faster paces, in a series of jumps and bounds, with all four legs off the ground.

Naturally all this does not deny that the horse, like anything else on earth, is subject to the force of gravity. We all know that; but we also know, or should do, that gravity is only one of a number of forces, and that, when more than one force acts upon the same body, that body will be driven in the direction determined by the Resultant of such forces. Now as long as the body of the horse, or rather the bodies of horse and rider, on whom these forces act equally, do nothing to counteract their effect, there will be perfect balance of movement. It does not matter in the least where exactly that unity of balance lies at any given moment; the only thing that does matter is the rider's ability to feel it and to be and remain one with his horse accordingly.

In a very general way, we can only say that the principal forces which act upon a horse-rider are: Gravity, which brings the horse back to earth and tends to keep the rider in the saddle; Upward Impulse, delivered by the horse in order to rise off the ground in order to move at all, which tends to throw the rider out of the saddle; Forward Impulse, which drives horse and rider forward; Momentum, gained by this forward speed, and a number of other forces still.

Again, in a general way, we may conclude that the Resultant of these several forces, whereby the direction of the coupled motion horse-rider is determined, is normally forward and downward, towards the point where the horse's leading foreleg will meet the ground.

We may conclude also, in the same general way, that the Unity of Balance of this coupled motion lies in the same direction, forward and downward, and this fact confirms that, in a general way, the rider's seat, previously described, down and forward in the saddle, is the one best calculated to maintain him in close accord with the resultant forces acting upon him and his horse alike, and therefore in the unity of balance.

Before closing our discussion on the subject of the seat, it is worthwhile reverting to the stereotyped expression, that we ride "by balance and by grip".

By balance, certainly, in the sense above referred to, that of unity of balance in the movement of the complex body horse-rider.

But by grip, certainly not, at any rate not in the normal course of events, affecting the skilled rider on a trained horse. Normally we sit and remain seated on the horse by exactly the same laws of gravity and adhesion whereby we sit and remain seated on a chair; to do that we need no grip, since the effect of our own weight will keep us there. The only occurrence liable to cause us to lose our seat, and to fall, is the sudden removal, by breakage or disappearance, of the object hitherto supporting our weight.

It is true that chairs are not, usually, in the habit of disappearing from underneath us, although they do, occasionally, break. If they do, no amount of grip will help us any. It is true, also, that horses do not usually break but that they can, occasionally, disappear from underneath us. Again, if they do, grip will not help us. But of course the horse, unlike the chair, is usually in movement, so that the foregoing comparison is rather an over-simplification.

None the less, the horseman's primary concern is that of retaining the horse's support underneath his seat, which he does by keeping him going in the direction of his, the horseman's, choosing. As long as he is able to do just that, the question of security of seat or of the need to grip simply does not arise.

Difficulties present themselves only when sudden divergencies of direction occur between the line of the horseman's progress and that adopted unexpectedly by the horse; it is in such cases that the horse tends to escape from underneath the rider's seat. But not, in ninety-nine out of a hundred cases, in any manner likely to cause difficulty to the skilled rider who, by sitting in the correct place on the horse's back, will find it easy and natural to adapt, on the one hand, his own direction to that of the horse, and by re-aligning, on the other, the horse's direction to his own.

The security of the rider's seat on the horse, in such cases, depends therefore on the re-establishment of unity of direction between horse and man. It is only in very rare cases of severe disturbance of unity of direction, that the rider may find it necessary to resort to the expediency of gripping the seemingly disappearing horse with his knees, in order to assist for one awkward moment in the re-establishing of unity.

Grip, then, in the normal course of skilled riding, is not necessary; it is not part of a good seat; more than that, it is, through stiffness, destructive of the basic principles of a good seat, which demand supple adhesion.

I feel that it would not be right to close this chapter on the seat without some reference to certain influences of the German School which have made themselves felt in this country, and I believe also in the U.S.A., increasingly since the end of the second World War.

Already, before the war, some impression had been created over here by the English translation, *Riding Logic*, of W. Müseler's book *Die Reitlehre*. But since the war a number of British and American officers of the occupation armies have been to school with some of the eminent masters which Germany undoubtedly still possesses. And a few of these masters have been over here a good deal and have been instructing both military and leading civilian riders. Accordingly certain typically German conceptions have begun to make their way in.

I approach this subject with some diffidence. I have myself been brought up in the French tradition and have never had the opportunity to make a thorough study of the German School. This, I realize, is a weakness in the armour of any author setting out to write a book of this type, and I can only apologize to my readers for the omission. However, there are certain things concerning German riding which are common knowledge. The first of these is that the German School has a great history behind it; its traditions are derived from acknowledged masters whose work did not suffer the interruption caused to the French by their revolution and the Napoleonic wars, as a result whereof French Equitation undoubtedly went through a period of temporary decline. We know also that the Germans, in the years preceding 1939, had brought their modern school to such a height that they were able to compete in all branches of riding on at least equal terms with all comers. These are great achievements, commanding great respect.

Having made this clear I would now like to examine a subject whereon the German School appear to lay great stress, that of "bracing the back" (*das kreuz anziehen*). French writers appear merely to ignore the matter; I do not think it wise to adopt the same attitude in this country, when the German principle is to a certain extent being taught, and has found some adherents.

I have already mentioned Müseler's book; it is well written, by an author who appears to have mastered his subject and who obviously has a good many interesting and sensible things to say; the assumption appears justified that what he has to say on this matter of "bracing the back" is a reasonably authoritative presentation of the German theory.

And he says a great deal about it; in fact in the first ninety or so pages it is almost the leading subject, reiterated again and again. What it amounts to is briefly that "bracing the back" has the dual purpose of maintaining the rider's seat in the front of the saddle and of forming a driving aid.

With the desire of keeping the rider's seat in the front of the saddle one can certainly find no fault. But why that should have to be done by tightening the muscles of the loins is difficult to understand. The arguments produced, to the effect that this tightening of muscles can be produced without stiffness, are far from convincing. The typical German position on the horse, with a braced back, certainly does not look supple; it is quite possible that such stiffness is more apparent than real, although it is difficult to deny that the apparent stiffness of the seat is almost invariably accompanied by an equally apparent stiffness in the rein-control. We do not seem to see that grace and lightness so much beloved, and in my opinion rightly so, by the French School.

It is not impossible that an explanation of this somewhat striking difference between the two schools of riding may be found in differing characteristics of the types of horses used in the two

CAPTAIN HANS MOSER (SWITZERLAND) ON "HUMMER". OLYMPIC GOLD MEDAL, 1940

LT.-COL. A. R. JOUSSEAUME (FRANCE) ON "HARPAGON". OLYMPIC SILVER MEDAL, 1948, BRON...
MEDAL, 1952

CAPTAIN G. A. BOLTENSTERN (SWEDEN) ON "TRUMP". OLYMPIC BRONZE MEDAL, 1948

"ALERT AND CHEERY". THE AUTHOR'S "WHITSUN" WATCHING HOUNDS

countries. The French, like we in this country, use a horse with much blood, of thoroughbred type, with an excellent sloping shoulder and with low action. On such horses there is no difficulty at all in retaining a relaxed position in the front of the saddle and consequently there is no need to brace any back. Possibly matters are somewhat different with the average type of German horses, with their straighter shoulders and normally higher action. Such horses may well be more difficult to sit down to without some special action. I offer this suggestion only on the ground, which in itself is undeniable, that considerable variations in the type of horse being ridden must account for some variation in the rider's technique.

In the matter of the use and value of bracing the back "as an aid", the German theory, as presented by Müseler, simply cannot stand up to examination. He presents pictures to show that an individual standing on the ground by a table, over the side of which a book protrudes, is able to push that book on to the table with his tummy; that, of course, is something nobody would care to query, however obscure the relationship of such action with horsemanship may be. He then goes on to make the amazing statement that, since it is easy to move a swing by bracing the back, we can make a horse go forward in the same way! This lighthearted assumption that the movement of a swing, which is a pendulum, and that of a massive body, such as the horse, are subject to the same laws and can be influenced by a human body superimposed upon it in the same way, denotes such a lack of appreciation of elementary physics as to amount to absurdity. If it were true that we could move a horse by bracing the back we could *a fortiori* make a bicycle go forward in the same manner, without the need to pedal!

However, Müseler's development of the argument goes on for the best part of ninety pages, wherein he seems to attempt to convince his readers, and himself, that there does lie in this bracing of the back some mysterious physical force whereby the horse can be compelled to go forward; that, in other words, this bracing of the back constitutes in itself a very powerful aid. It is quite possible that he may have succeeded in so convincing his readers; but it is quite certain, and most remarakable, that he has not succeeded in convincing himself. For what do we read on page ninety of the same book, where the entire long and involved argument is wound up with the statement that "Influences of the back without a supporting action of the legs are impossible "?

Quite; with that I am in entire agreement; obviously, through that conclusion, the entire theory of the value of bracing the back as an aid goes by the board. Or almost so; for Müseler could have pointed out that movements such as bracing the back, and many other movements of the rider besides, can, even though they are not truly aids in their own right, become "aids by association".

The horse, as pointed out repeatedly already, is exceedingly sensitive of every one of his rider's slightest movements, and if such movements mean anything at all he is very quick to interpret their meaning. He is also very quick in associating one movement with another; there are very few aids given by the rider which are not preceded by some introductory movement. The simplest example, probably, is the aid of the spur; this, provided the rider knows his job, is always preceded by a gradual tightening of the calf of the leg against the horse's flank; quite obviously then, the schooled horse will not wait for the arrival of the spur, but will act on the approach of the calf; or on any action usually even preceding the approach of the calf, such as for instance "bracing the back".

These "aids by association" are exceedingly important and it is mostly their use, by the skilled rider on the schooled horse, which makes it so difficult, or impossible, for the onlooker to see what the rider is doing or that, in fact, he is doing anything at all.

To give a few more examples. The rider who sits down at a collected trot, will usually rise when going into a more extended trot; if he be in the habit of rising first and then applying the driving aid of the leg, he will very soon find that it is sufficient to rise, in order to obtain extension, and that he can, in most cases, do without the leg aid altogether. The rider who is in the habit of bracing the shoulders when reining in his horse will find his horse stopping on the movement of the shoulder alone, without any need to touch the reins.

At any rate, reverting once more, and this time finally, to the theory of bracing the back as an aid, it is worth repeating with renewed emphasis that which has already been said before: there exists no aid of any kind whatsoever that is physically compelling on the horse; the horse is not a lifeless machine; the horse possesses a brain of his own and can only be made to do things through such messages as we manage to convey, by means of our actions, from our brain to his.

Incidentally, it is worth noting that Gustav Steinbrecht, one of Germany's most famous masters, of undisputed international fame, condemns the stereotyped stiffness of the regulation seat of the German cavalry; he refers in particular to the disadvantages of a too strongly braced back (*Das Gymnasium des Pferdes*, published posthumously, Potsdam, 1886).

CHAPTER VIII

THE LURE OF THE OPEN SPACES

T HE Horse is, by virtue of his ancestry, a creature of the wide open spaces. The deserts of Arabia, the endless steppes of Mongolia, the Hungarian Puszta, the prairies of the New World, are the countries of the type where one might expect to find his ancestral home. The type of country where safety against attack, on well-nigh defenceless animals, was to be found in numbers and in speed. Hence still our domestic horse's herd-instinct and his love of a gallop, preferably in company and preferably in the open.

The wise horseman will turn these natural instincts of the horse to his own advantage, and will do so the more freely since they so closely match his own ancestral heritage. For man too is the descendant of an ancestry that was wont to roam far and wide in the search of sustenance for himself and, later, for his domesticated animals. And what animal could he have found better fitted than the horse to help him in those wanderings and in the adventures inevitably attached to them, such as chase and war?

The long since altered circumstances of the domestic environment of the horse, and of man no less, may have done much to mellow the impelling fierceness of their original instincts; it may have made them, and no doubt has made them, more controllable; but it has not been able, and never will be able, to eradicate them! Horse and man we have been made; from the dawn of history and until the doom of history shall overtake us, man and horse we shall remain. And who shall regret it, that has ever tasted the thrill, the pure mad happiness of a good horse's hoofs rattling the turf, *quadrupetante putrem sonitu quatit ungula campum*, as Virgil described it, when horse's and man's pulses quicken and the blood of both rushes imperiously through their veins, rushing forward together and in unison, two souls and but one burning desire, the same that animates the hounds in front of them, the same that has come down to them, untainted and unchanged, from an age-old ancestry.

And what then is that passion?

None other, assuredly, than the urge of achievement, the thirst of adventure, that drives all men forward in whose hearts the sublime spark of the indomitable is aglow. The same spark and the same passion that has driven countless seafarers over uncharted seas and through unknown dangers to the four corners of the globe, that has, in more recent times, driven our pioneers in frail and preposterous machines to the conquest of that treacherous element, the air.

And is it not by the deeds of those very men of enterprise that nations have become great and prosperous, and oceans, air and continents conquered for humanity?

And is it not essential for the future of humanity that men and women capable of keeping that precious fire burning shall be enabled to do so, shall keep their identity and shall not lose themselves forever in the colourless mass of mediocrity so beloved of contemporary rulers? There is no goodness in bread without leaven, any more than there can be hope for nations without the spirit of adventure.

That precious spirit can be kept alive only as it was born, by the battle with nature and the elements, on the sea, in the air, and on the land. On the sea, there no longer is adventure in the modern steamship, though plenty may still be found in yachts and sailing vessels; in the air, in less than half a century, the thrill of early planes and airships, which depended on the skill and coolness of one man, has already given way to the modern airliner with its mass of instruments whereof man is largely the slave and no longer the master.

On land, there still is some adventure to be found and what adventure could be better than that enjoyed by our forbears for thousands of years? And again, what adventure could be better than that which we can share with our age-long companions, our horses and our hounds? And is not that the more true if we reflect that these trusted companions of ours are inspired by the same motives as our own? For of that I feel quite certain: so the high-couraged horse, as the intelligent dog, derives as real a thrill as we do from his battle with nature, and as full a satisfaction of achievement. And does not that very similarity of instinct between man, his horse and his dog explain better than anything, their age-long companionship and the bonds that hold them together?

That, to me, is the real thrill that draws me to the adventure of hunting when, on a high-couraged horse, every bit as keen as the keenest human and every bit as knowledgeable and understanding, we match our wit against that of a highly intelligent wild animal, with all his wiles, and those of nature itself, to help him. When we have the woods and the wind, and the scent and the sound, the ground and the going, plough or grass, sun and cloud and beasts and birds, hill and dale and a hundred and more things to consider quickly, and to decide on a hundred times in a hunting day, if we wish to remain with our hounds and yet not hinder them.

Without that thrill of the unknown there can be no true adventure, and without adventure, no true hunting.

The riding horse then, belongs in the open and it is there first and foremost that we have to fit him for his work. The covered riding school is not the horse's natural habitat and, though such an establishment has many advantages for certain specific purposes, it should not be made its destiny.

The modern riding horse should receive much of his education, and almost all of it in the earlier stages, particularly in the first year, out of doors.

As soon as we have him quiet to carry a rider and under reasonable control, he is ready to make his entry into the outer world, over the farm, through woods and fields, by roads and tracks.

The primary purpose is merely that of introducing the animal to the many strange sights, noises and happenings that occur as a matter of course in strange places. That is merely a matter of commonsense, of time and of patience. The company of a made and mannered horse as a schoolmaster, though not essential, will be found of very great assistance.

Initially the walk is the best pace, to give the horse time, to keep him quiet, and to get him fit. Incidentally the walk is such an important pace that any time spent on its development is time well spent. In that respect it is essential to concentrate on a free and easy walk, long striding, but natural and without hurry. The horse shall, as much as possible, be left the free use of his head and neck and be ridden, as much as possible, on a long rein or even on a loose rein. We do not seek collection in the early stages of a horse's schooling, particularly not at the walk; for reasons stated already in previous chapters, untimely attempts at collection may result all too easily in damage to the mouth and to the freedom of that forward movement that must become the very foundation of our future training.

It will be understood that trotting, cantering, an occasional gallop and jumping can all be introduced gradually into those outdoor rides. It is all a matter of commonsense, and the avoidance of any tendency to get the horse excited will be obvious.

It is assumed that the processes of elementary schooling involved will be familiar to readers of a book such as this; incidentally, I have discussed them at some length in my book *Equitation*, and other sound advice is available in other directions. There is accordingly no need to go into any further great detail concerning this elementary work, the more so as it raises no specific points that have not already been discussed in preceding chapters or that will be discussed hereafter.

A few generalities may therefore suffice.

The principal objects of our first year's riding should never be lost sight of. They are the creation of a calm, confident, mannered but courageous horse; a horse that carries himself naturally, freely, without fuss, with adequate natural balance; a horse that goes gaily, with pleasure, unconstrained and with great freedom, even with abandon.

Courage and self-confidence are of the utmost importance and no opportunity shall be lost to confirm the horse, quietly, sensibly and progressively in these qualities. The crossing of little streams, bigger streams, brushwood, thick places, ravines, all sorts of small obstacles, muddy places, steep places, queer places, can all become a matter of second nature to the horse, without fuss or trouble during his daily rides. Again, in all this, the presence of a schoolmaster will be found a definite help.

It will be obvious that some of these things may require some little amount of schoolwork that can better be done on the home ground, and there is no reason why some of the things to be discussed in the chapters that follow should not be undertaken during the same period.

All the same, any of the more advanced type of work, undertaken before the horse has been confirmed as a free moving, courageous, pleasant-tempered outdoor horse, is liable to do much more harm than good; and that is true in particular if the rider is not sufficiently experienced to notice at once any untoward effects on the horse's free, unfettered and pure movement, on his mouth and on his unruffled temper. Great care is therefore indicated and outdoor results ought to remain the principal object for the time being.

Once a horse has been well prepared on those lines, there is no reason why he should not be introduced to hunting. On the contrary, no matter what his destiny, hunting will do him a world of good.

But the introduction should be made sensibly, and ought not to result in the sort of initial excitement that may quite well prove difficult, and sometimes even impossible, to cure.

It is really quite simple. I take my youngster in the company of an older and mannered hunter. We hack quietly to the meet, where we arrive early; we look on from some little distance, from where we can see everything, but where we are safe from interference with other riders. Naturally an unimportant meet, a cub-hunting meet by preference, is the most suitable beginning, unless we are lucky enough to live near kennels and may have been allowed to follow hound exercise.

When hounds and field move off, we move off too, quite naturally . . . in the opposite direction! Having seen what we wanted to see, nothing to get excited about, we continue our customary hack, conversing ordinarily, our horses walking along peacefully, on an easy rein. We go on for a mile or two, describe some kind of circle, and presently we manage to get back to some suitable place wherefrom, at a decent distance, we can see, and hear, something of the proceedings.

If the hunt moves, we follow more or less, at a quiet walk and at a distance; by distance, I mean respectable distance, anything from a quarter to half a mile and not fifty, or a hundred or even a couple of hundred yards. After all, we must remember horses are gregarious and, if we try to make a high-couraged young horse walk with a number of other horses galloping away close in front of him, we are asking the impossible, and will ourselves provoke the very excitement that we intended to avoid.

However, in this manner we stay out in the neighbourhood of the hunt for an hour or two, just hacking and standing around. If our youngster is quiet, as he is almost certain to be, there is no harm in an occasional trot or canter, or even a jump or two, as we would do in normal hacking exercise.

We go about it in a similar manner for another hunting day or two; gradually we get closer to covertside, we mingle with other horses present, possibly find an opportunity of trotting up with them, and, if luck serves, a suitable occasion may be found for an inoffensive canter.

The day will not be far distant when we feel there should no longer be any risk of letting our youngster slip along easily, should favourable circumstances arise. By slipping along easily, I mean without undue need for control; to gallop along quietly in the rear is the feat of a made, mannered and settled hunter and we have no right to expect it, as yet, from the young horse. Consequently when we do decide to slip along, we are much better up in front, where there will be less need to check and a better opportunity to sit still and allow the young horse to settle.

CHAPTER IX

THE GAITS

I T is of the essence of all good riding that the horse shall move, in all his paces, with absolute purity of gait. The number of aberrations and irregularities that may occur is considerable, and the prevalence of such irregularities is much more frequent than is generally realized.

In dressage, which aims to lead to the most advanced forms of riding, this purity of gait is of absolute importance, and must not be overlooked, either by the rider, the judge, or the instructor.

In this respect the rider, provided he be both experienced and talented, is, in the saddle, in a rather favoured position; he will "feel" at once, any impurities that threaten to creep in, and his equestrian instinct may enable him to find the correction.

The same rider, out of the saddle, as a judge or as an instructor may be, is no longer in the same happy position; true, in many cases he may still sense that there is something wrong with the horse in front of him, though he may often find difficulty in laying his finger on the precise defect and might not then be able to give the rider adequate advice. But it is true also that the talented rider, who could not overlook even the slightest defect of gait from the saddle, will at times be found quite incapable of spotting such irregularities from the ground; I have seen striking examples of this from judges, and from instructors, whose outstanding ability in the saddle could not possibly be doubted.

Irregularities of gait in the dressage horse can never be passed over. They are sometimes congenital when, depending on their precise character and seriousness, they need not always be considered too severely. But as a rule, they are the result of faulty training or faulty riding, and, through habit or through wear, they may become habitual; they are then very grave faults indeed and require to be recognized as such.

That demands a thorough knowledge of the horse's gaits, in their regular form, and most certainly also in the many deviations therefrom which are liable to occur. I give it as my opinion that the first-class judge of serious dressage must possess this knowledge. I hold that the same opinion applies almost with the same force to the first-class instructor. And, though I recognize that the talented rider can get along without it, I would say none the less that everyone setting out to train a horse in advanced dressage will find in such knowledge a source of great strength. It is of immense help, when such troubles do arise, to be able, not only to feel them, but to analyse precisely what is happening; there will then be no need to grope in the dark in search of a cure.

Having said this much I am bound to add that the subject is an intricate one, which bristles with difficulties. It is much more difficult than may at first sight appear; true understanding of the laws that govern the horse's action is far from widespread, and reliable sources of information are very few indeed. It is true that numbers of riding books contain bits of information on the subject, nearly always of too superficial a nature to be of much value and, more often than one would expect, the information given is misleading, because incomplete, or even definitely incorrect.

On that account I have recently completed a special study, illustrated by Michael Lyne, published in 1954 under the title, *The Horse in Action*.

CHAPTER X

SOME IMPORTANT PRINCIPLES

*Language between horse and rider – Straightness – Control
of the quarters – The mouth – The "rassembler" – Collection – The "ramener" – The "mise en main" – Importance
of the mouth to forward movement – Combined effects of
legs and hands – Flexions – Acceptance of the bridle – Use
and purpose of the double bridle – Control of the quarters*

LANGUAGE BETWEEN HORSE AND RIDER

WHEN man wishes to carry his argument in a discussion
with other men he will have to select his words with care,
so that they may convey his meaning with the greatest clarity.

It is precisely so with the rider intent upon expressing his
wishes to the horse.

With one striking difference.

Man, who talks or writes to other men, has at his disposal a
device understood by all men: he can lay special emphasis on
some particular point, underline it, so as to drive it home more
forcibly.

That is not so with the rider!

The rider, to achieve his results in any form of advanced riding, can only make his point, in the end, by laying less and ever
less emphasis on the very thing he means to tell his horse.

A thesis to be argued amongst men may, with good effect, be
built up crescendo; the thesis to be worked out between rider
and horse, to be effective, can only be built up diminuendo.

The conversation between the rider, who aims at advanced
results, and the horse in never-ending; always, during every ride,
the rider asks little questions, the horse may query, the rider will
explain, the horse understand and improve his answers day by

day, until gradually the mutual conversation reaches higher and higher levels and becomes more and more interesting, light and pleasant to both participants. Riding, in this way, becomes an intellectual pleasure, wherein the rider weighs his every word and the horse his every gesture.

The language in this way spoken to the horse is usually designated as "the aids", and the language spoken by the horse as "obedience" or "disobedience". The aids are usually neatly catalogued, to the effect that "such an such" an action by the rider ought to result in "such an such" an answer by the horse.

But what a very crude approximation that all is!

It is true that one must, in teaching riding, try to explain to students the nature and the manner of the aids one uses, and to a certain extent this can be done. But only to a very limited extent. The aids, such as can be described, are no more than the mere A.B.C. of riding; he that knows the alphabet has still to learn to use it, before he can speak or write creditable prose and, in advanced riding, he will have to speak, and write, poetry.

The same word, in poetry as in prose, can have many intonations and as many meanings. Just so in riding, where the same aid can be given an almost infinity of meanings and intonations, whereby in the end a veritable language, and a reciprocal one, comes into being between rider and horse.

It is with the creation, and perfection of this language that, in this study, we are concerned. It would appear essential that before we begin to talk to the horse, clarity shall exist amongst as humans as to the precise meaning of certain important terms of horsemanship which will be constantly used.

STRAIGHTNESS

We all know that it is of the essence of good horsemanship that the horse shall be straight. Not all of us may know how difficult this requirement is, and why. So let us see.

Général L'Hotte adopted as motto for his book *Questions Équestres*: "*Calme, En Avant, Droit*", which means "Calm, Forward, Straight."

The essentials that the horse shall be calm and confident, trusting his rider, and that he shall always be ready to go freely forward have been dealt with at length in a previous chapter. I do not therefore need to repeat myself, excepting to say that these essentials are pre-requisite to everything else in riding, also therefore to straightness.

By straightness is meant that the horse, when moving along a direct line, shall be straight in body from the tip of his nose to his tail; it means also that front and hind feet shall follow precisely the same track; it implies finally that the horse, when ridden from one point to another, shall be able to go by the shortest route, without deviation.

It sounds simple enough, yet it is seldom seen. All authorities recognize the difficulty, but explanations vary. Some have held that the difficulty is congenital, that the horse is born imperfectly straight, due to the manner wherein the foal is carried in the uterus. Since dressage cannot, under any circumstances, alter congenital forms, this argument would, if we accepted it, close the discussion. Since, on the other hand, horses can be and can go perfectly straight, we must obviously discard it.

Général L'Hotte, and other authorities, have pointed out that straightness depends on the rider's control of the quarters. In that there is a great deal of truth, but it is not, in my opinion, the whole truth. I have pointed out, in Chapter VI, that the horse steers from his quarters, so that we cannot be truly master of the horse's direction unless we do possess control of these quarters. Without that control we shall not be able to ride on a straight line from one point to another because, to do so, requires accurate steering. That is elementary enough, if we will but reflect that it is not the normal practice, of man or beast, to be going on perfectly straight lines from one point to another; to do so requires a concentrated effort; without such effort we always wander more or less.

But the requirement of straightness also requires that the horse shall be straight in himself, so that hind and front feet may follow the same track. Very many horses are not so straight; they are liable to carry the quarters more or less to one side or the other, so that the track of the hind feet deviates from that of the front feet; *le cheval se traverse*, the horse goes sideways.

Here again it is true that control of the quarters provides a measure of correction; but a measure only, sufficient maybe to prevent, whilst the control is applied, and therefore temporarily, manifestation of the horse's defective bearing. But it does not go to the root of the difficulty, to the cause that makes the horse seek to go sideways; it does nothing, and can do nothing, to remove that cause, since if it did, or could, the horse would carry himself straight of his own free will and the control, in this respect, would no longer be necessary.

Where then do we look for the cause that induces the horse to seek a sideways escape with the quarters? I give the answer without any hesitation: that cause lies in the horse's mouth. In my opinion, if we desire our horses to be straight and to go straight we have to look, in as much as such things can be expressed in figures, as to 75% to the horse's mouth and as to 25% to all that follows behind the mouth, including the quarters.

In raising this particular question we are faced at once, and inevitably, with the main problem that is cardinal to every form of advanced horsemanship, namely:

The "Rassembler"
Collection, The "Ramener", The "Mise en Main"

The literal translation of the French word *rassembler*, is the English word "collection"; unfortunately the true implication of the two expressions is so vastly different that one just cannot use the one as a legitimate translation of the other.

The word "collection", as understood in English, has a strictly limited meaning; it describes the "attitude" or "bearing", assumed by the horse in certain of his exercises.

The word *rassembler*, used in the academic sense, has a far wider meaning; it embraces the entire demeanour of the horse in all his actions, the suppleness of his body, of his limbs and joints, the ease and generosity of his movements and, in particular, their rhythm and cadence; it embraces also the horse's absolute lightness, due to the perfect harmony of mouth and action; in effect, it embraces a high degree of all round perfection; it is at one and the same time the final object of the trainer's efforts and, as and when achieved, the crown upon his work!   It cannot be achieved, in full measure, except in the high-school horse and it is just that, in particular, which distinguishes the high-school horse from any other.

Results in riding, as we know, are only obtained progressively and step by step. That applies, evidently, to the *rassembler*, but it applies just as much to mere "collection", which is in itself an essential achievement on the trainer's road, before the *rassembler* can even be thought of. Similarly, other preliminary milestones must be passed successfully before a correct form of "collection" can be obtained.

We are here dealing with subtle differences, which tend at times to merge into one another without a clear dividing line; accordingly the explanation is somewhat difficult. It is probably best attempted by reviewing in brief the various stages which the horse must pass before he can achieve either.

A reasonable degree of "collection" is of course essential to any form of "horsemanship" worthy of that name, whether concerned with hunters, hacks, children's ponies or troop horses. It relates to the form wherein the horse is able, and willing, to go forward with his head in the right position, bridled, under reasonable control.

The accent is here on the word "forward", for there is no merit in an apparently correct head position, bridled, unless the horse be able, and willing, to move forward "freely" in that attitude. To achieve just that combination must remain the primary object of our training. It cannot be done all at once and it may well sound a great deal easier than indeed it is.

The first step is the attainment of a measure of acceptance of the bit, characterized by flexions of the jaw, accompanied by a measure of flexion at the poll, resulting in a measure of correct head carriage. It is what the French call *le ramener*, which I would like to translate as "obtaining head carriage". Actually the literal translation is "bringing the head back into position". And, unfortunately, that is more often than not the manner wherein this head position is obtained, with fatal results to the horse's further progress.

However, done properly, this position of the *ramener* constitutes already some degree of collection; we might perhaps call it "collection of the first degree". This time the accent is on "done properly", namely by riding the horse forward, towards his head and not by pulling the horse's head back towards his body.

Throughout our training of the riding horse it is our object to attain lightness in front through increased activity of the quarters; but lightness alone is of no value unless we maintain all the while, and improve, free and generous forward movement at the same time. In fact, if we had to choose between the two, free forward movement would be the more important quality. That is where the difficulty lies, and where it is so very easy to go wrong.

We have, in English, the descriptive saying "he, or she, cannot ride one end of the horse". However often that dictum may be applicable, it is undoubtedly much more current to find people who can ride, up to a point, one end of their horses without appearing to realize that the animal most decidedly possesses two ends, and that little good can come from attempting to ride only one of them! That is all the more true since such riders as concentrate on one end usually concentrate on the head and forget about their horse's quarters, his motive power, altogether.

In that way they may well be able to produce something superficially similar to a correct head carriage, but at the same time intrinsically detrimental in its final effect. For, whatever the head carriage may look like, it can be of no value unless it is based on increased energy of the quarters, resulting in free and improved forward movement. Neither of these can be achieved without a confident mouth, ready to go gently into its bridle, without hesitation, at all paces.

However, let us assume that we have achieved our first object, that of the position of the *ramener*, or collection of the first degree, correctly; we will have done so by pressing the horse gently forward towards his bridle, so as to feel him flex from time to time, as his mouth meets the bit.

We are then ready to continue working towards the achievement of "collection" in the English sense, which I would like to call "collection of the second degree" and which is known in French as *la mise en main* meaning the horse which "goes in hand". The accent is on "goes": the horse goes forward freely, with a perfectly balanced, energetic stride, with a nice soft pressure on the rein; the hocks are active and the shoulders move freely; it is obvious, above all, that the horse accepts his bridle, does not fear it and is not impeded by its action. Or that, at any rate, is the correct form of collection. Its achievement is a matter of time and of careful, very careful, work.

The basic principle of that work is eminently simple; it is merely that of gradually increasing the action of the hocks by getting the horse to engage these just a little further underneath the body; it implies the shortening of the base whereon the horse moves just a little; the horse brings his rump and quarters a little nearer to his head; to do so, the horse must of necessity lower his quarters a fraction, resulting in a relatively higher position of the forehand.

These results are achieved by the "combined effects" of legs and hands, working in unison on the same problem, in other words by riding "both ends" of the horse.

Though the principles may be simple, the correct application of them is the root difficulty in riding. That difficulty lies in the ability to create the right reactions in the horse, and above all in the ability of avoiding wrong reactions. One of these faulty reactions is the tendency of the horse to go sideways. Which brings us back to the very question leading up to this discussion, that of the horse's "straightness".

I have already said that we are aiming, in this work, at shortening the base whereon the horse moves; that implies in effect that we are aiming, to some extent, at shortening the horse himself. Which is far from simple. It cannot be done without an immense increase in the pliability and suppleness of all the horse's muscles and of all the horse's joints. That necessitates, in the first place, a course of carefully thought out and methodically applied gymnastic exercises. These will be described and explained in following chapters.

It will be understood that the horse's ability to shorten his base in movement, to collect himself, in other words, can only develop gradually and in the precise measure wherein the pliability of his muscles and joints increases. The horse will be ready enough to try and execute his rider's demands, aiming at shortening his base, in accordance with his physical ability. Beyond that, he obviously cannot go; so, if forced beyond his physical powers, he can do no other than take evading action; he does that by going sideways, "traversing himself".

That, in so far as the case has now been put, constitutes a problem in appearance wholly physical and therefore relatively simple, amounting in the estimation that I have already given to some 25% of the difficulty involved.

The remaining 75% is related to the horse's mouth. I have already mentioned the "combined effect of legs and hands", wherein the legs control the quarters and the hands control the mouth. Again, that sounds simple enough, considered from the rider's point of view. But the horse also has his point of view, and what is more a most decided one, about his own " combined effect of mouth and body "! The inter-relation between the reactions in the horse's mouth and the actions of the horse's body have been given prominence in the writings of all leading authorities. Explanations may vary and may not always be easy to follow, but on the existence and effect of the phenomenon all are agreed. In brief, what it amounts to is this: as long as the horse is happy, and yielding in his mouth, he will be happy and supple in his body; the moment anything occurs to disturb the happiness in the horse's mouth, sympathetic stiffening reactions set up at once in his body; such disturbances in the mouth may have a number of causes, maybe the rider's hands, maybe fright, emotion or temper on the part of the horse, maybe something quite extraneous to either horse or rider; conversely any discontent, pain or stiffness in any part of the horse's body will also, and at once, set up a sympathetic stiffening in the horse's mouth, which will cease to be yielding.

Now it must be clearly understood that in all the work undertaken to reach the *mise en main* or "collected movement" we must pursue, and cannot do other than pursue, two aims simultaneously: that of increasing the energy of the horse's action on a shorter base and that of creating a happy mouth; the two problems are inseparable.

The inherent difficulty posed by this work is undoubtedly considerable, but the trainer who realizes the cause and effect of the interactions referred to above, between mouth and body, is forewarned against his most serious troubles; actually, if he be truly observant, he will find that the state of his horse's mouth is a veritable barometer, and an extraordinarily accurate one, of his horse's feelings.

So, to revert once more to our problem of straightness, he will find an unmistakable warning in his horse's mouth, whenever he overtaxes the animal's capacity to collection; if he insists none the less, the animal will take evading action all round, in his mouth, in his quarters, in his forward movement and, of course, in his straightness.

Accordingly, we may qualify as correctly collected (in the English sense, collection of the second degree, *mise en main*) the horse that goes forward with energy (impulsion), well off his hocks, well up to his bit, with a correct head position, flexed at the poll, happy in his mouth and straight. If any of the factors here mentioned are missing, collection has not been fully achieved. We frequently see horses presented in collected gaits which lack all real impulsion and brilliance; their movements are merely slow and, in a sense, extinguished; such horses are not "collected" but, provided head carriage and mouth are otherwise right, merely in the *ramener* (collection of the first degree).

To attain really good collected gaits is already quite an achievement, whereof any horseman may well be proud, and beyond which very few ever progress. Collection as here explained is sufficient for all the exercises and competitions of the low school.

The horse is truly obedient, and has surrendered himself almost completely to the combined effect of legs and hands; the degree of control at the disposal of his rider has become very great; even though still short of the maximum obtainable in the true *rassembler* (collection of the third or highest degree).

The term "collection" is applied in a limited sense to describe the horse's correct bearing in collected forward movement.

The term *rassembler* is applied in an unlimited sense to describe the complete harmony of movement and bearing, whatever the horse is doing.

"Collection" is a limited achievement, wherein the horse goes truly up to his bridle; the rider feels the forward impulse of the horse come up to the tips of his fingers (*la mise en main*); the fingers and the bit are the limit whereto the horse can go.

The *rassembler* is an unlimited achievement, wherein the bridle, horse and rider have become absorbed into one entity; the bit possesses a limiting effect no longer, the forward impulse travels right through it, without let or hinder; actions of hands and bridle-effects have become mere messages to the horse's nerve-centre.

"Collection" is a form.

"*Rassembler*" a quality!

"Collection" can be taught, more or less to perfection, depending upon the degree of the rider's ability.

"*Rassembler*" can only be developed, on the basis of an already very good collection, provided the rider possesses, or is able to develop, an exceptionally sensitive feel for the harmony of cadence, movement, forward impulse and delicacy of rein-control. It is not, in my opinion, something that we can set out to teach the horse, but rather a quality which the horse may acquire gradually by himself, as a result of ever increasing resiliance, suppleness and muscular control. It is only the very finely schooled horse that can gradually attain this degree of perfection—for such it is—and then only in the hands of an exceptionally gifted and experienced horseman. The gifted horseman may be able gradually to feel his way towards the *rassembler*, to obtain glimpses of it from time to time in certain movements and at certain paces, but, unless he also possesses very great experience, he will find the status escaping him frequently; he will not be able to produce and to maintain the *rassembler* as he wishes. The experience needed can only be acquired as the result of many years of work, and the training of a number of horses.

The horse, once brought truly in the *rassembler*, has accepted his rider's mastery so completely, both in a physical and in a mental sense, as to make that rider's aids and wishes as near "compelling" as is possible (see page 49).

COMBINED EFFECTS

Everything in riding, from the beginning till the end, culminating in the *rassembler*, is dependent upon the combined effects of legs and hands: the two are completely inseparable, and it is not until this complete inseparability has been absorbed so fully in the rider's system as to have become part of his very nature, that he can begin to achieve harmonious results.

The limitation of the words at our disposal, spoken as well as written, makes it extremely difficult, if not impossible, to preserve this indissoluble entity in our descriptons. We are almost bound to describe certain actions as if they were separate entities; such expressions as "the legs create impulsion and the hands regulate its effects" are common and are descriptive and true enough in a sense, so long as the reader is made to realize that these effects cannot operate properly one without the other.

However, it is the primary effect of the legs to drive the horse forward, and of the hands to receive that impulsion through the medium of the horse's mouth; it is the secondary effect of legs and hands combined to utilize that impulsion to the best effect; this secondary effect cannot be obtained to the full until the horse has formed a good mouth; a mouth that flexes and is thereby able and willing to absorb the impulsive forces harmoniously.

The importance of correct flexions (page 65) is paramount. It must be the rider's first and permanent care. On that point, once more, all authorities agree. But not all of them attach the same meaning to the word "first". Some (Baucher, Fillis) advocate "flexions in hand", whereby the horse is taught, with the trainer on the ground, mostly standing still, to yield the lower jaw to the pressure of the bridle-rein. Others (Decarpentry) have pointed out the inconveniences of this method. These are, in my opinion, very real; the effect obtained is not harmonious, it is not the result of impulsion from the quarters; in reality it is an attempt at short-circuiting a difficulty in order to gain time; many of Fillis' photographs show horses with a wide open mouth, which is something very different from flexing, and very much against its principles.

When I say that flexions must be the trainer's first care, I really mean that they must be his first objective; but in my opinion there is not the slightest need to hurry; on the contrary, with patience and tact, flexions, and harmonious ones at that, will presently appear all by themselves.

Strength, in the bridle or in the hands, is not only not needed but deleterious; therefore we do not begin with a double bridle, but with an ordinary mild snaffle; we use the hands gently, avoiding all backward action; we just ride the horse on gently, requiring gradually, not more speed, but increased energy of gait without increased speed; in that way the horse must, and will, meet his bridle. In tactful hands he will very soon begin to show occasional flexions; tactful hands are hands that can feel the appearance of these flexions at once and that will encourage the horse to flex by easing him a little, and at once, each time these flexions make an appearance.

It must be understood from the outset that good flexions, offered by the horse himself, do not impede forward movement; on the contrary they improve it; it is only thanks to them that the best, the freest and the most generous forward movement can in the long run be obtained. In this, the true flexion, the horse accepts his bridle!

That is the quintessence.

All too often riders try to enforce flexions by pulling on the reins; naturally the horse will take evading action, either by sticking his nose out (ewe neck), so as to minimize the effect of the bit, or else by assuming a nicely bridled position, without true contact, behind his bridle! The latter is a position whereby many riders are misled; it is serious, because destructive of forward movement and consequently of reliable control.

The use of an ordinary snaffle, of light hands and of a sustained drive by legs and seat are quite sufficient to obtain the *ramener* (collection of the first degree) and of a very fair measure of collection of the second degree. The idea that horses cannot be made to bridle with the use of a snaffle alone is based on ignorance.

The use and purposes of the double bridle are largely misunderstood. It is a common belief that the double bridle is a sort of safety brake, and there is no denying the fact that, on account of its more powerful action, it is often fitted for just that purpose. In the more advanced forms of riding any form of bit assumes the role of a signalling device, used in conjunction with the legs to unify the rider's control of the horse's balance. In that respect the double bridle is more refined than the snaffle alone, because finer gradations are possible by means of two bits, working in different manners, than can be achieved by one bit alone.

Though sounds can undoubtedly be drawn from a violin with but one string, it is necessary to have all the strings in order to play a concerto.

For the same reason it is necessary, in the advancing stages of our dressage, to resort to the use of a double bridle. Once the horse flexes well and pleasantly in a simple snaffle, a double bridle may be fitted without any fear that the more powerful action whereof that bit is undoubtedly capable will be used, or rather abused, to enforce that which should have been forthcoming of the horse's own free will.

The finer effects which can be obtained by means of a double bridle are its great advantage; the force which can be, but should not be exerted by its use, is an equally great, or perhaps an even greater disadvantage. With the double bridle we have four reins, as against two with the snaffle; an infinite variety of effects can be obtained by the use of each of these reins, either singly, in combination with any other rein or, in combination with any one or other or both legs. It follows that the use of a double bridle makes little sense, excepting in the hands of a rider who possesses the ability to use any one rein independently of any other, as the case may seem to demand.

I say "seem to demand" on purpose, for there is no set rule as to which particular rein may fit any particular purpose; it is all a matter of tact, intuition and careful trial on the rider's part. The main purpose of our bridle is to obtain, and to maintain, peace in the horse's mouth and, by so doing, peace and harmony in the horse's movements. That peace and harmony are at all times as delicate as the horse's balance and rhythm, and constant slight adjustments are essential.

It is quite impossible to lay down any rule as to which rein is to be used for which purpose; sometimes a touch on one or both snaffle reins, at other times a touch on one or both bit reins, or again a cross effect of one snaffle and the opposing bit rein may be indicated; it is essentially the task of the rider handling these four reins to play such particular tune on them as seems best suited to the harmony of the moment.

The full development of the horse's powers are dependent on the rider's ability to harmonize the combined effects of legs and hands for the same purpose, that of forward movement. The difficulty, which is really very great, lies in the correct appreciation of the part which the hands have to play.

In order to obtain the maximum effect of the horse's motive power, it is essential to increase the activity of the horse's quarters by shortening the base whereon the horse moves. That can only be done by demanding increase of energy, or forward impulse, without allowing the horse to translate that increase of energy into greater speed on a longer base, as he would undoubtedly do if there were no bridle to restrain him from doing so.

Here we meet our real difficulty, that of "restraint by the bridle", which, misunderstood and misapplied, can so easily be fatally destructive of the very effect which we hope to attain. Well understood and well applied, that restraint must be passive; the rider merely indicates, by the length of his reins, the place whereat the horse will meet that bridle, and so regulates the amount of tension which the horse (not the rider!) is allowed to exert. Provided the rider is tactful in graduating his demands of energy and the passive resistance offered to the tension exerted by the horse, which should never be more than slight, he will gradually succeed in acceptance of the bridle, flexions, and a shortening of the base.

But if the rider pulls (backward action of the hands) or forces upon the horse more energy than the state of his mouth is able to absorb, he will provoke detrimental effects: the horse will shorten his stride, hurry it, reduce his speed, traverse himself, try to avoid his bridle, or do any or several of these things all at the same time.

It is only by the gradual perfection of the horse's mouth, through and combined with increased energy of the quarters, that the rider will ultimately be able to use that increased energy for the purpose of creating a longer, loftier, more cadenced and balanced stride. That, and not restraint, is the true purpose of the bridle on a well-schooled horse.

CONTROL OF THE QUARTERS
THE HORSE IS ONE AND INDIVISIBLE, REIN OF
OPPOSITION TO THE HAUNCHES

In our discussion of "straightness", I have referred to "Control of the Quarters", as an element in the establishment and maintenance of straightness. I must now make it clear that the expression, as used in that context, refers to lateral control, meaning the rider's ability to displace the horse's quarters away from the straight line, and the ability to prevent such displacement.

We will certainly discuss that particular subject, briefly under this heading, and more fully in following chapters dealing with all work on two tracks.

But before doing so, I would like to make what is, in my opinion, an exceedingly important point!

Expressions such as "control of the quarters", appear to refer to the control of one part of the horse; they, and the sometimes lengthy explanation appertaining to them are apt to lead to the fundamental confusion that the horse can be controlled in parts, that bits and pieces of the horse can be controlled independently of other pieces and bits of the same animal!

It is a very serious confusion, which, once it has taken root in the student's mind, is apt to lead to almost insuperable troubles. It is often difficult for a writer, or a teacher, to avoid creating that confusion; he is obliged, in order to teach at all, to go into very great detail on many aspects of horsemanship, and it is far from easy to convey the complete interdependence of all these details to the student's mind.

It is for that reason that I beg my reader never to forget that the horse is one and indivisible, so in body as in mind!

We can certainly teach our horse the use of our alphabet letter by letter, in fact we cannot do otherwise, but nothing that we teach him can be of any value except as an element in the control of the complete animal in forward movement.

The true answer always lies in forward movement, in front of the leg and on the bit! Other things only matter in so far as they help in improving that control itself and the uses which we shall be able to make of it.

Thus, I hope it will be clear to my readers that there is little point in attempting lateral control of the horse's quarters, unless and until we first possess, and can maintain, forward control pure and simple. By that I do not mean that lateral control cannot be obtained without this forward condition; on the contrary, we see, all too often, horses quite brilliant at moving in every direction of the compass bar straight ahead of them! But in such cases, if there can be any question of control, it is in the horse's and not in the rider's power, contrary of course to the very first principle of horsemanship.

However, lateral control is exerted, whether standing still or in movement, by a combined effect of legs and reins; both legs keep the horse up to his bridle; both reins keep contact with the horse's mouth; if it be desired to move the horse's quarters over to the right, or to prevent these quarters from moving over to the left, the left leg presses the stronger somewhat further behind the girth than the right leg, the latter merely maintaining "forward" pressure; the left rein is drawn towards the withers, acting as a rein of opposition to the haunches, whilst the right rein merely maintains pliable contact.

In the effect here described the action of the left leg and the left rein support each other; they are predominant but are of slight value in themselves unless forward impulse and contact are maintained by the opposing leg and rein.

The movement of the quarters to the right, in answer to the pressure of the left leg, is a conventional obedience by the horse to an aid which has been taught him. But there is nothing compelling about it; the horse is perfectly able to move against the leg, and against the spur, should he feel inclined to defend himself.

The effect of the left rein drawn towards the withers is a natural effect; the horse which has accepted its bridle finds it practically impossible to defeat it. It is natural for the horse to steer with his quarters and to turn around his centre; for instance, he begins a turning movement to the right by swinging his quarters to the left, the forehand following, obviously, to the right. Now the rein of opposition to the haunches, in this case the left rein drawn towards the withers in the direction of the right hip, prevents the horse from swinging his quarters to the left, and his head and forehand are prevented from following the pivot to the right.

If the horse were longitudinally supple, like a cat, or even, in a much lesser degree, like a dog, he would be able to bend his body so as to bring his quarters nearer to his head, notwithstanding the action of our reins. But the horse is longitudinally quite stiff and that type of evasion is not open to him.

The rein of opposition to the haunches can prevent the quarters from moving over against its effect and can also move the quarters over to the other side by its effect.

It is a very powerful aid on any horse that has accepted its bridle; it is the second example of an aid giving the rider almost absolute power over the horse's ability to turn away against the rider's will.

The technique of its use, and the schooling of the horse generally in lateral effects, will be discussed in a later chapter.

CHAPTER XI

CONSIDERATIONS FROM THE SADDLE

Objects – Muscular development – Reward and punishment(?) – Use of the whip – Use of the spur – Use of the leg – The hands – Surrender of the hands (la descente de Main) – Riding with one hand

OBJECTS OF SCHOOLING

THE objects of any schooling given to the horse may be summarized, in order of importance, as (first) keeping the horse calm; (second) confirming the horse in what he knows already; and (third) progress.

If the rider fails in the first object, he fails inevitably in all three.

The second and the third objects merge into one another to some extent, in that methodical confirmation is in itself a form of progress and is at the same time the only sound basis for still further progress.

With these objects in view, I follow invariably the same programme. I begin with five or ten minutes' free walk on a long rein, just airing the horse agreeably, without asking him any questions. I may then take a light feel on the reins, ask for a shade more energy and a flexion or two of the mouth. Subsequently I trot around a bit, varied with some walking in between, until I feel that my horse is beginning to supple up nicely. All this may take perhaps twenty minutes. For the next half-hour or so I get the horse to do basic work of mostly trot, some walking and perhaps a little cantering, in good form, but well within his limits and below the best standard of which he is capable. I see that my horse keeps cool. I follow this up with five minutes or so of walking on a loose rein. The next part of my lesson is then devoted to going through the same basic work once more, but this time I work my horse gradually up to the best standard of which he is capable and if, but only if, I feel he is going well, I may try for just a little further improvement in this basic work. I may, during this stage of the school, ask for a very great deal of energy, but I never do so for longer than a couple of minutes at a time. I see that my horse keeps cool. I ease my horse frequently, in fact every time he has given me reasonable satisfaction; that is the best form of reward, the one appreciated most and understood best by the horse. I follow this second period of my school by another rest of about ten minutes, walking on a free rein.

Finally I spend a few minutes, perhaps five or ten at the most, to practise any of the newer and therefore more difficult work which my horse has not yet mastered. I do this particularly carefully; I ask any new movement once only, for a few steps, ease my horse for many steps, repeat three or four times, and take him to his stable. My horses know this final programme very well indeed, and are fully conscious that they have only to do their best for a few minutes in order to secure a nice rub-down, a feed and a complete rest for the remainder of the day.

It is quite a simple method, logical, or so it seems to me, within the scope of any rider and applicable to any horse. Followed methodically it may save a great deal of quite unnecessary trouble. The greatest mistake any trainer can make is to attempt to rush his results! The less experienced are so easily misled into striving for spectacular results, such as changes of leg for instance, before a sound basis of balance and resilience has been laid.

MUSCULAR DEVELOPMENT

When *we* do some unaccustomed work, particularly if it is strenuous, we soon feel stiffness, and indeed pain, in such muscles as have been submitted to unusual strain. That pain and stiffness may well last for days. One has to think of the results of an excess of energy, suddenly setting out to dig, or even only to weed, the garden!

Now it is precisely so with the horse. Only, as we do not

feel it ourselves, we are apt to forget it. This may be quite serious. In bringing the horse on to new work, we are requiring efforts, sometimes quite strenuous ones, which bring untrained or insufficiently trained muscles into play. If, ignoring this, we prolong the strain on these untrained muscles just that much too long, and it need not be much either, we cause stiffness, pain, and quite possibly even actual cramp.

The whole idea of dressage is to increase all-round suppleness in every muscle, sinew and joint. So if, instead of improving pliability all the time, we induce stiffness, even temporarily, we go against the very principle that we wish to pursue.

Stiffness anywhere, as I have already pointed out, leads to stiffness everywhere and is, as has been pointed out also, reflected in the horse's mouth.

What is more, if the action of any particular muscle is uncomfortable to the horse, he will try to avoid using it, naturally, precisely as we would do ourselves. Accordingly we are in effect, by causing these evasions, teaching the horse the use of them!

Obviously then, we have to go steadily, always, in the practice of any new work, in order to bring muscular development along gradually and in careful steps. The horse cannot tell us in so many words that we are overtaxing his capabilities. None the less, provided we are observant and on the alert, the signs that we are doing just that are often clear enough. The horse may signal discomfort by laying back his ears, by obvious evasions and finally by obvious irritation and a show of temper. The rider who calls such conditions into being has lost sight of the fact, that "keeping the horse calm" is the very first object of any schooling.

Reward and Punishment(?)

Many books about riding make a great deal of play about getting results by means of reward and punishment. I don't know.

There are two forms of reward particularly appreciated by the horse; the first is a calm and confident rider to whom he can give his unmitigated confidence; the second is an observant and sensible rider, who eases him often, in prompt appreciation of an effort well done.   I can see no reason why these two forms of reward should not be always with the horse.

And as to punishment, well, I think I do know; or at any rate I hold a most determined opinion!   I have never yet seen any case of real punishment do any horse any good, but I have seen a goodly many horses ruined in the process.   A capable rider, who knows what he wants and who has the understanding, the tact and the patience to see that he gets it through quiet determination,   will   need   no   other   form   of   punishment. Naturally, any horse may be a little naughty at times, or a little cunning; he may suddenly get it into his head to sham inability to do some particular work which he finds especially strenuous, or for some other reason not very much to his liking; then, provided the rider is quite certain that the demand made by him is within the horse's capabilities, that the question has been put to him properly and that the horse is shamming, or naughty, he may certainly use a flick of the whip or a touch of the spur somewhat more severely than normal.   But such action is only a call to order and need not, and should not, degenerate into punishment.   Certainly, the well-trained horse must respect his rider, but it is of the utmost importance, in my opinion, that he shall not fear him, nor his spur, nor his whip!

USE OF THE WHIP

The use of the whip, as the rider's third hand, was referred to on page 35 in conjunction with work from the ground.   The use of the whip from the saddle is equally valuable in all stages of the horse's training, from the most elementary to the most advanced.   I never work without one, excepting of course in a competition, when one is expected to show results and not a school.

The horse understands the actions of the whip more naturally, and therefore more easily, than that of actions with the leg; for one thing he cannot only feel the action of the whip, but he can see it as well; provided the whip be always used sensibly, so that its action is not feared by the horse, the fact that he can see it is a decided advantage.   No aid, of whatever kind, ought ever to startle the horse; aids should always approach progressively, so that the horse knows that they are coming; it is only so that he can prepare himself to give the required answer smoothly.

In the first place then, the whip is used for the purpose of teaching the horse the meaning of the use of the leg. Later the whip may be used to support the action of the leg; in certain cases it is better fitted to do so than the spur, because the radius of useful action of leg and spur is very small, and that of the action of the whip almost unlimited; with it we can influence almost any part of the horse's anatomy.

Finally, in the advanced stages of training, the whip gives us a means of encouraging energetic use of the horse's shoulder.

Accordingly, I thoroughly recommend the carrying of a whip as a valuable aid for occasional use. But for occasional use only! It is meant as a support to other aids, mainly those of the legs, in cases where these might fail to achieve either the full, or the precise, effect expected.

The whip should be used sparingly; though I always carry one, I may go for days, or even weeks, without ever resorting to its use, other than as a fly-whisk.

Use of the Spur

The use of spurs is essential in all stages of horse-training, except in the most elementary ones. We cannot obtain refined results unless the horse learns to answer implicitly to extremely finely shaded actions of the leg; these may vary from the slightest squeeze with the top of the calf to a graduated approach of the lower leg, culminating in a touch of the spur. If there be no spur we would have none but the heel of the boot to rely on; the heel of a boot is much too clumsy an accessory to allow of its application with any precision, on the required spot exactly; moreover its effect on the horse is liable to be insufficient and undetermined, unless it be used with great strength, kicking, and perhaps doing so repeatedly.

There is nothing against the use of spurs; no harshness or cruelty should be involved, since spurs need not be sharp enough to pierce the skin and draw blood; only just sharp enough to be felt distinctly when they touch, or brush, the horse's coat. I never use spurs other than with the rowels well filed down.

Obviously spurs, in order to do any good, must, exactly as the whip, be used sensibly, with care, and in such a manner that the horse neither fears nor resents them.

Quite obviously also, the use of the spur and its meaning do not come naturally to the horse; he has to learn about them, as about everything else, by gradual steps. On the young horse, just broken, we use no spur; instead of that we use, when called for, the application of the whip just behind our heel and simultaneously with it. By and by we begin using a dummy spur, without rowels; this, which is never resented by any horse, is already a considerable improvement on the bare heel, since it allows of much greater precision. In time, we replace the dummy spurs with very blunt rowels, with points almost completely filed down or worn away. Generally speaking, these are all that we shall ever need, although it may be advisable occasionally, on horses already very far advanced in their training, to resort to slightly sharper spurs for a few days in order to obtain enhanced obedience to them in certain exercises.

The above describes my method of teaching the horse the use of the spur.

Some of the older books, and famous ones amongst them, teach a very different method, that of the "lesson of the spur" (la leçon de l'éperon). Briefly, the horse is submitted to a prolonged "attack" with the spurs, to drive him forward, whilst being held forcibly in place by the bridle, with a view to forcing him into a state of abject surrender, "enclosed" as he is between the combined effect of spur and bridle. The horse is overpowered into submission by helplessness. Such are no longer the methods of our time. Whether the results obtained by them in olden days were worth having is, to say the least of it, open to doubt. At any rate it was said of Baucher's horses that "they worked with clockwork regularity, but in a state of deadly sadness" (Aubert).

At any rate, "attacks" by means of the spurs, or by any other means, have no place in methods of training that aim at a bright and willing execution of the rider's wishes by a confident and happy horse.

The use of the spur, on the horse standing still, is sometimes advocated to cause a flexion. It is perfectly true that a light touch of the spur on the collected horse standing still will bring about a form of flexion very readily; the horse appears to say "yes", he will yield his jaw but, he will also bend the neck at about the third or fourth vertebra behind the poll. Not therefore at the poll!   Accordingly, we are not here dealing with a correct form of flexion; besides, flexions, except in movement, mean little and are of no real value. The practice is therefore not recommended.

USE OF THE LEG

The basic purpose of the leg is to cause, and to maintain, impulsion. To cause the horse to move forward, or to increase his energy during forward movement, the leg increases its pressure; the increase begins just below the knee and, as the need of the moment may demand, travels gradually down the leg, maybe until the spur touches the horse's flank. But not necessarily until then. It is of the essence of good riding that the rider shall be able to cease his leg aid as soon as the horse responds to the call that is being made on him. The rider's leg aid is in reality a force of pressure which travels down his lower leg, inch by inch, as more and more of that lower leg assumes a more intimate contact with the horse's flank.

I have spoken of "increase" of pressure; quite, because there is always some pressure, "dormant" if we like, due to the weight of the leg, or rather of the upper part of the lower leg, resting against the horse's flank and therefore "in contact" with that flank.

That form of contact should never be broken; it is just by that very contact that horse and rider "feel" each other's every movement.

This leg aid, by increased pressure travelling down the leg, is not given, at any rate not normally, in the form of a continuous squeeze, but rather in the form of a very brief momentary squeeze, just touching the horse's flank, culminating, if need be, in the briefest of touches with the spur. If necessary a succession of brief squeezes, or touches, may succeed each other.

The aid of the spur should never be any other than a mere fleeting touch; any continued squeeze with the spur is absolutely debarred; but a more continuous form of squeeze of the calf of the leg alone may have its uses and can then be used to good effect without detriment.

It will be seen that the leg is always in contact, active contact when a driving aid is given, passive contact so soon as the horse responds, and for so long as the horse delivers the precise amount of impulsion required by the rider.

Some authors have described the passive position as that of the leg being still; to appearances yes, but actually, no!   Since the leg rests in close contact against the horse's flanks, and since these flanks are always in motion, it follows that the leg itself is always in motion, be it passively, in sympathy with the movements of these flanks.   Or at any rate that is as it should be, if the rider is supple and his legs are supple.

At any rate, from the point of view of appearances, the leg should always appear to be still, or almost so, whether active or passive!   Moments of activity and of passivity are bound to follow each other more or less all the time, as rider and horse talk to each other, adjust their mutual balance and the effective amount of impulsion required to maintain that balance in the best form from moment to moment.

The better the horse is schooled, and the better the rider knows his job, the slighter and the more subtle will be the difference between the active and the passive use of the leg. And the finer these differences are graduated, the more smoothly will the horse answer to their effects.

THE HANDS

It is also one of the accepted truisms in riding that the hands shall be still.   Again, to appearances yes, but actually no!   The intricate task, which it is incumbent upon the hands to fulfil in riding, cannot possibly be fulfilled properly, or at all, by any positively still, and therefore rigid member.

The requirement that the hands shall be still is to be taken in the sense that they shall be quiet and restful and able to refrain from making any unnecessary or involuntary movement. The most common form of involuntary movement, wherefrom so many riders appear to suffer, is that of hands bobbing up and down, together with the body; it is a basic fault, very serious, which makes restful control quite impossible. Obviously, this is in the first place due to a faulty seat, since there is no need for any bobbing up and down, at whatever gait, if the rider's seat remains comfortably in the saddle. The fault is due in the second place to the rider's inability to hold and use hands and arms independently from the body to which they are attached; arms and hands are quite long enough, and equipped with a sufficiency of pliable joints, which ought to make it quite easy really, to obviate the necessity of transmitting movement of the body to the hands.

One of the reasons for this faulty interdependence of arms with hands and body is the teaching given in so many ordinary riding-schools, where the pupil is told to hold the elbows close to his flanks, in fact touching them. This causes stiffness in the shoulder, in the upper arm, elbow and hand and is therefore very wrong. The upper arm should hang down from the shoulder quite naturally, loose and straight; neither pinched in to the rider's sides, nor, of course, with the elbows stuck out away from the body, which is equally stiff and, besides, distinctly ugly. The forearm should be carried forward from a completely relaxed elbow joint; the forearm will point in the direction of the horse's mouth, usually therefore in a slightly downward direction. To avoid stiffness it is desirable that the line from the horse's mouth, through rein, hand, wrist and forearm, to the rider's elbow shall be more or less straight and not interrupted by angular joints. In that respect again, the position of the hands so often seen, and taught, with the wrists markedly bent inwards, is quite wrong.

The wrist-joint is nothing like sensitive enough, and too slow in its action, to be able to play a delicate tune on the reins. Only the fingers can do that! And even then only if no stiff wrist, elbow or shoulder prevents them from exercising the full measure of their agility!

The reins are handled by the fingers; the true role of hand and arm is limited to that of having the fingers in the appropriate place at the appropriate moment. Quite obviously that cannot be done without a certain amount of movement, now a little more forward, then back, a little higher, or lower, somewhat more to the left or to the right, and so on. But such movements need only be slight and should be quiet and unobtrusive, to give the onlooker the illusion that the hands are still.   Displacement of the hands implies movement of the arm, and even though such movement is comparatively slight, it must be unimpeded.   In other words the arm must be able to slide forward and backward, from the shoulder joint down, without meeting any obstruction from the body.   Once more then, the position so often seen, and apparently taught, with the hands held, wrists bent inwards, in front of the rider's tummy and frequently almost touching it, is quite incompatible with reasonable rein-control.

The position of the hand itself is perfectly natural, in prolongation of the forearm; exactly as when lifting the forearm to shake hands with someone, with the thumb uppermost.

The fingers, the hand, the wrist, the forearm, the elbow, the shoulders are all relaxed and remain relaxed.   The fingers handle the reins but do not grip them; if they grip they can no longer handle.

The action of the hands is the single most important element in the rider's armoury, because it is they that form the link with the horse's most sensitive element, his mouth.

It is through the medium of the reins that the hands receive the effect created by impulsion in the horse's mouth; the effect of that impulsion is always forward, towards a destination well in front of the horse's mouth, a destination which the good horse, well ridden, is eager to pursue; the hands are there, and the reins are there, for the sole purpose of tempering the effect of that forward impulsion just sufficiently to keep the resultant forward movement of the horse balanced.

That is the primary, the principal purpose of hands and reins, only just that: to regulate the balance, and with it the rhythm, of the moving horse; just as easy, and just as light, as adjusting the needle of a pair of scales which are almost equally loaded. Almost, but not quite.   The well-ridden, properly trained horse is by himself "almost" perfectly balanced, but never "quite" for any length of time; variations in pace or direction, variations in levels or nature of going, variations in impulsion and other factors all make for slight variations in balance; the needle has to be kept in the centre!   That is the primary purpose of the hands.

They fulfil that purpose through their effect on the horse's mouth.   But to fulfil that purpose well, their effect must never exceed the precise minimum needed for the maintenance of "forward moving balance"; they must never interfere with that forward movement itself!

Here lies the greatest difficulty. If the hand fails to accompany the forward impulse, the effect of that forward impulse will be impaired; if the hand actually counteracts the forward movement by backward action, that movement will be ruined. Any untoward action, backwards, on the sensitive mouth of a good horse, automatically restricts the movement of the shoulder and with it, of course, the movement of the hocks.

Actually, correct rein-effects, by the very fact of insuring the optimum of balance, assist the forward movement. But rein-effects can be correct only if the horse accepts them fully, freely and smilingly in his mouth. The hands must be able to keep the horse's mouth happy and to obtain flexion from that mouth as and when desired. It has been explained, in the description of "combined effects", that the hands cannot do all this without the help of the legs, that the two effects must work together. Quite so, but there is nothing in riding which ensures results automatically, not even the use of combined effects; it is not so much what we do, as how we do it; this is true in particular of anything connected with the horse's mouth. Force or mere restraint will not help.

The hand must be very tactful; more than that, the hand must be so tactful and delicate that it can cajole the horse's mouth into surrender by subtle insinuation travelling along the rein.

The rein itself, light, soft and pliable, is a wonderfully sensitive organ of control; it weighs hardly anything, yet any variation in the weight of a loose-hanging rein is felt instantly, so by the sensitive hand as by the sensitive mouth. Variations in weight occur through variations of length and through variations of slack taken up by mouth or hand. In all forms of riding a well-schooled horse there is contact through the rein between hand and mouth; even on a loose rein, when contact, though at its weakest, is still maintained by the weight of the rein alone.

It follows that the intensity of the contact between mouth and hand may vary almost *ad infinitum*, from the positive contact of a rein taut by a forward pressure exerted by the horse, to the minimum contact through the weight of a loose rein.

It is the function of the hand to "feel" the degree of contact commensurate with the horse's comfort, balance and action at any given moment; it is up to the hand to "feel" whether there shall be light tension on a rein just taut, or whether equally good or possibly better contact may be achieved on a rein somewhat less than taut; for, be it noted, the well-schooled horse can quite well go "on the bit", even though the rein be somewhat slack!   Finally, it is an important function of the hand to determine the best distance from the hand, commensurate with the horse's action and balance, whereat the horse's mouth shall make contact with the bridle; in other words the hands have to determine the best length of rein to be used, and with it the effective length of the horse's neck.   Again, be it noted, that the well-schooled horse shall flex equally effectively with a long as with a short rein and no matter at what distance from the rider's hand his mouth shall meet the bridle.

In this way, by means of variations of contact, of length of rein and of weight of rein, the rider may achieve the subtle insinuations suggested.   Usually the ability to make these simple variations of contact, according to conditions, in an even and progressive manner, is quite sufficient to maintain or to re-establish comfort in the horse's mouth.   But occasionally a tremolo effect may be more effective, achieved through sending a slight wave down one rein.

SURRENDER OF THE HANDS
(La Descente de Main)

In the preceding paragraphs I have endeavoured to convey the action of the hands in their function of controlling the horse. But in dressage there are moments when the rider may choose to abandon hand-control altogether, without affecting the horse's gait, balance, speed and bearing in the slightest; in fact, moments arise when this freedom from control may actually help the horse's performance.

It can only be done on the very well-schooled horse, who is so fully confirmed in his balance and paces that he will continue the work which he is doing in his best form, and without alteration, whilst completely free, for a time, from all perceptible control.

Normally, the horse is in a sense a prisoner, enclosed between the effects of hand and leg.   When the rider abandons these controls, the horse becomes, according to the picturesque description of Général Détroyat, a "prisoner on parole".

Assuming that the horse has settled to the rhythm and bearing required of him, the rider's leg will be passive, since there is no need to stimulate impulsion which is already there in the desired degree; the rider may now carry his hands frankly forward, and usually in a somewhat downward direction (*la descente de main*), so that there is no longer any direct contact between hand and mouth. The horse "on parole" will continue his work completely unaffected.

It indicates a very high degree of training and confirms that the perfection of balance under saddle has become completely natural to the horse, and effortless. It is mentioned by de la Guérinière, Baucher, and Général Decarpentry, but appears unknown in English literature.

The German school know the effect well, and cultivate it; they require its application, by way of proof, in their dressage tests in a form which they call *überstreichen*; in this the rider is required to bring his hand, holding the reins, right up and down the crest of the horse's neck, stroking his mane. Naturally this implies, and shows visibly, that there is no rein-contact between hand and mouth during this operation.

But apart from its significance by way of proof, this purposeful abandonment of rein-control, surrender of the hands, *descente de main* or *überstreichen*, has inestimable value as a means of calming the horse, keeping his mouth fresh and happy, or even overcoming slight disturbance in the mouth.

Even the very slightest degree of irritation felt by the horse will set up some stiffening of the jaw; the complete surrender of the hand described is usually fully effective in restoring complete harmony; the horse will at once flex with a smile and champ his bit.

The quintessence of this surrender of the hand is that the horse shall not alter his head carriage or his speed by one iota. The action and its effect is therefore totally different from that of lengthening the rein, in order to allow the horse to stretch his neck, to lower the head carriage and to extend himself. Two diametrically opposed implications therefore of almost the same aid; almost, but not quite; in the surrender of the hands, the leg remains inactive, telling the horse that the cadence of his pace, and the head carriage appertaining to it, shall remain the same; in lengthening the rein, the pressure of the leg which accompanies the gesture causes the horse to extend.

Naturally, we have here a finely shaded difference, which none by the very finely-schooled horse can learn to distinguish.

RIDING WITH ONE HAND

It will, I hope, be obvious that the function of the hands in riding is of the utmost importance and far from easy; there are two sides to every horse and two sides also to every horse's mouth; these two distinct sides are not, as a rule, evenly developed by nature; we will see presently that it takes a great deal of work to even-out discrepancies in that respect, and that in doing this work the hands play a preponderant part. The hands must play their effects by means of four reins on both sides of the horse's mouth in all sorts of combinations. Two hands and ten fingers are none too many for a correct and harmonious performance in this respect; the artist on the horse needs his ten fingers just as much as the artist on the piano.

So, in any serious riding, we use both hands; there is not the slightest merit in trying to do with one hand that which can be done infinitely better with two.

Naturally, in any work wherein the horse is at ease, one hand may be quite sufficient.

Riding with one hand only may be demanded, by way of special proof, during exercises requiring difficult transitions in advanced competitions (Grand Prix). It is to show, not that the rider can ride with one hand, but that the horse is so fully confirmed in extended and collected paces that the transitions from one into the other are light and effortless.

CHAPTER XII

THE TURN ON THE FOREHAND
(PRELIMINARY FORM)

T H E turn on the forehand, in its perfect form, is a small circle on two tracks described round the forehand in the position "shoulder-in" (*Epaule en dedans*); it is then the correct *pirouette sur les épaules*, which will be discussed more fully under "work on two tracks".

In its preliminary form it is a simple lesson, very easy to teach, whereby the horse learns to obey the lateral effect of one leg, in the first place, and at the same time the combined lateral effect of one rein and one leg used to the same side.

It is quite essential that every horse should acquire this obedience, for such simple everyday purposes as opening gates and so on, and it is so easy to teach that it can be undertaken in the very early stages of a horse's schooling. It is, in fact, something so utterly simple that every horse with stable manners knows it, and performs it, on the command of his groom to "get over". In "getting over" in his stall, or when racked up in his box, the horse does neither more nor less than describe part of a pivot round his forehand by displacing his quarters to one side.

Though the horse will learn this lateral displacement of the quarters quite easily, it is yet pertinent to observe that this type of movement is not natural to him; naturally, the lateral mobility of his quarters is limited, he does not normally use them in that way.

In dressage it is a basic exercise which the horse must know, since we could not get anywhere, in later work, without lateral control. But, apart from its necessity as an introductory lesson to lateral control, the exercise as such possesses definite values of its own.

In pivoting round the forehand, the hindlegs must step side-ways in a pronounced manner; in so doing they assist to a considerable degree in developing the elasticity of the muscles of the loins. And the development of these muscles, and their pliability, is one of our most important objects in training our horse!

One is so easily apt to associate movement with use of the limbs, that one is inclined to forget that the real source of power of the limbs lies in the muscles of the loins. Any development of movement must be based on development of the loins. That applies to the horse just as much as it does to humans; any impairment of the function of the loin-muscles impairs movement itself; any serious impairment may preclude movement altogether (lumbago!).

Mobility of the loins, in the horse, is also connected, perhaps mysteriously but none the less indubitably so, with mobility of the mouth; no good mouth is possible in a horse with stiff loins. Now, as it so happens, the exercise of the turn of the forehand is a preliminary means of exerting a beneficial influence on the loins and on the mouth at the same time.

For, let us see how the movement is done.

We halt the horse squarely, with the head carried in a normal position. We intend to move the horse's quarters over to the right. We shall use pressure of the left leg behind the girth. But we intend that the effect of the left leg shall be supported by the effect of the left rein; we mean to use this left rein in opposition to the haunches, by drawing it towards the withers, exerting a slight pull in the direction of the right hip. In order to be able to do so the horse's head and neck must be bent somewhat to the left. So, we begin with an even feel on both reins; relaxing the right rein enough to cause the horse to turn his head slightly to the left will place him in the right position to commence the movement.

We now touch the left snaffle rein gently, acting on the corner of the mouth, feeling our way towards a careful tension, intermittent if need be, in the desired direction. We support this action of the rein simultaneously by the action of the leg, also intermittent if need be.

Now it is a fact that flexions of the jaw are always easier to obtain by the effect of one rein than by the effect of both; a flexion of the neck itself is conducive to flexions of the jaw;

and so is mobility of the quarters! Thus, we have here a most simple exercise, easy to do carefully and quietly, wherein all factors conducive to creating a commencement of mobility of the jaw and of the quarters are about ideally combined.

It is the object of the exercise to obtain both effects. Simply pushing the quarters round by pressure of the leg alone is of little value; the rider performing in that way has not understood the purpose of the movement.

It is pertinent to add that the front legs are not required, as is so often believed, to stay more or less anchored on the spot; in fact, to be quite correct, the front legs ought to describe a very small circle round a point closely in front of them. This may well make the impression on an onlooker as if the front legs were slightly stepping back. In actual fact, they would not be doing that, as we shall see presently when it comes to discussing circles on two tracks. Suffice it for the moment to state that a turn on the forehand should not be faulted because the horse gives the impression of stepping back. But the movement is distinctly faulty if the horse steps forward, and of course also if he does not accept the rein-effect.

This movement is asked in elementary dressage competitions; a full turn (360°) is seldom required; more usually a half-turn (180°); in such a case the rider must show that he has the movement under complete control, by doing the turn quietly, evenly and neatly, halting the horse precisely in the required position. Frequently the horse is seen to do one or two steps too many, which is not up to requirements.

CHAPTER XIII

CIRCULAR TRACKS

---

*Lateral flexibility – Physical development – Rein-effects –
The direct rein – The indirect rein – Seat and position of
rider – Leg effects – Alteration of direction – Circular figures
– The volt – Riding through the corners – Other circular
figures*

T H E riding of circular tracks is the most important of all
training exercises.

Its purposes and effects are many.

Going on a circle the horse has to bend his body, from his head
to his quarters, to conform to the shape of the track. This is not
easy for the horse. His spine, between withers and quarters, has
but little lateral flexibility; in sympathy the muscles of the loins,
which lie to either side of the spinal column, are not used to that
sort of lateral flexion of the back either. If the horse circles
to the right, the muscles to that side of the loin contract
and those to the other side of the loin extend. The exercise
of extending and contracting these muscles is beneficial to
their flexibility, suppleness and strength. We know how
important those muscles are to the action of the quarters
(impulsion), so it follows that, by improving the muscular
structure of the horse's loins, we improve his capacity for
action.

Though it is much easier for the horse to bend his neck, in
front of the withers, than his back, it is yet true to say that the
horse comes none too easily to lateral flexions of the neck. Yet
again, a degree of improvement in that lateral flexibility is of
considerable importance. Hence once more we remark that the
attractor muscles, responsible for moving the forearm of the

front legs, are attached to either side of the horse's neck. Improved resilience of these attractor muscles benefits the ease and power of his movement in front.

I have here spoken of "a degree of improvement of the lateral flexibility of the neck" on purpose. I believe that ample improvement in this respect can be achieved by riding the normal circular tracks, and the exercises on two tracks to be discussed in a later chapter, without any need to resort to the special neck-bending exercises, standing still, advocated by Baucher and Fillis. Others have pointed out, and I share that opinion fully, that no advantage is derived from an excessively flexible "rubber" neck. I believe the disadvantages of that particular procedure to outweigh the advantages and, at any rate, I am not fond of any work not done in movement.

As will be discussed in a later chapter, the trot is the gait *par excellence* for most of our schooling. The trot is a pace of two-time, in which diagonal pairs of legs, near-hind and off-fore, off-hind and near-fore, function together, with a moment of suspension as each pair of legs leaves the ground. It follows that in any normal trot, on a straight line, each hind-leg and each foreleg belonging to the same diagonal pair, travel precisely the same distance.

Obviously, trotting along a circular track, this is no longer so!

On a circular track, say to the right, the right foreleg and the right hindleg follow the smaller, and the left foreleg and the left hindleg the larger of two concentric circles. It follows that the legs travelling on the outer circle have to take longer strides than the legs on the inner circle. This would be of little consequence, but for the fact that the left hindleg, which has to make a long stride on the outer circle, is a pair with the right foreleg making a short stride on the inner circle! And *vice-versa* for the right hindleg and the left foreleg! This discrepancy may not be very material on a large circle but it is most definitely so as the radius of the circle decreases. It requires a degree of adjustment in the horse's locomotion which is not inconsiderable; unless the horse make that adjustment, his balance and his rhythm will be affected. Hence the undoubted difficulty in maintaining unaltered rhythm, and unimpaired impulsion, in riding small circular tracks at the trot.

The difficulty is not so material at the walk, which is a pace of four-time, wherein all four legs move independently of each other, nor in the canter, which is a pace of three-time.

It will be understood also, that the legs to the inside of the circle carry a greater part of the horse's weight than the outside legs; this affects in particular the inner hindleg, which has to develop considerably increased energy.

Taking these various factors into consideration, the bending, the adjustment of stride and rhythm, the increased effort imposed on the inside hindleg, it is clear that we have, in the circular track, a physical exercise of the highest order.

It is not an easy exercise for the horse, and much time is required to perfect him at it. Naturally, we must begin with large, or even very large circles, reducing the radius only gradually, in accordance with the horse's proficiency.

I have mentioned several times already that flexions are obtained more easily by the effect of one rein than by the effect of two. In that respect also, the circles are most helpful in obtaining flexions, both from the jaw and at the poll, quite naturally.

Provided only that we use the correct rein, seat and leg effects!

Before discussing these effects, it had better be pointed out that the horse is not ready to derive benefit from work on circular tracks until he has achieved a fair measure of acceptance of the bridle, head carriage and collection.

Assuming that to be the case, we will examine these effects.

Most books on riding teach us to use the direct opening rein, when wishing to alter direction; so, to turn right, we shorten the right rein, and, to turn the other way, the left rein. And that, in effect, is what most people appear to do when attempting a circular movement. There are two serious inconveniences. In the first place, it is essential that, in a circular movement, the horse shall be able to bend his head and neck freely to conform with the parabola of the movement. And, however much we use the direct rein, the horse will be quite unable to bend to its effect unless we lengthen at the same time the opposing, or indirect rein, proportionately.

And that is precisely what any number of riders seem to overlook entirely. As a result we see a horse being more or less forced on to a circle, held tightly between a "pull" on both reins. Through the pull, or backward action, of both reins, impulsion and rhythm are destroyed, as also the possibility for the horse to bend; the exercise, done in this manner, is a travesty of the circle, and valueless.

The rider who uses the direct rein to "open" the turning movement of his horse, but who remembers to lengthen the indirect rein, so that the horse shall not be prevented from bending, does very much better, and can ride a quite acceptable circular movement. But even his action is by no means ideal!

Let us examine this proposition rather more closely.

Again, almost every riding book tells us that we have to use pressure of our outside leg, on the circle, to prevent the horse swinging his quarters out.

Now why is that?

In the system of lungeing that I use (Chapter IV), I do not get that trouble; I let my horse go freely on a very lightly held lungeing rein, which effects no pull on the horse's head. Precisely, no pull! Consequently, the horse flexes himself *without hinder* to the direction of the track.

And the circular track is a direction!

It is not a turn!

The way a horse turns naturally is on his centre; to turn his forehand to the right, he swings his quarters to the left (Chapter VI, p. 75). If the horse swings his quarters out, on the circle, he does so because he is ridden as if to turn. He is so ridden by the use of the direct or opening rein. Using that rein to bring the horse's head round, we have to shorten it, which cannot be done, however gently, without exerting some pull. Some pull in the direction of the quarters; the action of the rein in that position is so similar to that of the rein of opposition to the haunches (Chapter X, p. 122) as to make no matter; and, since we know that the action of the rein of opposition to the haunches causes the horse to move his quarters over, it follows that the use of the direct or opening rein has precisely the same effect.

Now it is perfectly true that this swinging the quarters out effect of an opening rein is not so strong that it cannot be countered by a contrary effect from the leg, pushing the quarters back again. But, surely, there is no point in creating effects that we do not want, even though we may be able to neutralize them again; particularly so, as all such contrary effects must affect the horse's rhythm and forward movement adversely. And, above all, why do so if a much cleaner rein-effect is at our disposal, whereby these difficulties can be avoided?

I refer to the use of the indirect rein.

I will explain.

The riding of circular movements is essentially a form of collected riding. Consequently, when riding to commence a circle, we have the horse collected, in front of the legs, straight, and on the bit with even contact on both reins. Now, to commence the circle, there is no need whatever to take any action with the direct or opening rein. Instead, we lengthen the indirect rein. In circling to the right, we lengthen the left rein. Since we take no action with the right rein at all, the question of setting up a force of opposition to the haunches does not arise. But we have our horse well in front of our legs, maintaining undiminished impulsion; the effect of this impulsion causes him to re-establish equal contact with both sides of his mouth; he does that by bending his neck to the right. Which is exactly what we want!

And our manner of obtaining it has many advantages, apart from that of avoiding opposition to the haunches.

We do not shorten the horse; we do not alter the length of his stride, nor his speed, nor his cadence. In fact, since the sum total of our two reins is greater than it was before, we lengthen him; we allow a certain amount of extension to his neck; this allows him to carry the head a little lower, encouraging him to flex. It lightens the extra effort imposed by the circular track on the inside hindleg. Last but not least, it is a method of confirming the horse in the invaluable habit of pursuing his bridle, of looking for it and of seeking, himself, to maintain contact!

This then, explains the principle in its simplest form. On a large circle, nothing else is needed. But on a small circle, the rein-effects become slightly more complicated. On a small circle, we require a considerable degree of flexion of the neck; to achieve it, we have to lengthen the indirect rein a good deal and, in so doing, the sum total of the length of both reins; too much in fact to maintain the horse's position and balance intact. Consequently, on the smaller circles, we are obliged to shorten the length of the direct rein sufficiently to cause the horse to contact his bridle in the right position. But, and this is important, whilst we lengthen the indirect rein to permit the degree of flexion required, we shorten the length of the direct rein just enough to insure continued contact by the horse on both reins. Without pulling on the direct rein. Merely enabling the horse to keep contact at the correct distance from our hand!

This lengthening of the indirect rein, to cause flexion to the opposite side, is its primary effect. It can be used on any horse, no matter what the stage of his training, provided only that there exists a fair acceptance of the bridle.

There is a secondary effect that may be used with advantage on horses that are far advanced in their training. It is the effect of exerting a light pressure with the indirect rein against the horse's neck. It is mainly useful in beginning a circle, in riding through corners and in gradually reducing the radius of the circle, as for instance in riding a spiral track.

To turn to the right then, we lengthen the left (indirect) rein, we adjust the length of the right (direct) rein, and we bring the left (indirect) rein to bear against the horse's neck, supporting the tendency to the right.

But we are here on dangerous ground! In the first place, the amount of pressure exerted must be so slight that the horse cannot feel any resultant effect of the indirect rein on his bridle; if he did it would be a backward effect, detrimental to his forward movement and to his flexion. In the second place the pressure must be so slight that it does not take the horse's forehand to the inside of the pure circular track intended. In other words the horse must not be neck-reined, and swung, as in polo!

Slight effects of this kind cannot be operative until the horse is already very well balanced, sensitive and light to the aids.

But, apart from that limitation, the secondary effect of the indirect rein is really a logical outcome of the use of the rider's seat and position in the saddle during circular movements. The horse's balance and rhythm, during these movements, is delicately adjusted and easily disturbed; it is most essential that the "unity of balance" between horse and rider be as near perfect as possible. The rider's seat, his body above the saddle, not forgetting his head, have to follow in sympathy with the horse; the rider must flex, just as the horse flexes; to lengthen the indirect rein, the rider's outside arm, hip and shoulder move forward; to adjust the length of the direct rein, his inside arm, hip and shoulder move backward; as the horse's neck flexes to one side, so does the rider's; as the horse's entire body leans over towards the inside of the circle, so does the rider's, precisely in the same degree; as the rider's body heels over towards the inside of the circle, so do his hands, both of them; the heeling over of the outside hands needs to be accentuated but a trifle to cause the indirect rein to bear against the horse's neck; as the horse looks where he is going, on the circular track, so does the rider!

In the beginning of the training, the rider "follows" his horse.

Later in the training, the rider "accompanies" his horse.

Finally in the training, the horse "accompanies" his rider.

The need for the horse, and the rider, to lean over towards the inside of the circle, requires some further clarification. The green horse, who lacks balance and sufficient suppleness to bend along the circle, will have to lean over very markedly (*le cheval se couche dans son cercle*). The well-schooled, balanced and supple horse needs to do so much less, and will retain a position nearer the vertical.

I have paid considerable attention to the various rein-effects on the circle, in an attempt to explain them clearly; the horse's performance is made or marred according to the delicacy of their precision.

Yet, precise and delicate rein-effects are impossible without full and frank acceptance of the bridle by the horse. And there can be no full acceptance of the bridle without generous impulsion, adequate for the movement with something to spare. There must be a measure of *brio*. The slower, and the more intricate the movement, the more difficult it is to maintain that *brio*, and the more necessary it is to have something to spare in the amount of impulsion produced by the horse.

That, precisely, is the primary object of the rider's legs, when riding circles; they cannot be ridden really well without sufficient drive to maintain the forward urge of the horse into his bridle. The circular track in itself demands from the horse an amount of energy considerably greater than a straight course; the inner hindleg in particular is taxed more severely.

The rider's legs have to be vigilant and allow of no relaxation in the forward contact, exerted by the horse on the rider's hand, not by the hand on the horse's mouth. That forward pressure may be light, certainly, but it must be positive, even when felt only through the weight of the rein! The entire horse must give the rider the feel of carrying him forward with a will, generously, with enthusiasm.

Whilst both the rider's legs have to play their part in creating and in supervising this impulsion, it is usually the inside leg that has to be the more attentive, since the more heavily loaded inside hindleg of the horse is directly influenced by it.

Now, whilst I stand by my opinion that there will be no tendency on the part of the horse to swing his quarters out if the reins are handled in the manner that I have indicated, that must not be taken to mean that the rider's legs have no role to fulfil in steering the horse! Most certainly they have. I have done my best to make it abundantly clear, in Chapter VI, that the horse steers himself mainly from his quarters. Accordingly, it is quite impossible to steer the horse accurately, whether on a circle or on a straight line, without adequate control of the horse's quarters. How this control is perfected will be dealt with in a later chapter.

Taking everything into consideration, the riding of a good circle taxes the abilities of both horse and rider to a considerable degree. The smaller the circle, and the more intricate the circular movements, the more these difficulties grow. Commonsense dictates that we shall start with large circles and simple movements and, as always, work for careful, methodical progress. A large circle, well done, is far more valuable than a smaller one leading to difficulties.

The peculiar difficulties met with in riding a circular track are met with in every change of direction of a circular character, riding round a corner for example or doubling back. In a sense, the difficulties are even aggravated at these moments.

Whilst it may be comparatively easy to maintain a level balance on a determined track, on a straight line or even on a circle, any alteration of direction is liable to unbalance the horse, causing him to lose impulsion, to change his rhythm, or to put in one or two uneven strides. This is a very real difficulty. The answer is to be found in demanding an increase of impulsion and firmer contact a moment or two before the alteration of direction is made.

CIRCULAR FIGURES
THE CIRCLE, THE VOLT, RIDING THROUGH THE CORNERS, OTHER CIRCULAR FIGURES.

In the first place we have the circle (*le cercle*), and the volt (*la volte*). Colloquially the two expressions, circle and volt, are frequently mixed up. Yet there is a most decided difference: the volt is a small circle of a determined size, whilst the circle may be of any size, larger than the volt.

In commencing to school a young horse in the open, we may select a circle of any diameter, provided it be a large one, to begin with. If we have a regulation school, then the width would be twenty metres (twenty-two yards). Obviously our horse will have to go at about eighteen inches away from the wall, so that the largest diameter of any circle possible in such a school would be about twenty-one yards.

That is quite a good size to begin with, and there would be no point, naturally, in reducing the diameter until our horse can perform really well on that large circle.

The volt is the circle of academic size; it is the smallest circle which the horse can perform either on one or on two tracks, the forehand turning round the quarters; in other words a turn on the haunches of 360% (*la pirouette*). Consequently the radius of the volt is equal to the length of the horse. This definition is given by Guérinière, and remains recognized as determining the correct size of the volt.

It follows that this radius is variable within narrow limits according to the size of the horse; but, since the average length of a horse is about three metres (ten feet), it is reasonably accurate to take the radius of the volt as being ten feet and the diameter twenty feet (six metres).

When circles are demanded in a dressage programme, the required diameter is always stated. But when a volt is demanded, or a half-volt, this information is frequently omitted; in such cases it is implied that the recognized radius of the academic volt, namely, the length of the horse or approximately three metres shall apply.

Incidentally, the size of the academic volt also determines the correct way of riding through the corners of the school. Each corner constitutes one quarter of a volt with a radius of three metres. The horse begins his quarter volt at a distance of one horse length before reaching the corner, and finishes the quarter volt at a distance of one horse length beyond the corner. During that movement the horse's body, from head to tail, is bent in precise conformity with the circular track.

It will be appreciated that the correct riding of so small a circle as the volt demands a very high standard of training; it is difficult enough at a walk, a good deal more difficult at a canter, and very difficult indeed at a trot.

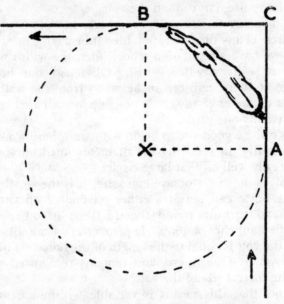

DIAGRAM 4. RIDING THROUGH CORNER

Distance AC and CB, also XB and XA equal 3 metres, or
one horse length. Going from A to B the horse describes
¼ volt of 3 metres radius

Circles of a diameter below ten yards do not really belong in the training programme of any horse below the standard of say the Prix St. Georges.

Once the horse has mastered circles of down to say ten yards diameter, he will be ready to undertake movements which, though based on the principles of the circle, demand changes of direction; these, as remarked upon in a preceding paragraph, constitute an added difficulty.

There is first of all the figure of 8; there are loops and serpentines, which the rider may compose at his own discretion, as long as he is careful that the radius of the various bends that compose his movements is within the horse's capability. The basic idea of these exercises is to promote the horse's balance and his rhythm. It is therefore essential not to push the horse into any exercise, which he is patently unable to perform without the loss of either.

It is the change of direction, and the complete change of bend of the horse's body, that constitute the major difficulty of these exercises. These changes require extreme smoothness of execution. To change smoothly from one bend to another the horse must pass through a moment of straightness. On the fully schooled horse that moment of straightness will be so fleeting as to be unnoticeable. But then the fully schooled horse is able to answer his rider's demands so quickly because his reactions have become intuitive and almost instantaneous. That is not so with the half-schooled horse; he needs a definite time-lapse to understand a demand, and a further time-lapse before he can act on that understanding. It is up to the rider's tact to see that his horse be left the appropriate time-lapse commensurate with his proficiency. It is advisable then, in beginning these exercises, to allow the horse quite a distinct moment of straightness, say a couple of strides to start with, before altering his bend. This is in accordance with the principle that our demands, whatever they may be, shall never surprise the horse; he must always be given a warning, and time to assimilate the warning, that a certain specific demand is coming. The inclusion of that warning, as a preliminary to the application of our aids, is the final refinement of the language spoken between horse and rider; it is the *demi-mot* sufficient for the good listener.

I will revert to this problem in greater detail in treating of the changes of leg at short intervals, which require almost lightning quickness of aids and which yet cannot succeed unless preceded every time by just such a warning.

An interesting exercise, suitable for the reasonably advanced horse, is the spiral, or the double spiral. We begin this exercise on a large circle, reducing the radius very gradually until we reach the smallest circle whereof our horse is capable; then, from the small circle, we increase the radius equally gradually until we are back again on the big circle. The measure of our horse's proficiency is in his ability to maintain the same balance, the same speed, the same rhythm, the same length of stride, throughout the exercise.

Finally, I suppose I ought to add, even though every reader of this book would probably know that already, that almost every horse is by nature more flexible to one side than to the other. Since we aim at equal proficiency on both reins, this implies that we may have to work to the difficult side rather more than to the easier one, until equality has been established.

CHAPTER XIV

WORK ON TWO TRACKS

*Objects – Difficulties – The shoulder-in – Corners – Circles –
The turn (pirouette) on the forehand (final form) –
Quarters-in (la croupe en dedans) – Quarters-out (la croupe
en dehors) – Circular tracks – The turn (pirouette) on the
haunches – The half-pass (l'appuyer or tenir les hanches)
– Effects of hands and legs – The pirouettes (definition) –
Counter changes of hand on two tracks – A powerful aid
in difficulties – Shying*

T HE term "on two tracks" refers to any movement in which
the horse's hind-feet follow a different track from that of
the fore-feet. This happens when the horse moves sideways.
It is not a method of progression used normally by the horse,
apart maybe from an occasional sideways bound when shying.
Obviously, to go sideways is not a normal way of progression for
the horse, or for other animals either. Equally obviously then,
the animal has some difficulty in acquiring smoothness of execution at this type of movement, to which he is not accustomed
and which is, in a sense, unnatural to him.

Dr. G. C. Simpson, Professor of Paleontology at Columbia
University, observes the following in his book *Horses*: The build
of the horse's legs "eliminates practically all rotating motion of
the feet. Along with other specializations in the joints of the
legs, the fact is that horses use their limbs only for locomotion
(or kicking) and not for holding, manipulation and the like as
do men, cats, squirrels, and many other animals that retain more
flexible limbs. Horses also walk or run in a peculiarly limited
and specialized, though highly effective, way. Within the leg,
the joints work only in a fore-and-aft plane and it is practically
impossible to rotate the leg or to bend part of it outward or in-

ward. The leg is a rigid machine for carrying weight and for moving forward. What side motion is possible comes from the shoulder and hip joints ".

I trust my informed readers will appreciate that the intrinsic value of the work concerned does not lie in the ability of teaching the horse to progress in a manner deviating from the straight and normal path, but in the physical and also psychological benefits to be derived from these gymnastic exercises.

In the first place these exercises, which are executed with a lateral bend, help to further perfect the horse's later flexibility, produced basically by the riding of circular tracks. It is here relevant to observe that these lateral movements are, as we shall see presently, derived directly from the circle; hence the study and practice of them follows logically after that of the circular movements.

In moving sideways the horse has to cross his legs; in going to the right for example, the near foreleg and the near hindleg are placed across and in front of the off foreleg and the off hindleg respectively. This entails a considerable sideways movement of shoulder and thigh and the physical development of the abductor and attractor muscles concerned. The horse is also obliged to raise the over-stepping legs rather higher and to bring them forward somewhat further than normal. All in all, freedom, elasticity and power of shoulder, thigh and loin muscles benefit considerably, important elements, all of them, in the general production of balance through ease of movement.

The better these exercises are done, the more beneficial will be their results. And, since they cannot be executed really well without considerable refinement in the control of mouth, forehand and quarters, it follows that it is the ultimate object of this work to seek for the gradual achievement of that refinement. In that search both horse and rider are bound to learn a great deal towards mutual unity in delicacy of effective control, which is the key to the ultimate goal of lightness.

THE SHOULDER-IN
(Epaule en Dedans)

In training the riding horse no exercise effects a full measure of usefulness unless it be conducive to the ultimate improve-

ment of free forward movement. That, as we know, is dependent on frank and energetic action of the hocks.

Accordingly, in practising all forms of sidesteps, the perfection of freedom and energy of hock action is at least as important as the perfection of shoulder freedom.

Now, when we begin with the attempt of moving our horse
on two tracks, we are faced with a difficulty; the animal, not
accustomed to this mode of progression, is bound to be clumsy;
he will have to place his legs sideways and forward at the same
time; this requires a considerable physical effort to which the
horse is not used. So, just as we do ourselves under similar
circumstances, the horse attempts to minimize the effect of our
demand on his muscular effort; he does that by evading the forward reach of his movements as much as possible.

So, since the ultimate value of all work on two tracks depends
largely on the achievement of this forward reach, governed pri-
marily by energetic hock action, it is essential to commence this
work in the form of an exercise which facilitates effective control of that action.

That exercise is the shoulder-in.

The exercise is best developed from the circle, perfected with
the help of the circle and, ultimately, on the circle. Our diagrams will help to clarify the descriptions that follow.

We ride our horse on a circle to the left.

The horse is appropriately bent and flexed on the circle.

The rhythm is perfect, and the horse's inner hindleg is
delivering its full measure of energy (see previous chapter,
page 143).

We select a suitable point whereat we desire to leave the circle;
probably the point where the circular track meets the side of
our school; when our horse's quarters have arrived at the selected
point, we push him away, sideways, along the tangent to the
circle, probably along the side of our school.

To do so, the aids are simple enough; we push him away with
our inside leg, aided by our hands and reins, which we carry
slightly towards the right.

We push the horse away in the flexed position of the circle;
we do nothing to alter that flexion, on the contrary we do our
best to maintain that flexion intact. Accordingly, the sideways
pressure to the right, effected with our reins, does not hinder
the horse's movement; actually it assists it, since the left-rein,

acting as rein of opposition to the haunches, helps in pushing the quarters to the right.

We now have the horse on two tracks; the tracks followed by fore and hind legs are entirely separate from each other and parallel to each other.

Done perfectly, we will maintain the horse's body at an angle of about 30° and never more than 45°, with the line of his progress.

Naturally, we do not begin with perfection, but with troubles. In the case under discussion, mainly, with the inner hindleg; we know from the previous chapter, that it is the inner hindleg which has to deliver the principal effort on a circular track. Now

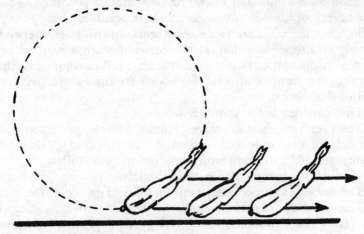

DIAGRAM 5.　LEFT SHOULDER-IN

in the shoulder-in we demand a much increased effort, since the inner hindleg (the left one in this case) is obliged to tread sideways very far underneath the body in order to receive the load. This entails increased flexion of the hock and a measure of lowering the left haunch.

To commence with, the horse is unable to deliver this action; he cannot help evading it; he tries to follow the action with the hindleg in question, instead of initiating it. Hence clumsiness, loss of rhythm and loss of impulsion, the main difficulties in all work on two tracks.

But, in this movement of the shoulder-in, we have the remedy at hand!

We simply re-take the circle, re-establish hock action and rhythm, and try again.

Obviously, to start with, we do a large circle and accordingly begin with but little flexion; and we also begin our attempt at shoulder-in at but a very slight angle. We make it easy for the horse.

It is quite unnecessary to have the horse truly on two tracks to begin with. It is sufficient, moving over to the right, if the near-hind treads approximately in the track of the off-fore, the horse thus making three tracks as it were. This movement, advocated by Steinbrecht, is well known in the German school; it is an excellent preparation. It is known as *schulter vor*, "shoulder-fore" or "shoulder in advance".

Incidentally, the names given to the various movements on

DIAGRAM 6. RIGHT SHOULDER-FORE (STEINBRECHT)

two tracks tend to be confusing; so let us begin by making the designation of the shoulder-in quite clear.

In the example discussed above, the horse was describing a circle on the left rein, flexed to the left. When we leave the circle, to follow its tangent, the horse, though side-stepping to his own right, remains flexed to the left; hence, we call this movement "Left shoulder-in" (*Epaule en dedans à gauche*). Similarly, when the horse is flexed to the right, whilst side-stepping to his own left, the movement is called "Right shoulder-in" (*Epaule en dedans à droite*).

Finally, it must be understood, that the shoulder-in is the only movement on two tracks in which the horse is flexed away from the direction wherein he is moving.

The shoulder-in is essentially a schooling movement, not used as a rule for exhibition purposes and not demanded in dressage tests. But its value as a sound foundation for all other two track work is great. De la Guérinière, and the classical school in general, lay great store by it.

Once the horse has become proficient, active and supple in

the position of shoulder-in on straight lines, there are several refinements of a circular character which may be attempted.

In the first place the horse may be taken right round the rectangular school, going shoulder-in all the time, on the straight lines and through the corners also. The correct technique of the shoulder-in through the corners may be described as follows. Assuming we go round the school anti-clockwise, with the horse in the shoulder-in position at an angle of about 30° along one of the long sides. When the horse's forehand reaches the track

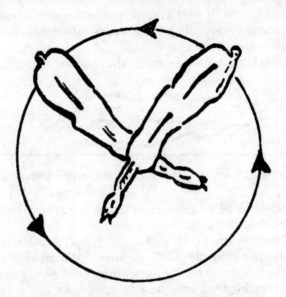

DIAGRAM 7. TURN ON THE FOREHAND

along the short side, we take a purely circular track; we keep this up for precisely one horse length, exactly until the horse's quarters reach the very point at which we have begun our circular track; at that particular moment we sidestep again, along the short side, in the position of the shoulder-in. The essence of the correct corner is that the quarters shall finish the corner at the precise spot where the forehand commenced it.

This refinement indicates the correct manner wherein to assume the position "shoulder-in" from a straight line. Assuming we are riding on a straight track along the side of the school; we commence a circle and as soon as the quarters reach the spot where the forehand has left the track, we begin the shoulder-in.

Lastly, the exercise may be practised on the circle, which demands considerable refinement of control. The horse is maintained at an angle of from 30° to 45° with the tangent to the circle. In the position of the shoulder-in, the forehand moves along an inner circle and the quarters on an outer circle concentric with it; accordingly, the quarters have to take a longer stride than the forehand; this difference becomes the more pro-

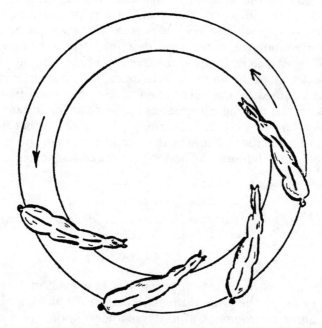

DIAGRAM 8.   SHOULDER-IN ON A CIRCLE

nounced as the diameter of the circle decreases, and reaches its maximum as we attain the smallest circle possible, which is the turn on the forehand (*pirouette sur l'avant main*). This is the turn on the forehand, final form; the horse is maintained in the position of the shoulder-in, the quarters describe a circle of one horse length radius; the inside foreleg moves almost on the spot whilst the outside foreleg describes a very small circle round it.

This exercise can be done only at the walk.

The particular gymnastic effects of the shoulder-in on the

circle increase the mobility of the quarters, hips, elbows and hocks; the loins are stretched and the back somewhat dipped.

Summarizing: The Shoulder-in is a movement on two tracks, in which the horse is flexed over his whole length away from the direction in which he is moving.

When the horse is flexed to the left (left shoulder-in), the near-fore and the near-hind are called the inside legs, and the off-fore and the off-hind the outside legs.

The shoulder-in makes its major demands on the inside legs (shoulder, loins, hip and elbow) and in particular on the inside hind leg (hock), which has to carry most of the weight in a very flexed position; the outer legs (shoulder, hip and elbow) are loaded lightly, so facilitating the freedom of the sideways reach.

The flexion of the shoulder-in, as described, corresponds to the flexion assumed by the horse when making a natural free turn on his centre, moving his quarters to the right for instance and his shoulders to the left. Accordingly he comes to that flexion easily, which is the reason why the shoulder-in, with this natural flexion, has been found the best two track exercise to begin with.

THE QUARTERS-IN
(La croupe en dedans, la hanche en dedans, travers)
ALSO CALLED HEAD TO THE WALL.
(La tête au mur)

The movement of the quarters-in is best evolved from the circle in much the same manner as that of the shoulder-in.

In this new movement, as in the shoulder-in, the horse moves obliquely sideways, flexed over his whole length. But the direction of the bend differs radically from that of the shoulder-in; in the quarters-in, the horse is flexed in the direction wherein he is going.

This makes a great deal of difference.

Firstly, because the movement as such is less natural to the horse.

Secondly, because, for reasons that will be stated, the handling of the reins is liable to lead to some difficulty.

Thirdly, because the radically different flexion permits us to exercise the same muscles and joints, as in the shoulder-in, in a completely different combination. Consequently, the greatest gymnastic benefit to the muscular structure of the horse and of his joints is achieved by the practice of both types of exercise.

Lastly, because the quarters-in prepares the horse for the execution in the correct form of the half-pass (*appuyer*), which is the ultimate aim.

In order to develop the quarters-in from the circle, we proceed then much in the same way as described for the shoulder-in.

Again we ride the horse on a circle to the left.

Again we select a point at which we decide to leave the circle.

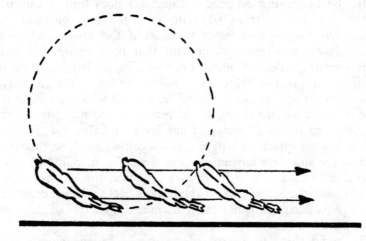

DIAGRAM 9.   THE QUARTERS-IN.   HEAD TO THE WALL

But this time it will be when our horse's head reaches the selected point that we push him away sideways along the tangent to the circle.

We maintain the flexed position, to the left, of the circle; so that our horse now moves obliquely sideways, bent in the direction of the movement.

Once more, if any difficulties occur, loss of flexion, loss of rhythm, clumsiness, or whatever it may be, we revert to the circle proper, re-establish bend and balance, and try again.

The aids, again, are self-evident; this time it is obviously the right leg that pushes the horse to the left, whilst the reins also move the horse sideways to the left.

At first sight one imagines that the action of the reins is the same, in principle, as that used in the shoulder-in. But indeed it is not, or at any rate the degree of difficulty is considerably greater.

We have seen, in the preceding description of the left shoulder-in, how the left rein, in maintaining the bend to the left, acted as rein of opposition to the haunches and thus assisted in pushing the quarters to the right. Now, in the quarters-in this is no longer so. This time, with the horse side-stepping to his left (see diagram), we use the left rein to keep him flexed to the left, looking in the direction wherein he is going.

Herein lies a considerable difficulty!

In the beginning especially, the horse does find it difficult to flex in the direction wherein he is moving; he tends to straighten his neck or even to bend it the other way. Of course, we can attempt to prevent that by keeping this rein taut, exerting a certain amount of restraint, perhaps even some pull, in the process. But, in so doing, we are liable to create two effects of opposition to the horse, both of which are destructive of what we are trying to achieve. In the first place, any pull exerted in the direction of our body, and therefore in that of the horse's quarters, will act in opposition to these quarters and to the sideways movement now desired. Also any distinct restraint by that rein will act as a brake on the energetic forward reach, the impulsion, of the horse's hocks. In other words these rein-effects can quite easily become destructive of the very aims pursued.

To avoid these untoward effects should be the rider's first objective. It matters a great deal, in the beginning, if the rider obstructs the horse's impulsion, and perhaps destroys it for ever, by his own action; it matters nothing at all, in the beginning, whether the horse goes with the correct flexion, with no flexion at all, or even with a slightly adverse flexion. Again the angle with the track whereat the horse is supposed to go is of no importance whatever and may be kept very slight to start with.

But to revert to the rein action.

The moment we leave the circle, to follow its tangent on two tracks to the left, it is our object to maintain the horse's flexion to the left. That can only be done by maintaining unaltered contact with the left rein; unaltered in the sense that the tension on that rein shall under no circumstances be increased. But there is no harm in decreasing the tension slightly, which will in fact facilitate the increase of impulsion demanded; and we

can obtain precisely that effect by lengthening the right, or supporting rein, slightly (see page 145).

So the action of the rider can perhaps best be described as
follows:

At the moment of leaving the circle, the rider himself moves
to the left!   He looks to the left, he flexes to the left, in so doing
his right leg presses his horse to the left, taking his left hand
and rein a little away from the horse's shoulder and his right
hand and rein a little closer to the horse's shoulder; the right
rein presses lightly against the horse's neck.   Lengthening that
rein slightly encourages the horse in maintaining his flexion to
the left!

It is not an easy effect to master.

THE QUARTERS-OUT
(La croupe en dehors, la hanche en dehors, renvers)
ALSO CALLED TAIL TO THE WALL
(La croupe au mur)

Since the riding-school is obviously the most convenient place
for the study and practice of the exercises of more advanced
horsemanship, it is logical enough that many such exercises
derive their name from the horse's position in the school whilst
performing any such particular exercise.

That this is not a general rule, we have already seen.   The
exercise of the "shoulder-in", described in a preceding paragraph, wherein the horse moves sideways with a bend opposite
to the direction of his movement, is always described as
"shoulder-in", no matter what may be the horse's position
relative to the walls of the school.

But the terms, "quarters-in" and "quarters-out", and the
various alternative names for these two movements, do relate to
the horse's position in the school specifically.

And the correct names to be used for such movements depend
on the relative position of the horse alone and on nothing else.

Technically, there is no difference whatever between the
movements "quarters-in" and "quarters-out"; the only difference is in the horse's position relative to the sides of the school.

In the "quarters-in" the horse moves with his "head to the
wall".

In the "quarters-out" the horse moves with "his tail to the wall".

Accordingly, all that has already been said with respect to the "quarters-in" or "head to the wall" applies equally to the movement "quarters-out" or "tail to the wall".

"Quarters-in" and "Quarters-out"
FURTHER CONSIDERATIONS AND REFINEMENTS

We have seen how, in these two exercises, the horse moves obliquely sideways bent over his entire length with the head flexed in the direction of the movement.

Let us consider this definition in detail.

The term "obliquely" refers to the angle of the horse's body with the line of his progress. In presentation of the "finished"

DIAGRAM 10.   QUARTERS-OUT.   TAIL TO THE WALL

horse, that angle should be of 45°. The horse cannot be considered "finished" unless he be able to show, at that acute angle, a full and convincing measure of untrammelled impulsion. The achievement, and maintenance, of this impulsion is the great difficulty in this work and the degree of this difficulty increases in conformity with the degree of the angle. And, since true impulsion must at all times be the trainer's first care, it follows that the angle chosen during training shall not be such as to hamper the development of that impulsion. Hence, it is advisable to begin these exercises at a very slight angle only! And, even with the "finished" horse it is usually better to concentrate, during practice, on impulsion above anything else and for that purpose an angle of about 30° is quite sharp enough.

When we say that the horse shall be bent over his entire length, we mean that the lateral bend of the horse's body in this work shall correspond to his bend on an equivalent circle. The circle which corresponds to an angle of 45° is the volt,

of one horse length (three metres) radius. Accordingly the
bend of the finished horse side-stepping at an angle of 45°
is fairly pronounced (see diagram). Obviously that is in itself
a reason why we should refrain from seeking so acute an angle
unless our horse were at least perfect in the execution of the
volt, which very few horses are. It will now be understood
that the bend of a horse side-stepping at an angle of 30° and
less becomes comparatively less and may become but very
slight indeed.

The flexion demanded of head and neck, in the direction of
the movement, is never more than comparatively slight. The
amount of flexion is correct if the rider, from his normal position in the saddle, can see the whole of the horse's eyeball.
But the form of the flexion is only correct if the head carriage
itself is correct; meaning that the axis of the head, drawn from
forehead to nose, is strictly parallel to the axis of the horse's
body, appearing perfectly vertical. Not infrequently, we see
this flexion attempted by a sideways and upwards pull of the
leading rein, which causes the horse's nose to come up sideways;
the head is then no longer vertical; it is a certain proof that the
exponent has not only failed to achieve flexion, but has also
failed to understand what is meant by flexion. As a fault it is
very serious, much more so than insufficient flexion, absence of
flexion or even wrong flexion.

CIRCULAR TRACKS

Assuming that we, and our horse, have mastered a really good
performance on two tracks along straight lines, in the position
quarters-in or quarters-out, we may then attempt these same
exercises along a circular track also.

It is observed that in the position quarters-in or head to the
wall, the forehand will describe a larger circle than the quarters.

This condition is reversed in the position quarters-out or tail
to the wall, when the quarters will have to describe a larger
circle than the forehand. This has inconveniences; in the first
place, the quarters are less easily mobile, sideways, than the forehand; in the second place, circles on two tracks tending towards
a push round the forehand dip the horse's back, the hindlegs
cannot tread under so well and additional weight is thrown on

the forehand; consequently, the exercise in this form tends to bring the horse more on to his forehand. Accordingly, circular exercises on two tracks are not done as a rule otherwise than in the position head to the wall.

Naturally, circumstances may arise when a trainer, familiar with this work and aware of the results he wishes to obtain, uses the tail to the wall position for his specific ends.

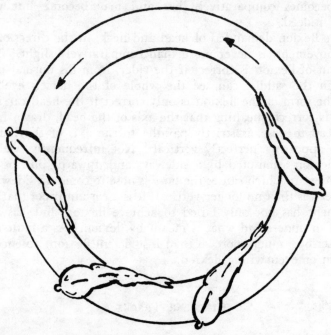

DIAGRAM 11.   QUARTERS-OUT OR TAIL TO THE WALL.   ON A CIRCLE

However, for our general purpose, we will discuss the quarters-in, or head to the wall, on circular tracks.

We begin with a fairly large circle, the horse in the position quarters-in, at not too acute an angle; the horse goes on two concentric circles, the hindlegs on the inner, smaller circle and the forelegs on the outer, larger circle, the horse flexed in the direction of the movement. Diagram 12 makes it clear that the forelegs have to cover a longer way, and to take longer strides than the hindlegs; yet forelegs and hindlegs march in time. The result is that the shoulders and front legs extend, whilst the haunches and hindlegs flex more markedly; the horse

DIAGRAM 12.   QUARTERS-IN OR HEAD TO THE WALL.   ON A CIRCLE

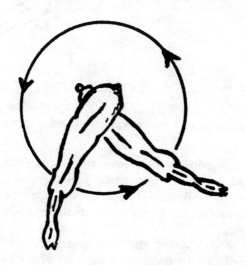

DIAGRAM 13.   TURN ON THE HAUNCHES

shortens on to his haunches. It is of the essence of the exercise that the position of the horse on the two concentric circles shall remain constant, that the flexion shall not change, and that the relative rhythm and the relative length of the strides with forehand and quarters shall remain constant also.

The exercise demands a nice degree of control and considerable lightness.

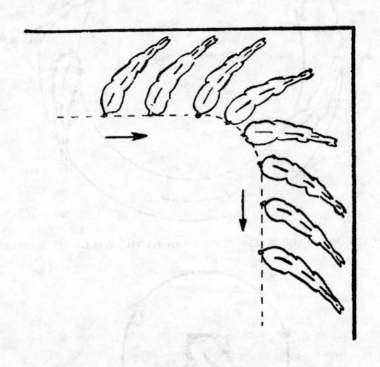

DIAGRAM 14. QUARTERS-IN ROUND A CORNER

Once these conditions have been fulfilled, smaller circles may be attempted, culminating gradually in the pirouette, or turn on the haunches. But this pirouette will never approach perfection unless delicacy of control has first been mastered on the larger circles.

And before attempting the pirouette itself, the horse ought to be schooled first in the correct manner of taking the corners of the school in the position "head to the wall". The above diagram shows the method; it will be seen that at the moment of almost pivoting round the corner, the movement approaches the form of the pirouette fairly closely.

The exercises head to the wall and tail to the wall on straight lines may be done at all gaits, walk, trot, passage and canter. On circular tracks, the exercise, tail to the wall, should be done at the walk only, but that of head to the wall at all gaits.

THE HALF-PASS
(L'appuyer or tenir les hanches)

The literal translation of the French verb "appuyer" is "to lean"; the term, as used in equitation, may relate to any movement in which the rider "leans against" his horse, pushing him sideways. All movements on two tracks already discussed, the shoulder-in, the quarters-in, the quarters-out, are forms of the appuyer. But, as each of these movements already possesses a specific name of its own, it is usual to call them by such specific name.

In general then, when the term appuyer or tenir les hanches is used, it refers to what in England is known as the half-pass (l'appuyer en ligne droite or appuyer sur la diagonale). In the half-pass the horse moves obliquely forward and not, as in the movements described previously, obliquely sideways.

In the half-pass the horse is not flexed over his entire length, as in the previous movements, but only in the neck and head. And that flexion is only slight. It has been explained that, in the quarters-in, the rider should see the ball of the horse's eye; in the half-pass it is sufficient if the rider can just see the corner of his horse's eye. It will be understood that, in the half-pass, the slight flexion required is always in the direction of the horse's movement. It is pertinent to add that, slight though the flexion need only be, it had better be distinctly visible to any officiating judges, who would be certain to fault absence of flexion severely. The form of flexion described is of the essence of the movement.

In the half-pass, finally, the horse should move obliquely forward, flexed as described, the position of his body parallel with the long sides of the arena, and the quarters should never lead, or appear to lead, the forehand.

At least, those are the requirements of the *Fédération Équestre Internationale*.

In England, the half-pass has frequently, somewhat light-heartedly, been considered as a fairly simple and more or less elementary type of movement. Done correctly, it is far from that; it is, on the contrary, very difficult. It is the culmination of all the work on two tracks described previously, and it is the ultimate form wherein that work is to be seen in demonstrations and competitions of the highest class.

Now let us consider the exigencies of this work in detail.

The horse is required to move obliquely forward.

The accent is, this time, very much on "forward".

In the quarters-in the horse was flexed in his body (see diagram 9); in that flexed position the outer hindleg had to take off from a position somewhat behind the inner hindleg; therein lay, to some extent, an impediment to the forward movement of that outer leg; which was not of much importance in a movement wherein the emphasis lay in going sideways.

But now, in the half-pass, the horse's body is no longer flexed, and so there is no longer any impediment to the forward movement of the outer hindleg. Precisely! Because it is the ideal that the horse, in the half-pass, shall, though going obliquely, be full of forward impulsion! As full of impulsion as he would be on a straight line, or even more so. His strides shall be roomy, balanced, rhythmic and even, each stride alike to the previous one and alike also to the one to follow.

That requirement is not easy!

And it is not made any easier by the required flexion, slight though it may have to be, in the direction of the movement. I have referred at some length, in discussing the "quarters-in", to the difficulty caused by the tendency of the leading rein to act in opposition to the haunches. Precisely the same difficulty is encountered in the half-pass; if anything, in an accentuated form. It is quite impossible to achieve anything like the degree of free forward impulsion demanded in a good half-pass as long as the rein whereto the horse flexes has the tendency to oppose the haunches.

Hence, we so often see half-passes, wherein the horse goes forward with hesitation, irregularly, with no defined direction and without brilliance.

It is a very real difficulty. It is curious that so few authorities appear to have referred to the question. The only exceptions, to my knowledge, are Général l'Hotte (*Questions Équestres*) and Général Decarpentry (*Équitation Académique*), who quotes L'Hotte: "The bend must be but slight in order to avoid that the rein, which calls the flexion into being, should oppose the haunches." Decarpentry adds that it is exceedingly difficult to avoid this effect, and almost impossible to do so completely.

I would go further.

I consider it quite impossible to avoid that effect completely, except in two cases:

(a) by holding the horse straight;
(b) by demanding this flexion only from a horse already so fully in the *rassembler*, so light, that he can give this flexion to a mere insinuation of the rein.

Consequently I advise the trainer to place first things first and to concentrate on well-defined movement, full of impulsion, obliquely forward, with the horse held straight; it is better to postpone flexion than to obtain it at the cost of destroying forward movement.

Perhaps I may be allowed to give it as my opinion that the flexion demanded in this movement is a relic inherited from the old masters, who were wont to ride with their horses looking at the public *dans la beau pli*, in the elegant flexion. Quite, but then the horses of the old masters were always trained to a maximum degree of the *rassembler*, sitting almost on their haunches. The more horizontal, more extended paces demanded by the modern school make this requirement even more difficult.

Finally, it is demanded that the horse shall maintain a position parallel to the sides of the arena and that the quarters shall never lead the forehand.

Firstly, let it be said that the demand to have the horse parallel to the sides of the school is an innovation introduced by the F.E.I. in 1950. The classical teaching has always been that the axis of the horse's body should be not parallel, but at an angle of about 13° with the sides of the school.

This makes a great deal of difference.

It is best explained by the accompanying diagrams.

These diagrams show, in stippled lines, typical trajectories normally demanded at a half-pass. It will be seen that these trajectories form an angle of 50° with the long side of the school.

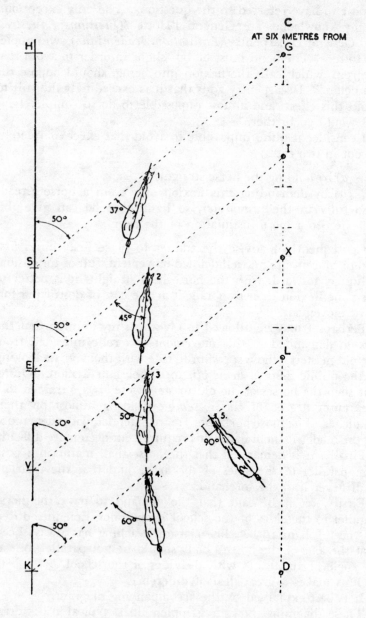

DIAGRAM 15. THE HALF-PASS

Picture 1 shows the horse's body at an angle of 37° with the line of his progress and consequently at an angle of 13° with the side of the school. This angle of 13° corresponds with the classical teaching and is incidentally the precise angle given in the regulations of the F.E.I. 1939. It may well be held that the angle of 37° with the line of progress is sufficiently acute for a movement calling for energetic forward movement.

Picture 2 shows the horse at an angle of 45° with his line of progress. According to all leading authorities that is precisely the maximum angle ever to be used. But it is still 5° short of being parallel with the side of the school!

Picture 3 shows the parallel position, the horse making an angle of 50° with his line of progress.

The law demands that the quarters shall never lead the forehand.

Rather a nice case this of the need to explain the law.

In fact, as far as the horse is concerned, the quarters will never actually lead the forehand unless his body makes an angle of more than 90° with his line of progress; pictures 4 and 5 show this.

But in these positions the quarters will appear to be leading viewed from C, where the judges are sitting. They will appear to do so immediately the horse's angle exceeds the position shown in picture 3, angle of 50°.

The judges see the centre-line of the arena, and the quarter-lines drawn parallel with it. The moment the horse's quarters look like reaching any of these parallel lines in advance of the forehand, the judges will conclude that such quarters are leading and will find fault accordingly.

This is the interpretation to be placed on this law.

Seen in this light, the new ruling of 1950 appears unfortunate.

Students will realize, of course, that it is much more difficult to judge the angle made by their horse's body with an invisible line of progress, such as from S to G, than when following a clearly defined line, such as, for instance, the side of the arena. Accordingly, it is my advice, given without hesitation, not to exceed the position shown in diagram 1, and certainly not that of diagram 2. And even that is difficult to control from the saddle, without the occasional assistance of someone viewing the proceedings from position C.

EFFECTS OF HANDS AND LEGS IN THE APPUYER

It is usual, in books on riding, to stress the use of the outer leg applied behind the girth for the purpose of pushing the quarters sideways; meaning, of course, that we use the left leg behind the girth to push the horse's quarters to the right and the right leg behind the girth to push them to the left.

The time has now come to draw attention to certain limitations and inconveniences of this use of the leg.

It is a powerful aid, easily understood by the horse and obeyed readily enough. In setting out to teach our horses this work, we certainly cannot do without it. Its first inconvenience is that its effect is predominantly sideways, and that this effect is gained at the expense of the purely forward urge which should always remain the basic purpose of the use of the legs. It is true that this loss of forward urge can be made up partly, but only partly, by effective use of the opposing leg for that purpose. But it must here be stated that few riders appear to be able to use their two legs in this manner; as a general rule we may observe that the rider who uses, say, his left leg behind the girth to push his horse's quarters to the right, will not use his right leg at all; in many cases we may see that contact between such right leg and the horse is completely lost; with fatal results, of course, to forward impulsion! Let it be said, in fairness to riders in this difficulty, that the effect of two legs, working each of them independently and to different purpose, is not easy to obtain. All too often the rider will find that the application of the right leg, to maintain impulsion, has the effect of neutralizing the effect of the left leg, applied for the purpose of going sideways. At any rate, even if well done, this application of both legs for different purposes remains a compromise yielding only partial results.

The aid, as we have said, is powerful and easily obeyed by the horse. Obviously then, as the horse becomes more and more proficient in this work, he will obey more and more freely to the sideward urge of the leg; much more easily so, in most cases, than to the sideways effect of the reins; hence the tendency develops to side-step more energetically with the quarters than with the forehand, resulting in a gradually increasing angle relative to the animal's line of progress. The quarters develop a tendency to assume the lead!

It is precisely for that very purpose that the rule discussed in the preceding paragraph is being enforced. The judges require to be satisfied that there is no tendency of the quarters towards an assumption of the lead; they require the lead to remain in the forehand, through the supremacy of rein-control!

And, in that, they are correct.

And in that direction also we must look for the ultimate solution of this and other difficulties referred to in preceding pages.

The answer then, lies in the gradual development of rein-control combined with gradual reduction of leg-control. As the balance of the horse improves, and his lightness, to be finally perfected in the *rassembler*, it will be found possible to dispense with the sidewards pressure of the leg almost completely and to rely on a sidewards effect of the reins alone. The horse is brought to this form of control, as always, gradually and by association of ideas. Once his rider's requirements have been thoroughly understood by him, it is possible to transfer the control from "leg and reins combined" to "reins alone"; naturally, such result can only be arrived at by most carefully graduated stages and even then the attempt will not succeed unless the horse, through lightness, balance and rhythm, be ready for it.

However, the improvement that may be achieved through this final refinement will be found to be very great, since the rider will now dispose of the use of both his legs for the maintenance of impulsion.

Accordingly, the trainer would do well to keep this ultimate objective in mind and not to use, during any stage of his schooling, any greater leg pressure than strictly necessary.

THE PIROUETTES
DEFINITION

The expression "pirouette" has been used already in some of the preceding paragraphs. Since the pirouette is essentially a movement on two tracks, it is relevant to include a clear definition of this term in the present chapter.

The pirouette then signifies any turn within the horse's own length, the shortest turn of which he is capable. The following forms are recognized:

Pirouette sur le centre, turn on the centre.
Pirouette sur les hanches, turn on the haunches, possible at the walk, piaffer or canter.
Pirouette sur l'avant main or *Pirouette renversée,* turn on the forehand, possible at the walk or piaffer.

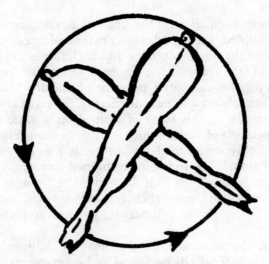

DIAGRAM 16. TURN ON THE CENTRE

The turn on the centre is natural to the horse. The two other turns are school movements.

Their execution will be discussed in greater detail when dealing with the paces at which they can be performed.

COUNTER CHANGES OF HAND ON TWO TRACKS

By crossing from one side of the school to the opposite side, along the diagonal, we perform a change of hand. If, part of the way across, we reverse the direction and return to the side that we had just left, we perform a counterchange of hand.

It will be clear that this movement, if carried out on two

SHOULDER-FORE (STEINBRECHT).
" BASCAR "

T SHOULDER-IN, WALK (MOVING TO
THE RIGHT). " BASCAR "

HALF-PAST, WALK (*Appuyer*) MOVING TO THE LEFT. "BASCAR"

ght: QUARTERS-OUT, WALK (*La croupe en ehors*) MOVING TO THE LEFT. "BASCAR"

FREE WALK ON A LOOSE REIN. "BASCAR"

tracks, requires a reversal of the horse's bend, flexion and side-ways movement.   This raises certain difficulties and calls for special consideration.

These difficulties increase considerably in the repeated counterchanges on two tracks, which require reversal of the horse's direction at intervals of every few strides.   Actually, repeated reversals of this kind, particularly at the trot and canter, belong to the high-school of riding; their discussion will have to be taken in connection with our consideration, in later chapters, of the various gaits.

A Powerful Aid in Difficulties
SHYING

It has been mentioned in Chapter IV, page 49, that we should come to dispose in time, as a result of our training, of a few aids which come very near to compulsion.

So, let us here examine a particularly effective example, resultant from the thorough schooling of our horse on two tracks.

I am thinking of the prevention of shying away from an object which inspires the horse with fear, or fright, and of overcoming his reluctance to pass such an object.

The occurrence is, of course, familiar to all horsemen; the horse's technique is invariably the same.   Let us assume the object of his aversion to have appeared on our right-hand side. The horse will suddenly stare at the object, lift head and neck high, so lightening his forehand and collecting himself on his quarters, preparing to swing round.   That he always does—away from the object of his fright, never towards it.   In so doing, he spins round on his centre; meaning that he swings his quarters, incidentally the seat of his armed strength, towards the object and his vulnerable forehand away from it.

So, having once grasped the technique of the horse's action, or rather proposed action if the rider is alert enough, the latter's technique to prevent the intended movement becomes obvious.

All he has to do is to prevent the intended swing.

He does that by placing his horse in the position shoulder-in, or rather shoulder-in advance (see page 157), more particularly, in the case under review, in the position "right shoulder-in"!

In other words, having the object of our horse's aversion on our right, we use our right leg to prevent the swing of the quarters to the right; at the same time we flex the horse's head to the right with the right rein which, acting as rein of opposition to the haunches, supports the effect of our right leg; in its turn, the effect of the right rein is supported by the action of the left rein against the neck; the reins, acting then together, prevent the forehand swinging to the left. All the while, the left leg, not so far mentioned, maintains impulsion and keeps the horse into his bridle.

It is a method that I have never known to fail on the trained animal and hardly ever on the semi-trained one.

Yet it is a method with which few horsemen appear familiar, even including many who have a quite reasonable experience of two-track movements. The instinctive reaction of most riders when their horse takes fright of an object to their right is to try and hold him to it by pressure of the left leg! Which has an effect completely opposite to the one intended, since it encourages the horse to swing his quarters to the right and so facilitates his turn!

CHAPTER XV

THE WALK

---

*A pace of four-time – The free walk – The walk on a loose
rein – The ordinary walk – The collected walk – The
extended walk – The driving aids – Uses of the walk*

IN schooling our horse, we aim, quite obviously, at attaining
an equivalent degree of proficiency at the three gaits of walk,
trot and canter. In a sense these three gaits are, like everything
in horsemanship, one and indivisible; they are all parts of the
same symphony; they complement each other, and, in many
respects, perfect each other. So, in schooling our horses, we
shall, in a general way, be called upon to seek for the gradual
development of all three gaits more or less simultaneously. It
will be understood, then, that the method of devoting separate
chapters to these three gaits has been adopted for the sake of
clarity only.

The walk, as we have already seen in Chapter VI, is essentially
a quiet and peaceful gait, which makes little demand on muscular and nervous tension. The rider, too, is at ease, comfortable and sitting still. There is plenty of time for carefree, quiet
and restful conversation between both. The walk serves equally
well for periods of rest and relaxation as for the quiet explanation
of new principles between tutor and pupil.

The walk is, in fact, a most useful pace.

Technically, it is a pace of four-time, in which four hoof-
beats are heard at precisely equal intervals. All four legs move
separately. Beginning with a hindleg, say the near-hind, the
sequence is: near-hind, near-fore, off-hind, off-fore. In the walk
the horse has never less than two legs in support at the same
time; there never occurs any moment of suspension.

Any variation from this, the form of the pure walk, is a serious fault in a dressage horse.

By nature, the walk is a relaxed gait, in which the horse's support varies constantly, but slowly and regularly, from one leg to another, from back to front and from side to side. The walk has a peculiar swing to it, with a variation of balance in which neck and head play an important part. In the natural, free walk, head and neck are never still; carried more or less horizontally there is a marked continuous swing, somewhat up and down and from side to side, in time and in sympathy with the movement of the legs.

It is of the essence of a good free walk that the rider shall do nothing to impede this natural movement of the horse's head and neck. And it is of the essence of good training that the natural aptitudes of the horse shall be cultivated, improved if possible, and certainly never suppressed.

The free walk then, remains basic, at all time, to all good training. In the free walk, under saddle, the horse goes on a long rein, with but the slightest contact and without any attempt at collection. The rider has to do no more than supervise, as far as necessary, the horse's direction and the maintenance of an even, completely natural pace, without laziness it is true, but most certainly without hurry. Horse and rider are both relaxed, at ease with each other and with the world.

The walk on a loose rein is essentially the same, with the sole difference that the reins are now dropped on the horse's neck, or held so long that there is no direct contact between mouth and hand, excepting through the weight of the reins alone. The horse is given complete freedom of head and neck and allowed to stretch and to drop them as much as he likes. It is an invaluable form of rest and of reward to the horse, in particular after any form of collected or strenuous work; the horse is able to stretch and relax all his muscles.

Whilst both these forms of walk should be free and easy, extension or speed should not be attempted in this form. In attempting to increase the speed of a free walk, which is easy enough in itself, the rider will find the horse to quicken the rhythm of his strides, or to hurry, but not to extend the length of them.

These forms of walk are, of course, absolutely elementary; but they are not, for that, any the less important! And if,

in attempting to do dressage, we ever lose sight of things that
are basic; if for instance we cause the horse to lose his natural
walk, we have, most certainly, taken a wrong turning some-
where.

There is little that the rider can or need do actively to make
or to perfect a good natural walk; but he can assist his horse,
passively, by not hindering him in any way. He can also select
for this work the sort of country which, by its nature and its
going, helps the horse's muscular development, his natural
balance under saddle, his attention and his interest. Hilly
country, with gentle slopes, woodlands and varied types of
natural going are most helpful in these respects.

It is characteristic of the free walk, and even more so of the
walk on a loose rein, that the rider effects a minimum of control,
leaving the horse "on trust" as it were, largely to his own
devices.

Obviously, there are many occasions when it would not be
wise, or safe, to do so, when it is necessary to have the animal
more readily under normal control. To that end we need a
more positive contact, a somewhat higher head carriage, a
slightly more compact bearing of the horse, in short, a degree
of collection.

We find these conditions answered, in a sufficient degree for
normal riding purposes, in the ordinary walk. In the ordinary
walk, we expect a measure of acceptance of the bridle, soft but
positive, on a rein of moderate length, the horse walking at a
natural pace, between our legs and lightly on our hands. In
reality the horse, at an ordinary walk, is not so much collected
as ready to be collected instantly, should conditions require it.

The subject of collecting a horse at a walk is of considerable
interest.

There is no pace at which it is easier to obtain a pretty-looking
head carriage, giving the impression of collection, than at the
walk; hence the popularity of the method with the general run
of nagsmen and dealers' men. There is no method either, by
which it is easier to ruin the horse. The reader will recall
from our discussions in Chapter X that no form of collection
is of any value unless as a result of lightening the forehand by
increased activity of the quarters.

Now the walk is essentially a pace which is by nature unsuited
for this purpose. By nature, the walking horse assumes a hori-

zontal attitude; in the walk, as we have seen, the horse has never less than two legs in support; in fact, support on two legs alternates with support on three. The distribution of weight varies constantly, from back to front and from side to side; there never is any concentration of balance, nor the degree of elastic muscular tension, of energy and impulsion, whereby alone carriage and lightness can be truly created.

Consequently attempts at achieving "carriage" by the use of the walk alone will fail, because the pace does not lend itself to the creation of compressed energy. Instead, a semblance of results will be achieved by shortening the forehand, pulling the head into the body and not by driving the body up to the head. That, as we have seen already, results in a closing of the shoulder, in the destruction of free forward movement, in a mouth behind instead of on the bridle and, more often than not, in destruction of the pure four-time gait. High-couraged horses may be induced to jog at the slightest provocation, or else the horse may tend towards the amble. The demanded increase of energy, which it is difficult for the horse to deliver at this gait, may induce him to approach the hoof-beats of each lateral pair of legs. Instead of the absolutely regular intervals, 1-2-3-4, of near-hind, near-fore, off-hind and off-fore, the horse may tend to near-hind and near-fore close together, a little interval, followed by off-hind and off-fore, such as 1.2-3.4.

Fortunately, all these difficulties can be avoided quite easily be allowing carriage, energy, rhythm and collection to develop at the trot and from the trot and, in conjunction with it, at the walk also. These matters will be dealt with more fully in a following chapter dealing with the trot more specifically.

Suffice it to say here then that the slight approach to carriage and collection required in the ordinary walk will develop automatically and without any special schooling during the early stages of a horse's career as a direct result of his work at the ordinary trot.

In the collected walk, the horse marches, in regular four-time, with great energy, with much carriage, with lightness and with a perfect mouth. Again, the qualities for this work can only be developed in conjunction with the trot.

The same applies to the extended walk. In this work the horse lengthens his stride to the greatest extent of his capabilities without hurrying his step. Success in this movement is not possible until the horse has formed a perfect mouth, ready to smile and to flex at the slightest contact of the rein. If we attempt to develop the natural free walk into an extended walk before the horse's mouth is ready, we shall only succeed in hurrying his stride but not in lengthening it; speed should not be confused with extension. The made mouth is essential because, as pointed out repeatedly, relaxation of the mouth and muscular relaxation are bound up together. And both are needed to achieve extension.

THE DRIVING AIDS

In the walk, as in all other paces, the amount of energy and impulsion required is controlled by the use of the rider's legs.

But not quite in the same way, at any rate not consistently so.

In most cases, at other gaits, the rider will use both legs simultaneously for the creation and maintenance of impulsion. To a certain extent the same method suffices for ordinary riding purposes at the walk also, but it can never be fully effective at that gait and most certainly not in its more extended horizontal forms.

The characteristics of the four-time gait have already been described. We know that impulsion, or forward drive, is delivered by the horse's hindlegs. We know also that the sequence of footfalls is near-hind, near-fore, off-hind, off-fore; that there is a definite time lag between the propelling actions of both hindlegs.

We need to be clear about it also that a driving aid cannot influence the action of any given limb after such limb has already left the ground; whilst this consideration may become largely theoretical in other gaits, with a much quicker succession of footfalls, it remains eminently practical in the case of the more leisurely walk.

It follows that in the walk, to be fully effective, the action of the rider's driving leg-aid must coincide with the moment in which the hindleg to be activated touches down. In other words, to be fully effective, the rider's driving leg-aids are used alternately, coinciding with the alternating footfalls of the horse's hindlegs. There is in that no difficulty, since the rider can feel these moments distinctly by the peculiar swing of the horse's body; he has but to follow that swing, from side to side, with each of his legs and, when a driving aid is to be given, accentuate the inward swing of each leg slightly; his aid will then synchronize with the corresponding footfall of the horse's hindleg.

The method described applies in particular to all forms of horizontal, non-collected walk, including of course the extended walk. It is less essential in the energetic, highly collected walk, which approaches the trot in outward form, because the horse so far advanced is already so saturated with the "forward urge" that drive from the rider's legs is hardly needed any longer; the horse will have reached the stage where the mere pressure of the rider's boot on the air is sufficient to send him forward (*le cheval fuit le vent de la botte*).

Even so, the trainer in advanced dressage needs to know the differing effects obtainable from the alternating leg-aid, at the walk, and the simultaneous leg-aid at the trot. As pointed out, there comes a moment when the horse's form and bearing in the highly collected trot and in the highly collected walk approach similarity. So, there may be moments also when the horse will become confused if his rider's simultaneous leg pressure, used normally at the trot or to move off from the walk into a trot, may at other times merely demand increased energy at the walk.

USES OF THE WALK

The usefulness of the walk as a peaceful and relaxed pace for the purpose of rest and for that of introducing and explaining new movements has been pointed out already.

In the latter respect the walk lends itself in particular to the initial study of all circular movements. The horse is relaxed, there is hardly any muscular tension, there is but moderate forward energy; there is, in consequence, hardly any risk of conflict between the effects of leg and rein. The horse is more horizontal; he is also longer. As a result it is comparatively easy for him to bend and to flex to circular movements and to alternate between flexions to either side.

Since the effect of speed does not enter the problem, the horse can do all these movements in a vertical position. Like-

FREE WALK ON A LONG REIN. "BASCAR"

ORDINARY WALK. "BASCAR"

COLLECTED WALK. "IBRAHIM"

COLLECTED WALK. COMMANDANT WALLON, CADRE NOIR, SAUMUR. "TAINE"

THE REIN-BACK. "BASCAR"

wise, there is no appreciable surcharge on the inner hindlegs as there is at the trot, nor does the variation in length of stride of the inner and the outer legs cause any problem, since these do not move in pairs but individually.

For similar reasons the walk should be chosen for the preliminary instruction of lateral movements. But there is one important factor to be borne in mind. To the effect that the walk is not, physically, the easiest pace whereat the horse can do this work! Rather to the contrary. We have seen, in the relevant chapter, that the horse possesses no lateral flexibility in his limbs themselves. Such lateral flexibility as there is, and it is in truth small enough, derives not from the limbs, but from shoulder and haunch; and the object of the exercises concerned is to develop the elasticity and strength of the muscles and joints of these parts.

Now in doing lateral work at the trot or at the canter, the horse uses the moment of suspension characteristic of both these gaits for the purpose of jumping sideways, and by so doing he lightens considerably the lateral effort demanded of his muscles.

At the walk there is no moment of suspension; moreover, the horse has never less than two legs and often three legs in support at the same time. Consequently it follows that, from a physical point of view, this lateral work actually imposes a greater muscular strain at the walk than at any other pace.

It is essential, therefore, to commence this lateral work carefully, and, having due regard to these difficulties, at only slight angles.

But it will be understood at the same time that the full benefits of lateral flexibility cannot be attained in the long run unless the work achieved later at the trot and canter be finally perfected again at the walk.

We have here the one example where work at the walk is capable of exceeding the gymnastic results obtainable at the more energetic and faster paces.

But apart from that, the work itself is not capable of producing the athletic results aimed at in dressage. For these we have to rely on the trot and canter, and particularly on the former.

CHAPTER XVI

THE REIN-BACK

I HAVE elected to treat the rein-back next to the walk because it is necessary, in my opinion, that a horse should understand this movement from quite early on in his training; I consider a horse that cannot rein-back a most awkward proposition to take out for a ride.

There are many authorities who would not agree with this opinion. They hold the view that anything that might tend to endanger forward obedience of the horse ought to be avoided at all costs until that forward obedience has been fully established and confirmed. With that I agree.

They consider that the use of the rein-back is such a danger. With that I do not agree. Properly used, there is no danger. But abused, well yes, that is quite a different matter! Probably my learned friends fight shy of advocating an early use of the rein-back because they know only too well that use degenerates so often into abuse! Well, that I imagine I know as well as they do. But then the whole purpose of this book is to try and clarify the distinction between what is good and what is bad, so that I would hardly be playing the game with my readers if I avoided subjects for fear of being misunderstood.

Frankly, it has ever been a source of amazement to me that so many people appear to experience such difficulties with a movement which is really so exceedingly simple.

However, let us examine the matter.

Although every horse, from a foal onwards, can quite well step back when he needs to, it is yet a motion which no horse ever uses of his own volition unless he cannot do otherwise, in order, for instance, to extricate himself from a position from which there is no other issue. Even then he will attempt to swing round, in order to move forward, as soon as he can see a chance, or even half a chance, of being able to do so.

In that respect then, stepping back is not a natural motion to the horse.

It appears unnatural also in that the horse cannot really walk back; he cannot use, in that motion, the normal four-time movement of the walk; in stepping back he must use the diagonal two-time motion of the trot, near-hind and off-fore together followed by off-hind and near-fore.

Now let us see how to teach our horse, and also how not to do it.

In the first place we have to explain, which can be done to any horse in a couple of minutes. We place ourselves, on foot, in front of our horse. We tell him to "back", stepping deliberately towards him and delivering some slight taps against his breast with our whip or effecting pressure with our fingers. Done intelligently, the horse will understand, and obey, almost instantly; one or two steps is quite sufficient. On no account are we to use any pressure by means of the bridle; we are explaining, not forcing (in other words ruining!).

We then continue precisely the same system from the saddle; the voice and a few slight taps with our whip against the horse's breast; back, just one or two steps; we then associate a feel on the mouth, not a pull, with the use of the whip and the voice.

After this simple explanation we may continue, gradually and as time goes on, with the proper aids, relying on the combined efforts of legs and hands. We are to teach the horse that the rein-back is in essence itself a forward movement, merely done in the opposite direction.

This is how I proceed.

My horse is standing still.

I close my legs and precisely at the same moment, or a fraction earlier, I bring my hands a little forward, lengthening the rein slightly. Answer: the horse moves forward.

Or, I close by legs without moving my hands. Answer: the horse makes contact, realizes the bridle does not yield, feels that the pressure of my legs ceases as he contacts his bridle, realizes that he has done all that is required, stands still in the collected halt.

Or, I close my legs, moving my hands forward just that tiny

fraction necessary to allow my horse to initiate the tendency to forward movement; at the very moment I feel that tendency, I close my fingers on the rein to prevent the development of that forward tendency, whilst my legs continue their pressure. Answer: my horse steps back.

And he does so the more easily because the forward tendency allowed him has been sufficient to mobilize his muscular and nervous system.

And, this being the essence of my answer to my learned friends, the horse is at all times between leg and hand, the action of the former always preceding the action of the latter and always predominant over it. Consequently, my horse is always ready to move in any direction desired, forward or backward, according to the appropriate action of leg and hand.

Admittedly, the explanation given above is not fully exhaustive. It is essential that the horse be ridden back, carefully, methodically and step by step; in such a manner that the movement can be terminated at any desired moment by a halt or be transposed, with equal ease and certainty, into a forward movement.

It is to be realized also that the rein-back is at all times so limited in its practical use that there is no sense, and there might well be some danger, in ever asking more than about half a dozen steps.

It is to be realized in particular that any attempt at pulling the horse back by means of the rein can be disastrous in its result, and it will certainly be just that if the rein is unsupported by the initial and continued pressure of the leg.

The essence of the system that I have described lies in the fact that my horses move back in front of the leg and on their bridle. The horse that is being pulled back is merely being taught to escape backwards from the pressure on his bridle. And that, of course, is liable to lead to very serious trouble indeed.

To sum up, I can see no danger at all in using the rein-back on the young horse, provided it be done in the right manner and with moderation for practical purposes, such as for instance opening and shutting gates.

But the rein-back has other purposes to fulfil as well. We make use of the movement in dressage for the purpose of strengthening the loins, and for suppling loins, haunches and hocks. In reining back, we shorten the horse from front to back, bring additional weight on the hocks, which are made to bend more, we cause the quarters to drop and the loins to rise. Combining this exercise with a strike-off at the trot or canter we release the bow that has first been spanned. Hocks propel the weight forward with increased energy, the quarters rise and the loins dip and lengthen. All in all, a potent muscular exercise.

Obviously, that type of use emphatically does belong to fairly advanced dressage and is not recommended during elementary stages.

Having thus described the method that I advocate, the details of a correct execution remain to be discussed.

The horse, in reining back, shall retain the form and bearing of a collected movement. Head carried high, bent at the poll, his face nearing the vertical but never behind it. He shall keep his head still and his mouth quiet, flexing but not open. He shall neither throw the head up nor overbend. There shall be no appreciable tension and certainly no visible pull on the reins. The rider's hands shall look, and be, relaxed and shall not have to make any discernible effort. The rider's legs shall be close to the horse; they shall maintain the horse's impulsion and shall at the same time guide him to move quite straight. The steps shall be equal, deliberate but slow. The horse shall bend his hocks markedly in order to be able to bring each hind-leg in turn backwards in a straight line, precisely in the axis of the horse's body. If the steps are hurried the horse will lack the time needed to lift his hocks and to bend them sufficiently; he will then not be able to step back straight, but will be forced to step back wide, dishing as it were with either one or both hindlegs. The rider shall be able to halt the horse smoothly with precision upon completion of any given number of backward steps.

CHAPTER XVII

THE TROT

---

*The gait, its advantages and its limitation – The rising and
the sitting trot – Development of the trot – The collected
walk – The extended trot – The mitteltrab – The trot on
two tracks – The passage and the piaffe*

THE GAIT, ITS ADVANTAGES AND ITS LIMITATIONS

DE le Guérinière spoke of the "utility of the walk" and of
the "necessity of the trot".

As far as dressage is concerned, the trot is indeed the fundamental gait.

The horse's natural carriage at the trot approaches quite
closely to the perfect bearing expected of the fully schooled horse;
in fact the best natural carriage of which the horse is capable
and the best carriage to be expected of the schooled horse are
identical.

However, the horse shows his best natural carriage but seldom;
only when he prances around in that spectacular cadenced gait
which can make him so beautiful to behold. It is that cadence
which is the essence of his beauty. It is that cadence then which
the trainer will seek to call forth at his bidding. But, whereas
the horse chooses a more or less specific speed for the expression
of this exuberant pride, the trainer will seek to make him produce it throughout the infinite range of speed possible at the
trot; varying from the piaffe, or cadenced trot on the spot, to the
most extended pace possible.

In his natural cadence, the horse is as light as a feather; and
why shouldn't he be with no weight and, be it noted, with no
bridle to mar the flight of his fancy? And, the trainer who
fails to preserve this airy lightness, given by God to the good

190

horse, fails in everything, since without that very lightness truly graceful cadence cannot exist. To succeed in these ends demands talent backed by experience. "Talent" is not a mere word, but an idea which it is often difficult to define. The term, used in connection with horsemanship, signifies to me the gift of understanding the horse, of truly loving him, of feeling him and of seeking success through co-operation with his remarkable gifts and not through domination.

Experience is needed because the work is not easy.

But it is easier at the trot than at any other gait!

The trot is a pace of two-time, by far the most regular of the horse's gaits; it is also the most easily balanced, and the form, the position, the attitude assumed by the horse at this gait vary but little throughout the wide variety of speed and tempo possible. In the trot the good horse goes naturally off his hocks, is naturally light in his forehand and carries his head high. And, above all, he keeps his head still. He does not need the play of his head and neck in anything like the same degree as at the walk and less also than at the canter.

This simplifies the rider's task enormously, since it enables him to hold his hands still, to avoid interference with the horse's mouth, be it voluntary or involuntary. In reality, all that the rider need do at the trot is to sit still, to cultivate, supervise and encourage the horse's natural rhythm and to avoid doing anything liable to disturb it. And the most certain way to such disturbance is interference with the horse's mouth. In answer to such interference the horse will, as we know, take evading action with the head, carrying it either too low, too high, too far forward or too far back; anyway, in some place different from where he would carry it in accordance with the natural laws of balance.

If riders could but realize how much damage they can do, and how quickly, by interference with the bridle and how extremely difficult, if not impossible, it is to do any good that way, there would not be the vast number of ruined horses to be seen around every day.

And it is all so unnecessary.

Carriage depends entirely on the development of the power and suppleness of the horse's muscles and joints, combined with the horse's free, voluntary and completely unperturbed acceptance of his rider's presence and of his help.

For of course the rider can help and can do so a great deal. He has but to supervise and cultivate, in sympathy with his horse, the animal's rhythm at the trot.

So easy, comparatively, at that gait.

The trot is by nature an absolutely rhythmic gait. And rhythm is the father of cadence. So by concentrating on rhythm cadence will, in the end, come all by itself, and with it perfection.

The rhythm of the trot is of itself of inestimable value for the horse's athletic development. It is by essence an exercise in which, like in Swedish gymnastics, rhythm plays a preponderant part. The trot is the only gait which is absolutely evenly balanced; in it, the horse goes with clockwork regularity, one diagonal after another, time for time, one hoofbeat matching the other. It is thus comparatively easy for the rider to supervise this rhythm, to cultivate it, to improve it and gradually to assume, himself, control over its tempo.

Meanwhile, in the trot, the horse works all his limbs, his shoulders and his hocks to an equal degree; no limb works more than any other, nor different from any other; his muscular development, the strength of thighs and forearm, the flexibility of hocks and knees and indeed of all joints is developed harmoniously.

In brief, no other gait presents so many gymnastic advantages.

Yet, the trot fails to some extent in one respect.

It has no great effect in suppling the back.

The horse's bearing is to a large extent static. The head and neck are kept still and there is but very little natural swing in the use of the back of a trotting horse. His back, as we have discussed in previous chapters, is stiff by nature. Now this stiffness of the back is presumably of no detriment to the horse in his natural state, but such stiff-backed horses are definitely unpleasant to ride. One cannot achieve the comfortable unity of movement looked for, it is uncomfortable, difficult and sometimes impossible to sit down to their trot; and, as long as that stiffness, or even a degree of it, remains, we shall never achieve the cadence, the balance and the lightness which depend so much on all-round suppleness of movement.

Frequently, this stiffness is pronounced in horses that are by nature strong movers, just the sort of horses therefore that are

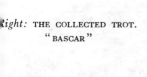

Above: THE ORDINARY TROT.
"BASCAR"

Right: THE COLLECTED TROT.
"BASCAR"

THE EXTENDED TROT. "BASCAR"

THE *Mitteltrab*. HERR RICHARD WAETJEN. "HAUSTOCHTER"

AL PASSAGE OF A RACEHORSE. THE CHASER "MONT TREMBLANT" (JOCKEY D. V. DICK)

THE SOFT PASSAGE (*Le Doux Passage*). " BASCAR "

likely to make into the best and the most spectacular dressage horses.

Now, the whole of the work discussed in previous chapters, and the methods to be discussed more particularly in this one, will all help to correct this stiffness of the back to a greater or smaller degree; but they would frequently not be fully effective, if the work were carried out at the trot alone. In dressage the various gaits complement each other and, basic and important though the trot undoubtedly is, we cannot complete our task without the help of the other gaits.

The walk, and particularly the free walk, is, as we have seen in a previous chapter, beneficial to the swing of the back. This is especially so if the nature of the going is chosen so as to include gradients and uneven going. Even so, the walk is not a sufficiently intensive exercise to exert a decisive influence.

But the canter can do so, in a manner which will be discussed in the next chapter.

THE RISING AND THE SITTING TROT

The rider may trot either rising *à l'Anglaise* or sitting *à la Française*. Both methods have their uses. It is not possible, nor necessary, to lay down hard and fast rules regarding the use of either one or the other of these methods during our work of training the horse.

Generally, the rider will use the rising trot for all ordinary work in the open country and for most extended movements, wherever they are made. Outside, on uneven ground, the rising trot is more comfortable, less tiring and therefore better for both horse and rider. On perfectly level going, in the school or elsewhere, the sitting trot may be equally comfortable for the rider, and therefore also for the horse, even at the most energetic and extended paces. But it will never be comfortable at any strong trot until the horse's back really swings and carries its rider as if on springs. There is no advantage to be gained, either from the rider's or the horse's point of view, by insisting on a seat which is uncomfortable to both, and so can only result in disturbance of harmony. So, when we are schooling our horse, it is sensible to take the rising trot whenever the sitting trot tends to discomfort. There are one or two specific cases, to be discussed presently, when it is sensible to take the rising trot also for the purpose of encouraging impulsion.

In making this statement, I assume of course that the rider does possess an adequate seat (see Chapter VII) and can sit down to a proper trot and not merely to a jog, which would be within the province of any beginner. If he did not possess that aptitude, he would not be able to judge, and would at any rate be, as yet, unfit to undertake serious dressage.

Before leaving the subject of the rising trot, I must crave my reader's indulgence for the inclusion of a few observations which are so elementary as to appear out of place in this book. Unfortunately, it is my experience that an astonishing number of riders whom one would expect to know all about it are quite ignorant of the simple principles involved.

In the first place then, and that everybody knows, we avoid, by using the rising trot, one bump in two. We come down in the saddle as one particular diagonal pair of legs meet the ground and rise from the saddle as the same pair leave the ground. We miss the impact of the other diagonal pair of legs altogether. We may rise either on the near fore-off hind diagonal or on the off fore-near hind diagonal. The fact which astonishes me is that any number of riders are in the habit of always rising on the same diagonal. They appear oblivious of the fact that one can and should rise on both diagonals alternately; in the sense that we trot away for the first ten minutes or so, we use, say the right diagonal (off-fore and near-hind) and that during the next period of trotting we use the left diagonal (near-fore and off-hind) and so on alternately. If we fail to do so we tire our horse, and in the end wear him out, one-sidedly. We also disturb the perfectly even rhythm of the gait in the long run, render our horse one-sided and tend to ruin his straightness. In that respect, the experienced horseman may at times be able to use the rising trot on one particular diagonal rather than on the other, temporarily, to improve unevenness in his horse's gait. If there be unevenness of gait it is usually the diagonal on which the rider rises and comes down which makes the longer stride. This is due to the fact that the driving aid of the rider's legs usually coincides with his return in the saddle and therefore influences the corresponding hindleg of the horse.

The dressage rider, of course, has to meet certain requirements expected of him in the arena with respect to the rising trot. This concerns the method of going round bends and corners, whether to rise on the outside diagonal or on the inside one. There are two schools of thought. The majority hold that it is preferable to rise on the outside diagonal. Others hold the opposite view. Neither side has ever been able to offer convincing argument. It is more a matter of "feel". My feeling is with that of the majority, but I am quite ready to admit that there may be nothing much in it. However, I make my practice accordingly. There is no rule about it, except that each competitor, free to choose his own system, must be consistent. In other words, once a competitor has ridden one bend on either the inside or the outside diagonal, he has to continue the same system; so, in changing from one bend to another at the rising trot, he must change the diagonal or be faulted.

The sitting trot unites the rider more closely to his horse; rider and horse feel each other more intimately; consequently the aids gain in delicacy and precision; the rider is much more conscious of rhythm, of swing and of cadence and is better able to work intelligently for their development; in fact, the sitting trot is a sensitive and accurate barometer of the degree of suppleness achieved in his horse's back; his comfort will increase *pro rata* of the progress made in that direction until, finally, he will be as comfortable at an extended as at a collected trot.

DEVELOPMENT OF THE TROT

No horse is fit to be taken into dressage work until his ordinary walk, trot and canter have been established on sound lines during his normal preliminary training in the open.

So, before we begin to talk of developing the trot, we assume that the horse is capable of a good, unspoilt ordinary trot. That means a trot with reasonably roomy strides, of even length, in regular tempo and therefore of good rhythm; it means that the head be carried still, in a normal position, neither high nor low, with the nose in front of the vertical, at an angle of about 45°. It implies that he is capable of reasonable variations of speed, within the frame necessary for ordinary comfortable riding purposes, and that he can be brought back to a walk or a halt gradually, without conscious effort. Obviously, he has a nice, naturally soft and unspoilt mouth, ready to develop into a made good mouth.

That then is the basis whereon to begin our work.

Our purpose is simple.

It is that of making the range of our horse's trot infinitely variable, from the maximum of extension to the maximum of collection, with perfect cadence and absolute fluency throughout the range.

By the time we have succeeded in just that, we have succeeded in everything!

We begin by developing the expressiveness of the ordinary trot. We wish to add a degree of brilliance, which means more energy. We begin the easiest way. The easiest way to create increased energy is by the demand of greater speed. But we must be extremely careful. The horse, also, is intent to answer our demands in the easiest way; he finds it easier to quicken rather than to lengthen his strides; and that we wish to avoid at all cost!

So this is how we proceed.

We have our horse nicely settled at his ordinary trot with a soft contact on the mouth. We have got him so far that the regular rhythm of that trot has become a routine; we are able to maintain him at it without effort and with hardly any aids on our part. At his ordinary trot the horse is pleasantly active and light.

We now close our legs gently, just enough to make him accelerate, just enough to do so distinctly but no more. The energy for this acceleration is delivered by a hindleg, which pushes with increased strength from a position behind the vertical. This action can have no other effect than to lengthen the next few strides. But only through the momentary effect of acceleration! That effect ceases as soon as the horse settles to his increased speed; the increased speed in itself does not really help our purpose; on the contrary it may very well spoil it; it may cause the horse to run fast with short strides, which is a disastrous form. It is for that very reason that we demand only momentary acceleration which must, as we have seen, produce a few lengthening strides. We demand this acceleration by action of the legs alone, without action by the hands.

But, as soon as we have obtained a few longer strides, the hands receive the horse gently on the bit, the legs cease driving, the horse is brought back quietly to his ordinary trot.

And here, in a nutshell, we have the entire principle for the development of the diagonal gaits, extension, collection, retardation! We extend the stride, we receive the increased energy on the bit (collection), we retard. It is all so simple. Provided always that we are content with very little at a time, that our aids are light and delicate, that we do not surprise the horse, that we do not startle him, that we do not call forth even the semblance of impetuous or rough reactions, that we do not upset the even rhythm of the pure diagonal gait, that we keep the horse straight.

The horse, meeting his bit gently through the effect of his own impulsion, will begin to flex and bridle, the retardation will bring him back on his hocks, be it ever so slightly to start with; both effects will gradually lead to collection and to all that this implies, suppleness, balance, lightness, and carriage.

So we work on gradually, as time goes on, along the same lines.

Our first line of progress is again to accelerate a few steps, receive the horse on the bit and continue for a few more extended strides on the bit, before we come back to the ordinary trot. Gradually, we begin working both ways, accelerate to lengthen the stride, hold the lengthened stride for a few moments, and come back to just a little slower than an ordinary trot. Soon we shall be able to produce the longer stride, softly on the bit, at a speed no greater than the ordinary trot. We have then achieved the addition of a measure of brilliance through increased impulsion without any further need for increased speed.

By that time the rhythm will have improved, and begun to tend towards cadence; the horse's back will begin to soften and his mouth to become more and more responsive.

The time has arrived to assume the sitting trot and to concentrate on the horse's responsiveness in maintained cadence during slight variations of pace, and without variation of pace.

It is desirable to achieve a fair measure of cadence, before risking any considerable variations of pace. If we demand more than the horse can do, we risk spoiling his rhythm and cadence. If we demand more than the rider can do we risk spoiling everything. If we proceed within the capacities of both, the horse will assume balance and correct still-head carriage quite automatically, as the direct consequence of correct movement, and the rider, if he be reasonably gifted and attentive, will perceive and feel the supreme ease and lightness of his own actions. The fluency of the horse's mouth, his quiet ease, the comfort of his paces are the rider's reliable guide; if he fails to read them, the horse will have to resort to clearer language still; if the rider hands be not gentle enough, or the reins too short, the horse will protest by his head carriage, too high, too low or too deep. These are certain signs that the rider is, or has been, at fault.

Having thus achieved a nicely energetic, rhythmic trot, always in impulsion, neither too fast nor too slow, the rider may now go a little further, again both ways; he will be able to go a little slower still and, at the same time, seek a degree of greater extension.

The time has now come to associate, in the horse's mind, the sitting trot with cadenced and comparatively slow work and the rising trot with more extended paces. So, to extend, the rider rises from the saddle and follows up almost immediately, but not simultaneously, with a pressure of the leg. The act of rising becomes an aid by association. Very soon the horse will need no other.

This response of the horse to the act of rising can be of great assistance in the execution, during the training, of certain exercises in which it may be difficult to maintain the desired degree of impulsion.

Meanwhile, the rider can now extend the range of his rhythmic trot gradually over an ever wider range.

In the sphere of the sitting trot, he will be able to vary, by frequent extensions and retardations, his actual speed from that of an ordinary trot to that of a very slow trot indeed. But such variations of speed will be of no value unless they lead to ever-increasing accentuation of rhythm and thus, gradually, to cadence.

Now, whilst rhythm is no other than keeping correct time, cadence is keeping time with a purpose, marking the rhythm with great energy, beating the drum as it were. To transpose rhythm into cadence the horse has to use great energy all the time, very much greater indeed than the untrained horse would use for comparable speeds. The trained horse delivers the maximum of impulsion all the time, whatever the speed, whatever the movement. But, being trained, he does that easily, without strain, without effort, in perfect lightness. That, precisely, has been the object of all his training!

Throughout that training, at the trot particularly, it is the rider's task then to seek for this state of energetic rhythmic action which is cadence; action with a "snap" in it, with what the French call *tride*. That action cannot be achieved but by a combination of absolute impulsion with absolute lightness. These qualities are inseparable and it is only the rider who can call them into being. There can be no lightness in the horse without lightness in the rider, who should need no more than a mere twitch of a leg muscle to create and to maintain impulsion and no more than a touch of a finger to control it. It is to that end that, in sympathy with his horse, the rider has to work until the good horse answers to indications so slight as to emanate from subconscious action. In that state, and in cadence the horse will be, truly, in the *rassembler*.

In working on these extensions and retardations, then, the rider will proceed so gradually that strength of rein is never, and strength of leg hardly ever, required. But he will have to realize that a good slow trot demands a greater degree of impulsion than a faster one. The slower the pace, the more the rider has to concentrate on the maintenance of impulsion.

It is difficult, of course, to arrive at this high degree of impulsion whilst being restricted, as the rider undoubtedly is, to such careful and delicate use of his legs. It is in this respect that the circular movements are so helpful. Here, as we know, the inner hindleg has to tread further under the body and to take a greater share of the weight, and also to deliver a greater share of the impulsion. Now, as the horse gets gradually fitter, more supple and more expert at this work, he will learn to deliver the extra energy needed all by himself and almost automatically. Circling to the left, we stimulate the right diagonal, the near-hind and, in sympathy with it, the off-fore. Circling to both sides equally, we develop the action of both diagonals equally. Circling to one side more than the other, we have the means of concentrating more on one particular diagonal as may be in need of extra stimulation.

Work on two tracks, and in particular the shoulder-in, has similar effects.

All the work so far described, at the sitting trot, is work in collection leading up by stages to the highest degree of collection, the *rassembler*.

Lastly, the rider has to study the transition from trot to walk, and from walk to trot, by delicate means, and ultimately also from trot to halt and from halt to trot. Actually the transition from trot to walk, and vice versa, is a most valuable exercise. In ordinary riding, and consequently also in the earliest stages of our dressage, the only correct way to perform this transition is to slow up gradually and to let the trot subside naturally into an ordinary walk. This is done by loss of impulsion in an uncollected form; it could not be done otherwise, so long as the horse lacks the balance needed to retain impulsion and lightness at a very slow trot.

Gradually, as his proficiency in this respect improves, we shall be able to obtain this transition with but a stride or two of subsiding impulsion and without loss of collection. Finally, we may obtain the transition to a walk, and even to a halt, without loss of either impulsion or collection and without any intermediate subsiding stride; the horse changes directly from a cadenced slow trot, full of impulsion, to a lively collected walk.

Before discussing this important subject further, I ought to devote a few words to the handling of the reins in these collected exercises. Actually, this aspect ought not to cause the rider any difficulty. It is of the essence of the collected trot that the horse shall keep his head still; his entire attitude and bearing remains almost unaltered throughout the range of speed possible at this gait. Variation of speed is effected by extension of stride, without affecting either the horse's carriage or the cadence of movement. Thus, the variation of rein-action is but slight, and limited to almost invisible adjustment for increases and decreases of pace.

The Collected Walk

The F.E.I. have defined the collected walk in the following manner: "The horse moves resolutely forward with his neck raised and rounded. The head approaches the vertical position. The hindlegs are engaged. The horse moves vigorously while still maintaining the walk, placing each of his legs in regular sequence; each step covers less ground and is higher than in the ordinary walk, because all the joints bend more markedly. The mobility is greater. The collected walk is necessarily slower

PASSAGE. COLONEL DECARPENTRY. "PROFESSEUR"

PASSAGE. COMMANDANT WALLON, CADRE NOIR, SAUMUR. "TAINE"

PASSAGE. "BASCAR"

PASSAGE. CAPITAINE LAVERGNE, CAVALRY SCHOOL, SAUMUR

than the ordinary walk, as otherwise it would become a hurried walk"

The quintessence of this definition is:

(a) that the horse shall go in the walk's regular four-time tempo;

(b) that the horse shall carry its head high, in a position almost identical to that of a good collected trot;

(c) that the pace shall be full of energy, and expressive.

That, in other words, the horse's bearing shall derive from mobility, impulsion and lightness.

It has been pointed out in Chapter XV that it is extremely difficult to obtain these effects by way of development of the walk.

Good head carriage can only be obtained naturally, without effort and without detriment, as the result of lightness through mobility of the quarters. That mobility is not a natural characteristic of the walk.

But it is of the trot. Especially the cadenced, highly energetic collected trot. And the whole of the horse's bearing at that trot, his grace, his lightness and his mobility are precisely the attributes we wish to preserve in the collected walk also.

So, it is plainly indicated that we should develop the collected walk, the really collected walk that is, in the *rassembler*, light, expressive and graceful, from the collected trot.

Once we have progressed so far that the transitions from the collected trot to the collected walk have become fluent and light, it will be easy to maintain the horse's bearing, and his mobility, at the walk also. It would be descriptive, even though not entirely correct, to say that the collected walk has all the characteristics of a collected trot in four-time.

The collected walk, once achieved, can be used in itself as a means to achieve further refinement in controlling the use of each one of the horse's individual limbs. As we have done at the trot, we can vary the speed and length of stride of the collected walk almost infinitely from pronounced movement to hardly any movement at all, to no movement at all, to the rein-back and vice-versa. It is the very shading of these movements which will, through leg and bridle, convey to the rider a feel of the co-ordination of individual limbs and muscle groups, which will establish between him and the horse a degree of intimacy of aid and response which will be of inestimable value in the more difficult work that is to follow.

THE EXTENDED TROT

The use of the rising seat in conjunction with the extended trot has been referred to in a preceding paragraph already. Again, the development of the more extended forms of trot benefits, as all other paces do, from variations of speed with particular attention to the preservation and the gradual improvement of the length of stride. Naturally, the development of collection and of extension proceed more or less simultaneously.

But with one proviso.

The school is not an ideal place for the practice of extended paces. The straight lines are much too short, and the many turns and corners make it impossible for the horse to persevere for any length of time in the right type of action with the hindlegs.

These legs, to make the horse trot at all, have to deliver a dual type of effect. In the first place they have to throw him upwards, off the ground; this they do from a position near the vertical. In the second place, they have to drive him forward; that they do from a position behind the vertical.

In the collected paces, we strive for cadence, tending towards a moment of suspension; consequently we concentrate more on the lifting effect of the hindlegs than on the driving one. The collected form of the horse, short, with head carried high, favours that effect.

In the extended paces, on the contrary, we concentrate on the driving effect of the hindlegs more than on the lifting one. The extended form of the horse, long, with head carried lower, is essential for that effect.

It will be understood then, that the continuous variation in type of action imposed by the many corners of a school make extended action round them so difficult as to tax even the fully schooled horse to the utmost. It is impossible to develop truly extended action under such circumstances.

The place for this particular work is in the open country, on good going, on long straight lines.

The reader will have noticed that the horse has to assume

a long, extended form, that he has to leave the collected shape. This means that he is to be allowed to lower his head and to extend his neck, things which he cannot do unless the rider allows him the appropriate length of rein.

That then, is the rider's first care.

His second care is the amount of contact which he shall allow the horse to take. It follows from the extended form itself that the horse must transfer more of his weight from his quarters on to his forehand. Consequently the contact he will take, must, of necessity, be more positive, even though it need never be heavy. So long as the horse urges forward there may be distinct contact, but not weight. Weight will only be felt if the horse urges downward as well as forward. Which, if it occurs, is a certain sign that the rider has either given insufficient rein or else, as often happens, that the rider himself is pulling, even though he may not realize it.

But, without positive contact, the rider would not be able to regulate the increase of forward impulsion, which may be very great, into evenly regulated, absolutely equal strides.

And that is of the utmost importance!

The training in extension then has to proceed just as gradually as the training in collection. Only, in a sense, it is even more difficult, because it is so easy to drive the horse beyond his rhythm. And an extended trot without rhythm degenerates just as easily into a valueless "run" as an indifferent collected trot may go to waste in an equally valueless "jog".

The method then, is to concentrate on rhythm and on length of stride, relying again a good deal on the effect of momentary accelerations for the production of that length (see page 197). In that way, progressing methodically, always within the horse's capabilities for the time being, we are certain to reach the maximum of which the horse can be made capable, in time.

Though the rhythm of the extended trot is of a different character to that of the collected trot, and tends towards cadence in a lesser degree, it is yet certain that the capacity to cadence acquired in the shorter gait, based as it is on increased power and elasticity of the hocks, is an important element in the full development of extension. I will go so far as to say that one cannot succeed fully without it.

In general, the high-couraged horse delivers his extension generously, without needing any great amount of drive from his rider; with such horses there is no need to use any other than the rising trot. But there are other, more cold-tempered horses, who require a great deal of sustained driving power from their riders. With such, it is more effective to resort to the sitting trot, which gives more power over the horse. It has been observed already that the sitting trot presents no problem, even at extended paces, once the horse's back is supple.

THE MITTELTRAB

Before closing this subject, mention should be made of the *Mitteltrab*, practised by the German School, unknown and practically never referred to in French literature; it is not a movement demanded by the F.E.I. or defined in its regulations. It is neither an extended nor a collected trot, but a form in between the two, with some of the characteristics of both. In it, the horse goes much in the position of the collected trot, head high and nose nearing the vertical, with a form of action resembling that of the extended trot, but delivered with marked cadence; the speed is more or less equal to that of the ordinary trot, but delivered with much increased energy; the hindlegs deliver their main impetus nearer the vertical than at the extended trot; the horse is light in front, light in hand and the extending action of the front legs is spectacular.

THE TROT ON TWO TRACKS

The work on two tracks has been discussed in detail in Chapter XIV. The following notes refer specifically to the trot.

It is essential to concentrate first and foremost on the maintenance of impulsion. Two methods will be found helpful in this respect. As long as the horse finds difficulty at this work, particularly in doing the half-pass, it is advisable to take the rising trot. In the earlier stages it is better not to insist on the correct bend. Progress is usually quicker and much more satisfactory if we are satisfied with a few good steps, delivered in impulsion. It is very difficult for the horse, in the earlier stages of his training, to do a good half-pass right across the school; if we insist, he is bound to do, and so to learn doing, a bad half-pass; the horse will lose impulsion, position, rhythm and everything else that matters; carried out under such conditions this work is not only without value, but definitely detrimental. A good half-pass comes at the end of the training, not at the beginning.

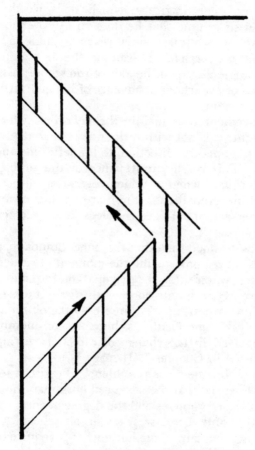

DIAGRAM 17. COUNTER-CHANGE OF HAND

However, developed on the right lines, there is no other work so effective as the trot on two tracks for the creation of cadence. In these exercises the hocks tread far under the body and deliver their impulse from a position near the vertical; the upward thrust of the hindleg begins to equal the forward thrust, hence the tendency to a marked cadence, which is the approach to a moment of suspension.

Once the horse has mastered this work fully, the time has come to embark on the counter-changes of hand on two tracks (see diagram). This movement places the horse before a physical problem of some intricacy, which it is worth while to examine. Let us assume that he does an *appuyer* towards the right; he moves on two tracks, sideways, at an angle to his line of progress; since his forehand is leading, the axis of the horse's body is at an angle also with the axis of the school; his forehand crosses the axis of the school in advance of his quarters; his head is flexed to the right.

In this movement it is mainly the near-hind which pushes him to the right; it is not within the power of that near-hind to push him in the opposite direction, to the left; only the off-hind can do that. This is the quintessence of the problem which the horse has to face when a sudden reversal of direction is imposed upon him, even though there are further complications, involving the action of the forelegs and the change of bend.

It will be understood then that the horse cannot change direction, for physical reasons, during the moment of suspension, nor for that matter, when the right diagonal, off-fore and near-hind are in support. He can only do so whilst the left diagonal, near-fore and off-hind are in support, since only the off-hind can push him to the left. The difficulty is therefore considerably greater than that involved in the change of direction during circular figures, discussed in Chapter XIII, page 151.

I have called this the horse's problem! Precisely, for, though I consider it essential that the advanced horseman should realize the nature of these problems and the degree of their difficulty, it is yet not he, but only the horse, who can solve them. All that the rider can do is to explain to the horse what is required and leave the horse plenty of time to study the question and to supply the answer. The rider's talent is taxed to the full by the need to build up his question gradually and clearly with complete avoidance of any risk of being misunderstood.

So, armed with this knowledge, we proceed in the same way, but with still greater care, as we did when studying changes of direction on circular tracks. Side-stepping to the right, we stop going sideways in the middle of the school, straighten our horse and proceed on a straight line. Nothing else. It seems easy. Done approximately it is easy. But done as it should be done, absolutely fluently, without any break in rhythm and impulsion, and perfectly straight, it is far from easy. So, we practise for just as long as it may take our horse to find the answer.

Obviously, we will do this same exercise from the right half-pass and from the left half-pass.

With this exercise under smooth control, further progress is comparatively simple. We can now side-step in one direction, straighten the horse, do a number of steps on a straight line, then side step in the opposite direction. Provided everything goes smoothly, we can reduce the straight line gradually to two steps, which is already difficult for an unfinished horse in the hands of a rider who may not yet himself be an expert at this delicate work. However, in due course we reduce to one straight step, and finally we reach the point where the horse can change smoothly from right side-step to left side-step direct.

This involves simultaneous change of bend and flexion, of lead to forehand and of side-step, and constitutes a feat of advanced horsemanship.

The ultimate refinement of this work, which belongs to high-school riding, is in the repeated counter-changes at regular short intervals, say six strides to the right, followed by six strides to the left and so on. This work is shown on the centre line of the school. We begin with three steps to the right, followed by six steps to the left, six to the right, and so on, finishing up on the centre line again with three steps to the left. The whole of the changes must be accurate and smooth, all strides the same length and the same width, always finishing at precisely three steps from the centre line, effortless, with perfect balance and in unbroken rhythm. It is a very elegant movement.

THE PASSAGE AND THE PIAFFE

DIAGONAL AIDS, OR "INFLUENCES", OF LEG AND
REIN. THE "SOFT" PASSAGE. THE REAL PASSAGE.
THE TRANSITIONS. THE PIAFFE.

The Passage and the Piaffe are the great classical "airs" of the high-school. They constitute the highest degree of cadence, balance and controlled impulsion which it is possible to achieve.

The Passage is a spectacular trot, in slow motion, in which the horse moves with much elevation and with great cadence; there is a definite moment of suspension, appearing almost prolonged, as one diagonal pair of legs reposes on the ground, with the opposing diagonal suspended in the air. The horse dances from one diagonal on to the other, progressing slowly but majestically with purely rhythmic steps. The distance covered at each stride is no more than about a foot.

The Piaffe is the same trot, with the same slow cadence, executed on the spot, without advancing.

The old masters would not consider the horse's education at the trot complete until these airs had been fully mastered. They laid down that the length of each stride at the passage should not exceed thirty-three centimetres, or just over a foot, that the foot of the foreleg in suspension had to reach about the middle of the canon bone of the front leg in support, and the hind foot in suspension to the fetlock joint of the other hindleg. They held that the elevation in the piaffe had to be markedly higher, knee high for a front foot and to the middle of the canon bone for a hind foot.

These indications could apply to their type of riding horse with much knee action. They can apply no longer to our modern horses, different in build and with the modern riding action nearer the ground. Where the old type of horse showed higher action at the piaffe than at the passage, the reverse is the case with the modern horse.

However, *mutatis mutandis*, there is no essential difference between these airs as executed then and now. The fundamental merit lies in the achievement of absolute regularity of cadence, combined with a marked degree of elevation commensurate with the build and action of the horse performing these movements. The greatest and final difficulty lies in the co-ordination of both airs in such a manner that transitions from passage into piaffe, and vice-versa, become easy, smooth and fluent.

The initial difficulty lies in the production of that maximum of cadence which makes the marked moment of suspension possible.

As we have seen, all our previous work at the trot has been calculated to perfect the horse's natural rhythm by ever increasing energy of action into cadenced rhythm. If we have been

PIAFFE. LT.-COL. PODHAYSKY, THE SPANISH RIDING SCHOOL

PIAFFE. "BASCAR"

PIAFFE. CAPITAINE LAVERGNE OF THE CAVALRY SCHOOL, SAUMUR

successful, the horse's action at the trot will have become timed and marked with great precision. The horse will go in a cadenced trot, *trot cadencé*, or even in a *trot passagé*, a trot beginning to assume a resemblance to the passage. The action of each diagonal has become so well marked by cadence that a moment of suspension, although not actually achieved, appears to be hinted at and indeed almost indicated.

That, and that alone, is the foundation whereon we may now attempt to build passage and piaffe.

Both airs can be taught entirely from the saddle.

But the initial difficulty, the creation of the peculiar cadence with its moment of suspension, is considerable and demands exceptional tact, much patience and a good deal of time.

Accordingly, certain schools employ means calculated to circumvent some of the difficulty and to save time.

The Italian Schools of the Renaissance made use of "the pillars", a system which spread to France and other parts of Europe and found general favour for a considerable time. The pillars are two tall posts firmly fixed in the ground in some convenient place of the school. The horse can be tied up between these posts by means of special reins fitted with spring hooks for quick release; one end of each rein is fixed to one of the posts and the other end to one of the bridoon rings; much in the same manner as horses, saddled up ready to go out, are turned around in their stalls and made fast to the pillars of their partitions, until needed.

The horse, fixed in this position, can obviously not move forward. But he can, urged on gently by a competent trainer, be rendered mobile on the spot and this mobility can be developed into a piaffe. That result can be obtained a good deal quicker in this way than from the saddle and it does make the rider's task easier.

But not without introducing other difficulties and inconveniences.

In the first place this work in the pillars requires itself very great skill from the operator. It is all too easy to spoil a horse in this manner, to upset him thoroughly, and even to cause serious accidents. It has the inconvenience that the horse cannot go forward, which is against the fundamental principle of riding. It is often difficult, with horses so trained, to achieve, later on, a smooth transition from the piaffe to the passage.

The system is still in general use in central Europe, and in particular in Vienna, where it is applied with all requisite skill. In France, the pillars have disappeared from current use almost entirely. Saumur still preserves them, but only for the training of the *sauteurs*. The *sauteurs* (literal translation " jumpers ") are not "ridden" high-school horses in the ordinary sense. They are trained specially for the spectacular jumps of the "school above the ground", comprising the Croupade, the Courbette, the Ballotade and the Capriole. It is extremely difficult to retain one's seat during these exercises, and these horses have no other real purpose than strengthening pupils' seats. It is essential to teach these horses the piaffe first, since they could not, without that, acquire the essential balance.

I have never used pillars myself, so it does not behove me to give a description of this work, other than the above brief note. But I have seen enough of it to realize its special difficulties and its dangers; the novice should tread warily! Général Decarpentry offers an excellent description in *Équitation Académique*.

Instead of pillars, other trainers use work from the ground, leading the horse from his bridle and using a polo or a light lungeing whip. This method can be very helpful and, provided it be done skilfully, the inconveniences inherent in the use of the pillars are avoided. The system is essentially the same as described by me in earlier chapters, when used for the purpose of explaining elementary principles and aids to the horse. But the system's adherents continue the horse's education "from the ground", used in conjunction with simultaneous education from the saddle, right through the whole of his training. The method is much used in Germany. In France it has also been used by a number of great exponents, such as Raabe, Gerhardt, Guérin, Montigny and Dumas. Authorities to consult are Capitaine J. B. Dumas (*Équitation Diagonale*) and Decarpentry. The method is no longer in general use in France to-day, though it is quite likely that individual trainers may still resort to it. After all, when it comes to this advanced and difficult work it is only logical that individuals should resort to the methods best suited to their style and temperament.

However, the procedure most generally in favour in France to-day is to teach these airs entirely from the saddle, as a logical sequence to preceding work. It is the only method that I have ever used and it is accordingly the method that I propose to try and describe.

I said " try ", on purpose.

Quite a number of leading authorities have attempted to analyse the aids used in this work in considerable detail. Yet, I must confess that I have invariably found these explanations obscure and, to me at any rate, unintelligible.

The reason for this apparent obscurity is not, I think, difficult to assess.

By the time the horse is ready to come to this work, he will have to have reached a state of perfect lightness. By that time the rider's aids too, will have reached a stage of extreme delicacy; they will have become indiscernible to the onlooker; they will, in fact be almost indiscernible to the rider himself! Indeed they will, for the most part, resolve themselves into finely shaded little actions produced largely from the rider's subconsciousness, from his feel and from the feel which now exists between him and his horse. Reins and legs no longer convey defined aids to the horse; they have resolved themselves into means of thought transmission along which the rider's and the horse's thoughts flow to and fro. One could speak of " influences " rather than of " aids ". The latter can be defined, the former cannot.

Accordingly, I will not attempt to define the indefinable.

What I rather hope to be able to do is to paint a picture of the development of intimacy between rider and horse from which these airs may gradually be born. But the precise ingredients for that development I cannot name, since in the absolute sense, they do not exist. Each individual rider will have to find his individual way; ultimately, he can only learn with and from his horse.

However, to come to facts.

A description of these two airs has been given at the beginning of this chapter.

In reality there are no two distinct airs, but only two different expressions of the same air, the suspended trot. The peculiar slow motion rhythm is characteristic of both forms. The combination of slow motion and great energy is the basic difficulty. The slower the motion, the greater the difficulty. Consequently the piaffe, done on the spot, is more difficult than the passage, done in movement.

The opinion, sometimes advanced, that the piaffe can be

taught first is not logical, not, that is to say, if the training is undertaken entirely from the saddle. Attempts to do so usually lead to difficulties; besides, the attempt is in flagrant contradiction of the principle of the forward urge, on which we have been working so conscientiously and for so long during the whole of our training.

We must, surely, remain consequential in our methods.

Accordingly, it seems more logical to search for the passage first, through the final perfection of the slow cadenced trot.

This cannot be done without the perfection of aids into influences.

In the ordinary rhythmic trot the rider has the feel of a perfectly level pace; the diagonal character of the gait does not usually strike him, he does not clearly perceive the swing of diagonally opposed sets of muscles. Thus, he feels it as natural to use both legs when required, and also both reins, simultaneously; it probably never dawns on him that they could be used otherwise; and of course, there is no real reason why they should; at any rate, the succeeding diagonal hoofbeats follow each other at such brief intervals that it would be difficult to diagonalize these aids.

However, as the rhythmic trot changes into a cadenced trot, the strides will become more marked, the interval between the footfalls with lengthen and the diagonal swing of the movement will gradually emerge upon the rider's consciousness. It is only then that he will perceive the possibility of harmonizing influences of leg and rein with the horse's diagonal swing; he will become able to diagonalize these influences in conformity with that swing.

It is the final revelation of unity at the trot between horse and rider.

Having discovered this harmony, which enables him to control the energy of each diagonal in turn, and without the use of any force, the rider may now concentrate on the gradual slowing up of the cadenced trot.

Without any force!

This is of paramount importance.

The basic merit of any passage or piaffe lies in the absolute regularity of individual strides; that regularity in turn depends on the preservation of the horse's equanimity, in perfect peace and lightness. We are not attempting to force the horse into a new and difficult movement. We are, as always, intent on explaining to the horse. Provided we succeed in doing precisely that, our faithful friend will never fail to oblige.

In this case, we know that it is bound to be particularly difficult for the horse to realize our intentions. Accordingly, we are particularly anxious to leave the horse plenty of time to discover, by himself, precisely what we have been asking him, so patiently, to do.

Yes, to do, by himself, of his own volition!

Only the horse can produce the passage, never the rider.

Thus, we concentrate on slowing up the cadenced trot, gradually and by stages. It will be understood that there can be no cadence without much energy; our leg influences will maintain the energy. Yet we must go slower and slower and we must achieve this by rein influences used without any strength. Opposition between leg and rein effects would create opposition in the horse, loss of patience, equanimity and rhythm; loss of everything in other words.

Again, the gradual reduction in speed must be realized by explanation!

So we commence with a reasonably slow cadenced trot which the horse can already do without much difficulty or strain. We continue for fifteen or twenty strides and reduce to a walk. We walk on a long rein! In this work it is essential to cultivate absolute calm. On that account we do not maintain the horse in a state of continuous collection, which might unnerve him; on the contrary we encourage relaxation each time. We thus walk twelve or fifteen strides and retake the cadenced trot for a further fifteen or twenty strides. We do this work daily, for fifteen minutes or so at a stretch. The horse will not take long to understand, from the regularly repeated transitions from free walk into cadenced trot and vice-versa, that there is no hurry and that speed is not required. Accordingly, transitions will become lighter and easier as time goes on; the need to use any perceptible strength in the opposition between hand and leg will simply not arise.

Gradually, as the days or weeks pass by, we may reduce the number of cadenced trot strides and the horse, through his understanding of our wishes, will himself offer to reduce the speed of his cadenced trot to very little more than that of a walk.

We are then within measurable distance of the passage.

We may now keep up this very slow cadenced trot for somewhat longer distances, say up to a couple of hundred yards, without constant reductions to a walk; even so, each time we do walk, we keep on relaxing on a long rein. Soon, we can introduce a few exercises which tend to accentuate cadence, small circles and side steps. But we do so naturally, calmly and without any attempt to achieve by force any distinct movement of suspension, which the horse will presently offer all by himself.

We bide the time when the horse will go at this very slow, but inherently energetic and markedly cadenced trot easily, without effort and in perfect lightness.

We then revert to frequent transitions to the walk. But this time we do only a few steps at the walk, reducing gradually to two or even to a single stride. This time we keep the horse collected at the walk also. As we make the transition into the walk, we endeavour to maintain cadence just as long as possible and to resume cadence as soon as possible on retaking the trot. This will result presently in a cadence so slow, that a moment of suspension must be indicated. As soon as we feel this indication of suspension, and not a moment later, we caress our horse and recompense with a free walk. The horse must be kept completely calm.

We may now defer our victory, and make it more complete, by the exertion of the greatest patience. Continuing on the same lines for a few more weeks, we will succeed in obtaining several steps, up to half a dozen perhaps, with this moment of suspension marked. They will be quite low steps, without much elevation, but they will be all the better for that, since calm and regular.

In fact, we have laid the solid basis of our victory in the achievement of the " soft passage ", *le doux passage* as the French call it.

The further development of these airs is now merely a matter of careful systematic progress at this soft passage only. As time goes on, we increase from six to seven steps, from seven to eight, and so on, until the horse can do say twenty.

Success or failure at this work depends entirely on the trainer's patience, and on his tact.

The trainer should realize that it is the horse himself who is learning this work, and not the trainer who is teaching! If the horse be given the time to do so quite unruffled, he will make smooth progress, without upsets. His steps will be regular. If he be hurried, or forced, he is certain to produce irregular steps or jumps and to acquire faults which it may be difficult, or impossible, to eradicate. The passage is a form of trot throwing great strain on the animal's hocks. That is true even in the case of the soft passage. It is only gradually that hocks and fetlocks can develop the strength and elasticity needed to stand that strain. If we overtax the horse's muscular power, the animal will, naturally, find ways of avoiding that strain; he does that by taking very short and low steps with the hindlegs, whilst moving more or less well in front. But the gait is no longer truly diagonal and, of course, quite worthless. It is a very grave fault, difficult to cure, entirely of the trainer's own making.

Tact is needed for the creation and development of the special language between rider and horse whereby these steps can gradually be produced at the trainer's bidding. How, in other words, we can make the horse move off from a walk into a soft passage or come back from a cadenced trot into a soft passage.

Each rider and each horse must discover and develop that language together. It is impossible to describe the precise form which that language shall take. But it can be said that the rider has to be very gentle and has to find the answer in slight conventional signals agreed between him and his horse. There is no such thing as a circumscribed aid which is bound to produce the result. The signal that I develop between my horses and myself can be described as follows.

When I take the trot from a collected walk, I use my legs first, without any perceptible hand effect.

When I want to take the passage from a collected walk, I use a hand effect first, without any leg. I take a slight feel on the corners of the horse's mouth, my hands a little higher than normal. My horses know that signal and accordingly move off at the passage as soon as I close my legs.

When I reduce from a collected trot into a collected walk, I use a slight hand effect and no leg until the horse walks.

When I reduce from a collected trot into a passage, I reduce the pace by a retarding hand effect without legs; I raise my hands a little, give the conventional signal on the corners of my horse's mouth, followed by diagonal leg effect. My horse assumes the passage.

In this way then we can time our work at the soft passage. Never more than fifteen minutes a day, never more strides than the horse can do easily, always with plenty of walking in between and always without strain, exertion or excitement. Proceeding thus quietly, progress will be both rapid and secure. The soft passage becomes merely another form of trot, at which we can do fifty or a hundred or more strides. And at which we can now undertake all the work, circles and side-steps, that are possible at other forms of trot.

Automatically, the horse will himself, with slight encouragement, come to the real passage, energetic and with considerable elevation and, which is most important, with absolute regularity.

Once we have achieved that, we may start thinking about the piaffe.

It is usually stated that the horse can be brought to the piaffe by slowing down the passage gradually, until that exercise can be performed on the spot.

That is certainly true, but with some important reservations!

It is the great and final difficulty in this work to master a smooth transition from passage into piaffe and vice versa.

Now, if we concentrate on slowing up the passage into a piaffe, we shall hardly ever succeed in mastering these transitions. And we shall meet other difficulties as well. By continuously working on a slower and slower passage, down to the piaffe, the horse will naturally conclude that it is this very slow passage which is wanted and we shall presently have very great difficulty in extending him forward again. We are in fact well on the way to destroying the forward urge! Incidentally we are, in so doing, losing our control over the horse's impulsion. And, without a very great deal of impulsion, within our easy control, a good piaffe is quite out of the question.

So, instead of seeking the piaffe by slowing down the passage in the hope that the transitions will also come, we set about it the other way round and seek to create transition first!

After all, the passage is a form of trot at which variations of pace, transitions from shorter to longer strides, are just as possible, within certain limits, as at any other form of trot. There can be, even though within a limited range of speed, an almost infinite variety of expression, from the soft passage, through the passage, to the *trot passagé* and back to the piaffe. There is not always a clear dividing line between these various forms of the same air; they merge one into the other.

Accordingly, we develop the passage in precisely the same manner as we did develop the trot, by variations of pace. We do not want the horse to think that he has to go slower and slower! What we are out to make him understand is that the passage is, like any other gait, a pace infinitely variable according to his master's wishes.

Thus, we begin, as we did in the trot, by going a little faster, and coming back to our normal pace. Gradually we come back to just a little slower than our normal pace, and accelerate again. The differences in pace need, and can, only be slight, but that is of no importance. It *is* important that the horse learns to make these slight transitions, and in particular that he remains always ready to move forward at our slightest bidding.

Once that principle has been established, we may then concentrate rather more on retardation, very little at a time, followed always by acceleration. Proceeding in this manner, the horse will presently do one step nearly on the spot and, a little later, on the spot. That is the piaffe!

Only one step, it is true. But from one step on the spot to two or three steps nearly on the spot, and presently on the spot, is only a matter of logical progress. And of course each time we are careful to move forward again before the difficulty of the steps on the spot causes the horse to lose the correct tempo of the gait. After that it is merely a matter of time and practice to obtain from twelve to fifteen steps at the piaffe in between two bouts of passage, and more should not be asked for.

The good piaffe then is a suspended trot on the spot. But a completely regular trot, wherein hind and forelegs both take part in absolutely regular diagonal sequence. Hindlegs are clearly lifted at each stride, somewhat higher than the hoof of the leg resting on the ground. The forelegs are lifted easily and fairly high. In this air the forelegs carry but little weight. The hindlegs carry a maximum weight. Hindlegs will not be lifted properly, or at all, unless the horse maintains, throughout this exercise, the forward urge, the wish to move on at any moment at his rider's bidding! That is why it is so important, in my opinion, to work first and foremost, and always, on the forward transitions. It is a grave fault if the horse keeps his hind feet on the ground, or nearly so. The trot on the spot shall always be perfectly straight, without any sideways swing of forehand or quarters. The movement is visibly easy and comfortable to the rider, who sits quietly and perfectly still in the centre of his saddle. Horses trained by artificial means, sometimes used for circus purposes, may be seen to throw the quarters up; there is no true suppleness and that form is without value.

Finally then, it is the maintenance of the horse's forward urge which constitutes the greatest difficulty and the greatest merit of this air. On that, once more, all authorities are agreed. It is difficult, and sometimes almost impossible, to preserve this forward urge to the full unless we allow the horse to trot, not on the spot, but nearly on the spot, allowing him to advance an inch or two at each stride. In the view of the ancient masters, and of many modern ones as well, to do so would not be a fault, but a quality. With that view I concur.

The regulations of the F.E.I. state that "if the horse does not remain absolutely on the spot, but advances only a few centimetres each step, his rhythm being well marked, regular and brilliant, his piaffer can be considered no more than sufficient". This means that a brilliant piaffe, under the conditions stated, deserves no more than five out of ten marks. Some consider this to be bad law.[1]

It has been observed that the airs of passage and piaffe make very great demands on the strength and suppleness of the horse's hocks, and also on his fetlock joints. It follows then that animals with weak hocks, and incidentally with weak loins, are unsuitable for this work; they cannot be schooled successfully in these airs, because they lack the physical power. It will be understood then also that this work should not be attempted before the horse, however strong his hocks may be, has achieved the high degree of suppleness and resilience which is prerequisite. He will show that himself by beginning to offer truly cadenced trot strides when the time is ripe.

The most notable difficulty frequently met with in this work is the so-called *saut de pie* or "magpie jump". In this the horse uses both hindlegs together, or almost so, instead of moving each

[1] *The F.E.I. have annulled this regulation since this book went to press.*

hindleg in turn and in proper diagonal sequence with the corresponding front leg. More often than not he does this only occasionally. It is obviously an ugly fault, destructive of the pure rhythm of the movement. It has been stated that the strain imposed on the hindlegs is great; the irregular movement described is an attempt by the horse to take that strain on two legs instead of on one.

The reason for this evasion is lack of forward impulsion or demands by the rider in excess of the horse's true capacity for the time being.

The maintenance of forward impulsion, of the forward urge in this work, is its greatest difficulty. We shall never succeed in obtaining the soft cadence and swing required for these movements unless both horse and rider are mentally and physically completely relaxed; and we shall never obtain that relaxation unless the aids are so light and delicate as to be almost nonexistent. But yet they must be positive! The horse must remain in front of the legs and on his bridle. It is the easiest thing in the world, in this most highly collected work, to get the horse to perform behind his bridle either by carrying the head too low and overbent or else by carrying the head so high that the bridle cannot act properly either. In both cases the magpie jumps are liable to creep in.

They will occur when the rider upsets his horse's equanimity by trying to force him through the use of strong aids or by demands for elevation and brilliance which as yet exceed the horse's capacities. Finally, they are liable to appear by attempts to slow up the passage, and to search for the piaffe, before the horse is ready or by doing so without keeping the horse on his bit. It is essential never to lose the forward urge, even in the piaffe on the spot.

The cure then is indicated:

Whenever this trouble arises, we will suspend the work and the methods which brought it about. Instead of attempting any slow and high passage, and *a fortiori* any piaffe, we will ride the horse forward gently, using soft and careful leg aids and no spur or whip, and bring him back to a slow collected *trot passagé*, softly but positively on the bit.

The things we concentrate on are calmness and regularity of gait.

We obtain or re-establish calmness by asking little; we do only short stretches of *trot passagé* with plenty of walking; we do not keep at it long and avoid tiring the horse.

We obtain regularity of gait by keeping the horse on the bit and in front of the legs; control in that respect can only be exercised by the combined effect of hand and legs and never by either legs or hand alone.

It is only by time and patience that such faults can be cured but if these are employed conscientiously the cure will not, as a rule, be unduly difficult.

CHAPTER XVIII

THE CANTER

The gaits of canter and gallop – Aids for the canter – Slowing the canter – Starts at the canter – Transitions from canter to walk – Transition from halt into canter – Transition from canter into halt – The simple change of leg – The counterlead – The changes of leg in the air – The canter on two tracks – The pirouette

THE GAITS OF CANTER AND GALLOP

THE canter and the gallop are two distinct forms of what is basically the same gait. The difference between the two forms lies in the sequence of the footfalls. The cause of that difference lies in the varying attitudes of the horse.

The natural canter of the horse, in freedom, is a comparatively slow pace in which the horse assumes a collected attitude. He carries head and neck fairly high, which has the effect of taking part of his weight off the forehand and transferring his centre of balance somewhat nearer the quarters. Consequently, in order to take their additional share of the weight, the hindlegs tread well underneath the body. That attitude, head and neck carried high and hindlegs treading well under is, of course, characteristic of all collected gaits and results in lightness in front. The horse's living and moving weight is about equally balanced between forehand and quarters.

It will be seen, I think, that the footfalls of the canter and the sequence of the supports afforded by the horse's legs are ideally suited to the weight distribution described.

The canter is a pace of three-time. Assuming the horse to be cantering with the off-fore leading, then the sequence of the hoof-beats, beginning with a hindleg, is as follows:

(1) near-hind,
(2) off-hind and near-fore together,
(3) off-fore
(4) in the air.

And the sequence of the supports is:

(1) near-hind alone, pushes the horse forward,
(2) off-hind and near-fore together carry the weight forward, until
(3) near-fore takes over and lifts the horse into the air, to come down again on
(1) near-hind, etc.

As in all collected gaits, the effect of the driving legs is delivered from a point near the vertical position and that effect is more lifting than driving forward. Hence the perfectly easy balance of the gait and the comparative lack of speed.

In the gallop matters are very different.

The gallop is essentially an extended pace, in which the horse stretches himself to his full length; head and neck are carried low and stretched forward. In order to develop the greater speed, the driving effect of the legs is delivered from a position considerably behind the vertical. This affects the weight distribution of the horse and the three-time gait of the canter no longer suits the altered conditions.

The footfalls of the gallop, again with the off-fore leading, are: (1) near-hind, (2) off-hind, (3) near-fore, (4) off-fore, (5) in the air.

Thus, there are four hoof-beats; accordingly, the gallop is a pace of four-time.

And the sequence of supports is:

(1) near-hind alone
(2) near-hind and off-hind
(3) off-hind and near-fore
(5) near-fore alone
(6) near-fore and off-fore
(7) off-fore alone
(8) in the air
(1) near-hind alone, etc.

It will be appreciated then that the difference in footfalls, sequence of supports, and in form between canter and gallop is considerable. It will be appreciated also that these varying forms are perfectly natural to the horse and need not be taught him!

Both are pure gaits, provided only that they are used for their specific purpose.

This point requires to be emphasized here.

Because it is of the essence of good riding that the horse's gaits shall be pure.

In dressage, we are concerned with the canter.

It is essential that the canter of the well-trained and well-ridden horse be pure and therefore in three-time. It is in that form alone that the horse can go in the appropriate attitude, with the hindlegs treading well under. It is only so that the horse can deliver the impulsion and the balanced energy without which the natural collected form of this gait cannot exist.

The moment the horse starts trailing his hindlegs instead of placing them far under his body, he will cease to move in three-time; he will assume a four-time canter. This is a lazy gait, without impulsion, which can never achieve the rhythmic swing of the real canter. It is undoubtedly a serious fault, which is usually acquired through faulty methods of schooling; it is then very difficult to alter.

The sequences of the footfalls of canter and gallop described above refer to "united" gaits. It will be obvious that any dis-united gait is a fault so serious as to be inconceivable in the case of a properly schooled and ridden horse. I am giving full details of these and other faulty gaits in *The Horse in Action*.

Aids for the Canter

There is no general agreement amongst authorities as to the precise system of aids most suitable to obtain a strike-off at the canter.

The question is somewhat complex.

By nature, the horse does not carry himself straight at the canter. He moves somewhat sideways. When cantering with the off-fore leading, he will flex his head slightly to the right and will carry his quarters somewhat markedly to the right also. This deviation from the straight appears to be common to all four-footed animals when cantering; it is particularly noticeable in dogs.

The system most generally recommended is that of the diagonal aids. This means that, to obtain a canter with the off-fore leading, we use the right rein to obtain a flexion to the right and the left leg to activate the near-hind leg which must initiate the strike-off. It will be understood that the action of the rider's left leg must have the secondary effect of pushing the horse's quarters slightly to the right.

In other words, these diagonal aids have the effect of placing the horse in a position which conforms with the natural form of the canter; it is easy and natural for the horse to assume the canter from that position. In that respect these diagonal aids are logical and fluent and, in my opinion, we cannot do without their use in schooling our horses.

But there are inconveniences.

It is impossible to obtain a perfectly straight start, or for that matter a perfectly straight canter, by the unmitigated use of the aids as described. The ancient masters were quite unconcerned about cantering somewhat sideways; in fact they delighted so much in cantering on two tracks that they were going sideways most of the time anyway.

But, and this is the quintessence of the matter, they did not practise the changes of leg! And, to obtain satisfactory changes of leg, especially at short intervals, the horse must canter straight.

So, it is a basic requirement of the modern school that the horse shall start straight and shall remain straight at the canter.

Let us then examine these aids a little more closely.

The use of the right rein causes a flexion to the right. But it also acts to some extent as rein of opposition to the haunches, tending to prevent the quarters from swinging to the right. However, that effect is only slight and insufficient to offset the effect of the left leg, particularly if that left leg is applied behind the girth.

Accordingly, when our horse is sufficiently advanced in his ordinary training to warrant us thinking about straightening his canter, we have to incorporate some gradual modifications and refinements in these aids.

Since the horse is so very observant, there is in that no great difficulty, provided we proceed step by step.

IRREGULAR PASSAGE. THE "*Saut de Pie*" OR "MAGPIE JUMP". A NOT UNCOMMON DIFFICULTY

COLLECTED CANTER. "BASCAR"

In the first place then we concentrate, if we have not already done so in our preliminary schooling, on using the rein-aid as a preliminary warning signal only. To obtain that effect we introduce a slight time-lapse between the moment when we touch a rein and the moment of applying our leg. Incidentally, this time-lapse is in truth always essential because it would be difficult, without it, to avoid a restraining effect of the rein at the very moment when the horse strikes off at the canter; this is so in particular when the strike-off is demanded from the walk or from the halt because it is then an acceleration.

However, our main object now is to agree with our horse that a slight touch on the right rein means that an order to strike-off with the off-fore leading is about to follow; and similarly, of course, a touch on the left rein precedes a left canter.

Once that convention has been established, there is no longer any need to apply the directing leg anywhere but quite close to the girth. For instance, to obtain a strike-off on the off-fore, we touch the right rein, followed by a touch of the left leg close to the girth.

That is already some progress, though still insufficient to insure straightness.

Accordingly, we progress further by using both legs close behind the girth, exactly as we would do for moving off at a trot. Risk of confusion does not arise, since the canter, and the particular leg to canter on, have already been determined by the preceding rein-signal.

Continuing in this manner, we will soon be able to use one or other of our legs more predominantly than the other, again without risk of confusion, thanks to our rein signal. This implies that we can now use both legs, or any one of them as occasion may demand, for the dual purpose of obtaining the strike-off and/or for dressing the quarters straight before, during and after the take-off.

In other words, we are now so far that we can use diagonal or lateral aids or a mixture of both, according to circumstances, without fear of being misunderstood.

It will be possible, finally, to obtain the strike-off by the use of the rein alone, provided the horse be in a state of collection and impulsion. But that requires the ability on the part of the rider of expressing a clearly dual effect with his rein-aid; first the conventional flexion effect as a warning followed by, or rather merging into, a slight lifting effect to determine the strike-off. This rein-effect is of particular value in obtaining and controlling the changes of leg at close intervals.

For the sake of clarity, we have, so far, only considered the horse's tendency to deviate from a straight line of progress at the canter and the actions of hand and leg which are at the rider's disposal, subject to careful progressive schooling, to obviate that tendency.

It is still necessary to mention a further peculiarity of the gait which influences the rider's seat.

When a horse canters with the off-fore leading, his off-fore and his off-hind leg will always touch down well in front of the hoof-prints made by the near-fore and the near-hind legs, and vice versa when the near-fore is leading.

Accordingly, when cantering with the off-fore leading, the horse's right shoulder and his right hip are somewhat in advance of his left shoulder and left hip. The feel of this position is transmitted to the rider's seat by the action of the muscles which determine it. Accordingly, the sensitive rider will adjust his seat by intuition in conformity with the feel given him by his horse. This means that, when the horse is cantering to the right, the rider will assume a position in the saddle with his right seat bone slightly in advance of the left. Obviously, to do that implies some muscular action, however slight. And, just as much as the rider can feel his horse's position under the saddle, so the horse can feel his rider's position in the saddle.

In so doing, the rider assists unity of balance.

But apart from that he will never be able, unless he does so, to achieve the nice refinements of aids that have been explained above.

More than that, this refinement of the rider's position in the saddle, clearly perceived by the sensitive horse, becomes an aid by association and finally almost an aid in itself whereby to determine the leading leg and, later on, the change of leading leg.

The study of these refinements of the aids with one's horse is quite fascinating. Its success depends entirely on the rider's tact and patience and on his ability to understand his horse. Complete calm and peacefulness are important in all stages of training the horse, but never more so than in this work at the canter. There is no other work which can upset and spoil a horse more thoroughly and more quickly than an injudicious approach to the inherent difficulties of this gait.

It is essential to seek response to discreet and careful aids and it is essential in particular to find that response without the use of any force, ever. The better, the more generous and the more high-couraged one's horse, the more carefully one has to proceed.

In this work in particular, the use of the voice can be of inestimable value. When I do this work, I touch the rein and say "so"; I follow up with the leg, or legs, and say "canter". Very soon my horse will strike-off at the word "canter" and not very long after that at the word "so". I then discontinue using the voice.

Slowing the Canter

The canter is one of the natural gaits. There is no difficulty in obtaining it. Every normally broken horse will soon canter well enough for such ordinary riding purposes as hacking or hunting.

The natural canter is a fairly slow gait, as compared with the gallop; it is also, as we have seen, a form of gait with a certain amount of natural collection; the horse carries head and neck fairly high, places his hindlegs well underneath his body and moves in an easy balance with fairly long strides in three-time.

But, in dressage, we require the school-canter, which is very much slower and demands a much higher degree of collection to insure accuracy, ease and lightness of control. The horse's carriage, his bearing and the rhythm of his gait are much more defined than in the ordinary canter. He presents a more elegant and more impressive picture altogether.

Provided always that he has lost neither the pure three-time form of his canter, nor the comparative length of his stride, nor his impulsion. In fact, the slower the canter the greater the impulsion needs to be to preserve these qualities.

Our problem then is to achieve a slow canter without losing any of the attributes of a good natural canter.

It is all too easy to fail in that respect.

Riders all too frequently attempt to obtain a slow canter by pulling on the reins. Pulling on the reins implies the use of a backward action of the hands which is always, under any circumstances, fatal. The effect of that action on the horse's mouth must destroy the freedom of his forward stride and its length. It is quite possible to keep the horse cantering, notwithstanding that pull, by driving him on at the same time; certainly, but in what form?

The French call this type of riding *tirer dessus et taper dedans*!

The front legs are prevented from reaching out, the hindlegs from treading under and the mouth ruined in the process; loins and back, instead of swinging more and more into the delightful undulations of a real canter, become cramped and stiff, causing the rider to sit on top of that back instead of into it; the horse potters with his forelegs and is prevented from placing his hindlegs well under his body; as a result he is forced to throw his quarters up too high, with his rider bumping out of the saddle, or else to drag his hindlegs and canter in four-time.

That form is a parody of a slow canter.

Examples of it can be seen in almost every hack class in our show rings.

And, unfortunately, even in the dressage arena!

How then to set about it?

As always, by explaining to the horse without using any force and without any hurry. As always, acting on the principle that only the horse, and never the rider, can deliver the movement, whatever it may be.

The following is my method.

My horse, trained in the open, hunted, goes a good natural canter with a nice long stride. Too fast, of course, probably a good deal too fast for what I now require.

He is familiar with the ordinary aids for a strike-off.

I take him for a ride, in a field, in the woods, during a hack or anywhere. I ride him quietly, mostly walking on a loose rein; I keep him perfectly cool and wait until he is quite relaxed.

I then pick up my reins and collect him only just sufficiently to be able to make him strike-off at an ordinary canter.

I am particularly careful that the horse shall meet no obstruction at all from his bridle during the strike-off. Obstruction with the bridle at that particular moment will mar the strike-off, it will upset the horse and it will make him nervous of this work.

Naturally, he will assume his habitual ordinary canter, which is too fast. But I do nothing to restrain him. I just let him canter on peacefully, perhaps for a hundred yards or so to begin with. I then bring him back to a walk. I could do that perfectly well by resorting to the use of the reins in the normal way. But I do not want to do that. In the initial stage of this training the outdoor horse is not accustomed to being pulled back to a walk every hundred yards or so. Yet this is precisely what I intend to do. But I reflect that to do so is liable to upset a high-couraged horse and to make him impatient. And that I wish to avoid at all cost. So I am particularly careful to use but very little rein-effect; I rely mainly on the use of the voice and bring my weight a little more back in the saddle. These means will suffice to bring my horse back to a walk presently; it may well take twenty or thirty strides; it may well look un-impressive; but it will achieve what I require without any risk of upsetting my horse; which is the only thing of interest to me at the moment.

I then talk to my horse, pat him and walk for fifty yards or so on a very long rein. I then repeat. I go on doing this work for a couple of weeks at the rate of about fifteen minutes a day.

It is extraordinary how soon the horse will have understood that I only intend to canter a short distance slowly and he will accordingly comply. And he will have come to this slower canter without any restraint from his bridle. So he will canter slowly with a perfectly unhampered, free and long stride and with his head carried naturally. There will be nothing forced in his position, nothing to prevent him from bringing his hind-legs well under nor anything to force his head into an unnatur-ally high or cramped position. All qualities these which I must preserve in order to be able, later on, to succeed with the change of leg.

Naturally, I practise this work about equally with the near-fore and with the off-fore leading. But not alternatively, at least not regularly so; if I did so, my horse would quite likely begin to anticipate; horses are so observant that they can become routined very quickly; routine, once established, can cause considerable difficulty; so, we ought to avoid any tendency to routine in our training.

However, working in this way, my horse will fairly soon canter very nicely and quietly and his transitions from the canter into a walk will at the same time become light, fluent and easy.

We can then begin to use the slow canter for considerable distances and enjoy the delightful feel of this mode of loco-motion during our hacking expeditions. All the while, we keep our horse on a very light rein; the weight of the rein and the strength of two fingers should be amply sufficient to control our horse. As long, that is, as everything goes according to programme. But it may not always do that. There are various reasons why the horse may get it into his head to increase his speed; he may see another horse in front of him, a partridge may jump up in front of his nose or anything similar may excite him.

Naturally, it is easy enough to restrain the horse by means of the reins and keep him cantering. But that I never do, not, that is to say, until my horse is really reliably schooled. Instead, I take him back into a walk on a very long or loose rein and keep him like that until he feels completely settled again. He is then ready to recommence cantering.

I would like to enlarge a little on this, in my opinion, very important subject of rein-control.

A great many riders seem to be under the impression that a positive, tight and fairly strong rein-control is unavoidable, necessary and good. It is, on the contrary, evil, quite unneces-sary and easily avoidable. This observation applies, of course, to all paces and not to the canter only. After all, we search for lightness in our horses, for balance and for fluency of move-ment. The two principal factors whereby these qualities are determined are impulsion and confidence. Confidence that is, between horse and rider mutually. Where that confidence exists, the horse can be ridden most of the time " on parole ", " on trust ", that he will not abuse his apparent freedom. The horse deserves that confidence and will act honourably in accordance with it. But, of course, we must do our part in creating this feeling of mutual goodwill. It is on that account that any powerful use of the reins should be avoided when there exists another way out. In the case considered above, there is an-other way out; we can walk!

If we act on these principles for a time, we shall presently find that we can control our horse, even under the most exciting circumstances, with but a touch of the rein and with but a couple of fingers. But such results are not achieved in a day, nor without patience. If we have no patience, they are never achieved.

This work at the canter is exceedingly beneficial to the suppleness of the horse's back and loins. Provided we possess reasonable tact and patience, and are prepared to learn with and from our horse, it is not difficult. It can be undertaken in the fairly early stages of our dressage and, by improving the horse's suppleness, will help to improve the trot.

Starts at the Canter

It will be obvious that the work described in the preceding pages entails the use of numerous starts at the canter and the opportunity to perfect and to straighten these starts in accordance with the principles discussed under the heading "Aids for the canter".

In ordinary riding it is often customary to start at the canter from a trot.

In dressage riding it is not advisable to do so.

The disadvantage is two-fold.

If the horse becomes accustomed to starting at the canter from a trot, it may become very difficult to achieve a good extended trot. It is much easier for the horse, and more natural, to canter when sent on faster than to trot out. So, the horse used to cantering from a trot will be inclined to break when asked to extend his trot.

It is also true that the rider who starts his horse from a walk has much more time to place the horse and to study, with his horse, the niceties of the aids. Both rider and horse will feel more finely that way and will learn more.

The practice of these starts, on either leg, is an essential preparation for the changes of leg. It is folly to attempt the latter before the former has been mastered completely. Complete mastery entails in the first place that the changes be smooth, fluent and restful; that the horse has absolute confidence and shows no sign of excitement at this work, all of which is merely a matter of equestrian tact and, accordingly, of quiet and reasonable progress. Mastery entails also, but only in the second place, that the horse is almost completely reliable in starting on the desired leg.

The word "almost" is here inserted on purpose.

In all stages of schooling, we and our horse are learning and progressing together. We, in studying these starts at the canter, are no doubt attempting to polish the use of our aids, to make them finer and lighter; we may be concerned also with straightening them. It follows that occasions must arise when our aids, or what we intended to be our aids, are misunderstood by the horse, causing him to strike off on what we will consider the wrong leg. Such misunderstandings are neither ill-will nor disobedience on the part of the horse; it is even conceivable that we ourselves have not been very clear in expressing our wishes! Obviously then, any form of punishment, roughness or even impatience are out of the question. We just pull up gently, walk a few strides and begin again.

It will be clear that the study of starts at the canter is bound up intimately with that of transitions from canter to walk, and from canter to halt, and vice versa, so let us consider these transitions first before we finalize the subject in discussing the changes of leg.

Transitions from Canter to Walk

In preceding pages the need has been stressed to begin these transitions very gradually. More or less by allowing the canter to subside through diminishing impulsion, through a few trot strides, into an ordinary walk on a fairly long rein. It will be understood that subsiding impulsion entails subsiding collection at the same time: collection without adequate impulsion cannot exist.

As the horse's understanding of our wishes grows, together with his experience, he will begin to offer easier, more fluent, and briefer transitions all by himself. We may then commence by making a more positive use of the rein, but always carefully, supported by use of the legs.

This presupposes that the horse is already cantering reasonably slowly "in impulsion". By that I mean that the horse will accept our leg-aids for the purpose of maintaining impulsion without tending to increase his speed, and that without any noticeable resistance of the reins.

Progressing in that manner, we shall presently be able to slow up "in impulsion" and "in collection", continuing to canter until the moment of transition. Again, we will understand that consistent success is not achieved at once. There will still be occasions when one or two trot strides slip in. That is of no importance and should not induce the rider into any attempt at using even faintly forcible means. In this work the horse becomes automatically more and more lightly on the aids and, in a state of true collection, equivalent to the *rassembler*.

LAST CANTERSTRIDE   **FIRST WALK STRIDE**
DIAGRAM 18. TRANSITION FROM CANTER TO WALK

It is only then that we can be certain of a smooth transition every time.

There is only one moment or "time" of the canter at which the horse can make the direct transition from canter to walk. That moment occurs at the so-called "third time" of the canter, when the horse has three legs in support, namely both front legs and one hindleg. That moment corresponds almost precisely with the "second time" of the walk, when the horse also has both front legs and one hindleg in support. It is at that particular moment that the horse is able to follow up towards the "third time" of the walk via "lateral support on two legs". This lateral support will be given by the hindleg which was in support during the last "third time" of the canter and the front leg on the same side. (*The Horse in Action*.)

This is a fleeting moment and it will be obvious that the real aid for the transition, which is the by now conventional one of arresting the canter in collected impulsion, must precede the actual transition by the time-lapse necessary to give the horse time to execute the order. This may sound complicated but that, actually, need not worry the rider. His primary responsibility ceases when he has given his order: the horse will quite well know how to execute it. The rider is bound to learn the slight time-lapse needed from experience.

Yet, to make certain of an invariably correct execution, there is one more "feel" which the rider needs to acquire.

To make that clear, I have to enlarge a little on the description of the "third time" of the canter already referred to. At that precise moment the leading leg on which the horse was cantering will be placed out in front of the other front leg and the hindleg in support will be on the same side as the leading front leg.

That is a moment which the rider can see and should learn to feel.

For that is the precise moment at which his aid to check the canter should cease and be transposed into an aid for continuing at the walk. This aid corresponds with the moment when the non-leading front leg is lifted to commence the first walking stride. The aid consists of a slight yielding of the rein, followed almost simultaneously by a slight squeeze of both legs; the effect can be felt distinctly as the horse lengthens somewhat and the altered rhythm of the gait is transmitted through the reins to one's finger-tips.

With growing experience, the rider should be able to acquire this feel, which gives him the impression that he is able to influence and control the movement of his horse's individual limbs. Which, in fact, he is, but within the precise limits of the horse's natural gaits.

TRANSITION FROM HALT INTO CANTER

By the time horse and rider have proceeded thus far, the start at the canter from a halt will cause no difficulty. Provided always that the horse be able to stand still in perfect collection and absolutely square. If he is not in perfect collection, the fluent transmission and execution of the aids is not possible;

if he does not stand perfectly square he is not in a position to strike-off indiscriminately right or left; he may not be able to strike-off at all without some preliminary fumbling. And there must be no preliminary fumbling!

The horse shall lift himself from the halt directly into a pure stride of the canter.

Assuming the horse to stand square and that a strike-off with the off-fore leading is required.

The horse will lift the diagonal off-hind and near-fore together,
subsequently he will also lift the off-fore
and be supported only by the near-hind (first-time of the canter),
to commence the regular stride *(The Horse in Action).*
Any other or additional motion is incorrect.

The aids are precisely the same as those for the strike-off from a walk; but the value of the preliminary rein-signal grows in importance and its significance must have been assimilated by the horse fully and unmistakably before he can be deemed ready for this exercise.

TRANSITION FROM CANTER INTO HALT

The transition from the canter directly into a halt is not in itself difficult to achieve with a horse which can already do the transition from canter into walk perfectly.

But the transition into a correct halt, with the horse standing square on all four legs, is quite difficult.

We have already seen, in a preceding paragraph, that the cantering horse, at the moment of checking, can do no other than place his leading foreleg well in advance of his other foreleg; likewise his hindlegs must touch down one in front of the other.

Obviously then, if we check him into a halt at that particular moment, which is comparatively easy, the horse will stand anything but square. Even so, that type of dead-stop is a spectacular type of halt which appears to impress the public. But it ought not to impress the judges! Because a horse standing in such a position as physically not able to execute every sort of movement which might conceivably be demanded next. Only the square-standing horse can do that.

Accordingly, the halt executed in this manner, however impressive it may appear to be, cannot be held to be correct.

In Chapter VI, I have given a full description of the halt from a walk.

The principles involved in the halt from a canter are precisely the same, but considerably more difficult of execution. As in the halt from the walk, the horse should, upon being checked from a canter, be allowed to round off his stride until he stands square.

The horse, upon being checked from a canter, even from a school canter which, though slow, is full of impulsion, will, if brought to a spectacular but somewhat abrupt halt, stop with his hindlegs very far under his body in a sort of sitting position. It is then almost impossible for him to assume a square stand fluently, however adroit the rider may be.

In my view then, the halt from the canter is best achieved by making the transition exactly as if going into a walk; the horse is then checked gently, or in a sense half halted in the position "third-time" of the canter, equivalent, as we have seen to the "second-time" of the walk; in that way the horse does not assume a sitting position but remains level; then, as the horse follows up towards the "third-time" of the walk, via lateral support, he is checked finally. Assuming that he were cantering with the near-fore leading, he will, at the moment of the transition, be with the near-fore in support in advance of the off-fore whilst the off-hind will be in movement. The final faint check, applied at that moment, causes the off-hind to cease its forward reach whilst allowing the off-fore to take its place by the side of the near-fore.

In other words the horse, after being checked from the canter, completes a mere beginning of the first walk stride, just enough but no more than is necessary to enable him to come to a square halt.

The intricacy of the movements is here given because it is of considerable help if the rider understands what his horse must do in order to answer his rider's requirements; the rider is then less likely to interfere with these movements and to thus make them impossible.

It is not expected, and in my opinion impossible, that the rider should actually control these movements from the saddle. That is, besides, quite unnecessary. As long as interference is avoided, the horse, once he has understood by experience what is wanted, will control his own movement much better than the rider could ever hope to do.

It is only by experience that horse and rider can find the mutual feel without which the nicety of this transition cannot be mastered.

THE SIMPLE CHANGE OF LEG

The correct simple change of leg is done by a transition from canter into walk, without any intervening trot stride: a couple of strides at the walk and a fresh start at the canter, on the other leg, from the walk.

This presents no difficulty to the horse and rider who can do these transitions and starts.

In competitions of a more or less elementary nature, the judges will usually overlook one or two intervening trot strides in the transition from canter to walk; such an execution might still be considered "fairly good", but it could never rank for top marks.

But the use of any trot stride in the strike-off from the walk could not be overlooked and would qualify the movement as insufficient.

Some riders, who are probably able to do a "change in the air", are in the habit of barely marking the transition into a walk; they strike-off again before the strides at the walk have been clearly defined. That type of execution, though perhaps more difficult in a sense, is clearly "insufficient" in that the rider has failed to answer the question demanded.

A "change in the air" would rank as "bad", since it would not even approach the answer expected.

THE COUNTERLEAD

The counterlead, or false canter, fulfils two purposes.

In the first place it is the means to make the horse understand that he is never to change his leading leg excepting upon the rider's implicit instructions. As such it is an absolutely indispensable preparation before the changes of leg in the air and particularly before the repeated changes are attempted.

In the second place it is a powerful suppling exercise, since it requires the horse to find his balance in a mode of progression which he would not use normally, entailing the use of muscles in unusual combinations.

A horse is said to be in the counterlead, or to false canter, when he describes a curve to the right with the near-fore leading, or a curve to the left with the off-fore leading.

It is not natural for him to do that. In the ordinary way of nature the horse will assume the canter to the right, or to the left, or change from the one into the other in accordance with his natural balance and his natural judgment.

Instead, we now want him to understand that he must give up acting in accordance with his own sense of balance and that he must in future submit to our judgment in the matter.

We have the means to do this at hand since the horse is already thoroughly familiar with our aids for the canter and is obedient to them under normal conditions. But we have now to obtain this obedience under the abnormal conditions of the counterlead also.

It is not difficult to succeed in this at the appropriate stage of the horse's training, but it does require tact; it is, again, an exercise in which we can only succeed by explaining to the horse's brain and not by acting forcibly on his anatomy.

We need plenty of room to begin this exercise.

Let us assume that we are going round a sizeable field in an anti-clockwise direction. We strike-off at the canter with the off-fore leading at the beginning of a long straight line. We sit quite still, keeping the horse quietly but markedly on the aids; we are careful in particular to maintain the feel on the right rein which causes the flexion whereby the correct leading leg is determined. We then begin a very faint curve to the left. We do that by using the left rein, quite carefully, as direct or opening rein; but without changing our aids for the right canter or our position in the saddle.

If the curve be slight enough, that should cause no difficulty. We continue this exercise by forming the curved line into a serpentine; we ride this serpentine without changing leg, so that the horse is alternately cantering true and cantering false.

These are, for the reasons already stated, difficult exercises for the horse. This means, in the first place, that it will take time to develop these faint serpentines into more defined serpentines, into circles and into figures of eight without change of leg.

It means also that the horse will frequently change leg of his own accord; he may do a true change or change only in front and continue disunited. When this happens we bring our horse gently back to a walk, walk a few strides and strike-off again, equally gently, on the required leg.

The accent here is decidedly on "gently"!

We are "explaining" to our horse.

If we use punishment, roughness, or even impatience, we shall also explain, certainly, but with the wrong result! The horse will conclude that it is wrong to change, under any circumstances, and that to do so leads to unpleasant consequences. The horse never forgets. So, once that conclusion has become fixed in his mind, we shall meet with considerable difficulties when it comes to obtaining the changes on demand.

It has been stated that it is necessary, in false cantering, to maintain the aids for the required lead clearly. These aids comprise the flexion. It is essential therefore to maintain right-flexion when cantering on the off-fore and left-flexion when cantering on the near-fore. But it is as well to be quite clear about the meaning of the word "flexion".

Flexion, in this context, refers to the relaxation of the horse's jaw to the action of the rein which determines the leading leg; that flexion causes the horse's head itself to look slightly in the direction of the leading leg; but this flexion of the head, limited almost to a tendency, affects the head alone and not the neck! There is no bend in the neck.

To derive the full benefit of this exercise, and to do it correctly in the long run, the horse, when false cantering on a circle or bended track, should be able to bend over his whole length round the rider's inside leg, whilst maintaining a flexion of the mouth to the outside rein. Thus, when describing a circle to the left at the counterlead, with the off-fore leading, the horse's body and neck shall be bent in conformity with the circular track; precisely as would be correct for the true canter, but with the exception of a right flexion of the mouth, maintained by the outside rein.

THE CHANGES OF LEG IN THE AIR

The change of leg in the air, or flying change as the Germans call it (*fliegender galoppwechsel*), is a perfectly natural movement to the horse; it causes him no difficulty.

Yet it is far from easy to obtain a correct change of leg on demand. But the cause of that difficulty lies entirely with the rider and not with the horse. It is not easy to apply the aids which are required without hindering his execution of this delicate movement. Even the slightest degree of hinder is sufficient to spoil the purity of the action.

The change is called "in the air" because the horse, not hindered, does the change during the fourth or silent time of the canter, which is the brief moment when he has all four legs off the ground. During this minute fraction of a second, he reverses the relative position of all his limbs. He does that with such unfailing accuracy and smoothness that the action is barely discernible in the saddle and has no effect whatever on the rider's comfortable adhesion. He does it without acceleration or deceleration; the rhythm of the canter is undisturbed; it is merely the lead which changes; he does it perfectly straight and without any need to swing.

Particulars of the canter gait have been given at the beginning of this chapter.

If the horse be cantering with the off-fore leading we remember the footfalls to be (1) near-hind, (2) off-hind and near-fore together, (3) off-fore, (4) in the air, and so on if there be no change.

But after a change, the sequence alters into: (1) off-hind, (2) near-hind and off-fore together, (3) near-fore, (4) in the air, and so on.

The lead at the canter is determined by the hindleg which initiates the movement; it is on that hindleg alone, not in combination with any other leg, that the horse lands to initiate the new stride, each time after he has been "in the air".

The near-hind determines the canter with the off-fore leading.

The off-hind that with the near-fore leading.

Cantering with the off-fore leading it is the near-hind which touches down alone; cantering with the near-fore leading it is the off-hind.

The purity, or otherwise, of the change under consideration, from off-fore to near-fore leading, is determined by the change of initiating hindleg, in this case from near-hind to off-hind.

This change of hindleg is the quintessence of purity; if that fails, everything fails!

Now let us examine the rider's difficulties.

They lie in the application of the aids.

The aids themselves have been described in preceding pages; the use of the determining rein-effect has been made clear; it has been stressed that any resistance by the bit to forward movement will mar the strike-off at the canter; it can now be added that any resistance by the bit during the moment of the change will ruin the change.

It is not always easy to avoid resistance of the rein during the take-off; it requires great delicacy to avoid it during the change; it is the rein-signal which controls the canter, so it must be used; it is the presence of that same rein in an unyielding form which mars the strike-off and destroys the purity of the change, so that must be avoided; but the time-lapse between rein-signal and strike-off is brief, so the action of the hand, which must merge from signalling into yielding, almost instantaneously, is difficult.

In the strike-off, the difficulty is caused by the momentary acceleration.

In the change there is no acceleration. But in changing, the horse lengthens momentarily; head and neck stretch somewhat forward and dip to some extent from side to side. Hence, though the causes of the difficulty in the two movements are not identical, the need to avoid rein-interference is the same.

The rider's second difficulty is to select the correct moment at which to give the aids. That moment must precede the execution of the movement by some time-lapse; of sufficient length to leave the horse time to obey our order when next he is in the air; he can do it at no other moment. Precisely how long this time-lapse should be cannot be stated; it depends to some extent on the quickness of the horse's reactions and therefore on his experience. But it cannot be long at the best of times, for the aids must be applied after a specific stride has commenced and before that stride is ending "in the air".

By way of general guidance, I advise to apply the aids for the change during the "second time" of the canter; at that particular moment the horse holds the leading front leg stretched out in front, above the ground, whilst his other three legs are all in support, on the ground. It is easy to ascertain that moment from the saddle.

The horse who has been taken conscientiously, and successfully, through all the stages described previously in this chapter, should now be ready to come to these changes. He should be able to start correctly, and unfailingly so, from a collected walk or from a halt into a canter, canter a few strides, make a perfect transition to a collected walk, strike-off again, and so on. He should by now, as a result of all his training, be in the *rassembler*, in perfect collection, use his hocks energetically and be very light in hand. He is perfectly balanced.

The state of "perfect collection" implies that we are able to collect our horse on an easy rein. For the changes of leg at the canter this is essential. It has been stated that the horse stretches head and neck forward to some extent and dips them from side to side during the change. The canter is a horizontal pace; the horse's back is mainly parallel with the ground; though the hindlegs tread well under, they do not do so with exaggeration; the horse assumes no "sitting" position, with the forehand carried higher than the quarters.

To succeed with the changes, the horse must be collected, it is true; but in the natural form of the canter and not pulled together; if the rein be too short, the neck has insufficient freedom and the horse will be hindered in the liberty of his stride; if the stride be too short, the execution of the change will become very difficult. It will be appreciated that these hindrances, all, are of the rider's making.

Lastly, it has been stated already that the horse neither accelerates nor decelerates when changing in freedom. Deceleration, whilst under saddle, is fatal. It will rob the horse of the possibility to complete a pure change. He will be forced to land, not on one hindleg, but on two, or on three legs perhaps; there will be a jolt, through interruption of the smooth movement; the horse will extricate himself somehow, but not without demonstrating publicly, by bumping his rider about in the saddle, that the change has been bungled.

However, the rider forewarned of these difficulties and bent on avoiding them should have no undue difficulties in obtaining these changes and in perfecting them gradually. The horse, prepared as outlined, will do a correct change at the first time of asking. Naturally, we make it easy for him in the beginning. We begin by asking the changes during a change of direction. We do not swing the horse; that is quite unnecessary, it is bad form and leads to disunited changes. We simply reverse the aids. We realize that each change is in essence no other than a new start at the canter with the other leg leading. We do one change only, and walk for a while. If we fail, we also walk for a while before we try again. We are quite satisfied, and pleased, with but a few successful changes every day. We avoid always asking the change in the same place; in so doing, we avoid routine.

As the days wear on we ask more changes, but never very many, not more than a dozen or so; and we keep up the practice of walking for a while after each change, for several weeks; we do that for the sake of calmness, which is absolutely essential for this work.

We help the horse by not cantering too slowly; the change is easier from a long stride than from a short one; we are particularly careful that we do not cause any deceleration during the stride of the change; but it can do no harm and may well help us, and our horse, if we accelerate. The change requires plenty of impulsion. In fact, if we feel that we, or our horse, are bungling the changes, acceleration will usually bring the cure. If the change is correct there is no jolt whatever; if we feel a jolt, we can be quite certain that the change has been bungled; we must feel our way towards a change without a jolt; we are likely to find it through acceleration.

It is essentially an exercise which horse and rider have to learn together. It is the rider's main objective to perfect the timing of the aids so that he obtains the change precisely during the intended stride. If he fails in that, but gets a delayed answer during the next stride, he will know that his aid has been mistimed.

He may either have given the aid too late or, which is perhaps more likely, he may have failed to warn the horse that the aid was coming, by preparing him for its execution. The horse cannot execute precision movements unless he be on the aids with precision. Now it is true that the well-schooled horse is always on the aids, but not all the time with precision. On the contrary. Once we have put our horse at the canter, say, with the off-fore leading, he remains lightly on the aids; we are more passive than active; we need do no more than regulate impulsion, if necessary, and keep our horse straight, if necessary; in reality, whilst we remain observant all the time, we actually do very little; there is no need to; the horse himself knows the work and does it to a large extent "on parole". It has been the whole object of our schooling to bring the horse that far.

But the horse is not, in that state of free and pleasant partnership, able to execute totally unexpected commands which appear like lightning from the sky. So we have to draw his attention before we start speaking. We do that by accentuating the aids for the movement which he is doing, in this case the aids for the canter with the off-fore leading. This action is taken before the new aids are given. In the earlier stages, some moments before, perhaps a couple of strides; as progress is made, a moment before, perhaps during the preceding stride; finally, as horse and rider become very experienced, warning and aid almost merge.

I have said that the horse is brought on the aids "with precision"; quite, but of course not abruptly, nor with any roughness; just enough to draw his attention, and no more. Whatever we do on the horse, including this warning, should never surprise him. But we may well use the opportunity, when circumstances seem to demand it, to obtain a little more impulsion or a little more speed, or both, before demanding the change.

When the changes done with the help of a change of direction have become established, are smooth, easy and fluent, we will ask for a change on a straight line. I prefer to do this work in the open, away from the school. In that way the horse can canter on long straight lines and there is nothing to encourage anticipations. We canter along quietly, bring the horse on the aids, do our change and walk. I attach very great importance to the use of the walk throughout the whole of this training; it keeps the horse relaxed; thus, he will not contract the habit of being on the look-out for these changes, which produces tension and leads to anticipation and related difficulties.

It is only when I am really satisfied that the horse does his one change perfectly, with absolute precision on my demand and with complete calm, that I keep him cantering on a little longer and ask for two, or perhaps three changes at intervals of perhaps twenty or thirty strides.

The whole basis of this work is purity of change, on demand, calm. The entire further progress is built up on just that. We will not succeed if we attempt to hurry progress and repeat the same exercise too often or for too long a time during one lesson. A lesson in any specific, difficult work should never last more than a quarter of an hour; most of that time the horse should walk and at the end of that time he should be cool.

Once the horse changes well, accurately and calmly every twenty strides or so, there will be no difficulty in reducing the number of intervening strides to ten or even to eight.

We have by now reached the stage for the repeated changes at close intervals, say every six strides to begin with, every five, and eventually every four. It is then advisable to revert first to perfecting our control of the counterlead and secondly to perfecting the starts from the walk.

We begin by asking changes on a circle of adequate size, changing every ten or twelve strides, cantering true and cantering false alternately. In practising starts from the walk at this stage we keep the horse collected. Six strides at the collected walk, six strides at a right canter, six strides at the collected walk, six strides at a left canter, and back to a walk. We repeat a few times, but we vary our demands somewhat. The horse can count as well as we can, and if we use precisely the same number of strides every time he will be learning a lesson by heart instead of relying on our aids.

The horse which can do these repeated starts from a walk accurately, will be found to be able to do his changes in the air every six strides equally well. We then study this work at the canter, changing with some variation, after six strides, after seven strides, after five strides. But never more than a few changes consecutively, followed by some walking. Calmness is and remains the number one requirement in this work.

In this manner it is fairly easy to come down to changing at every four strides.

Changes at every three strides are already more difficult. We attack these changes at short intervals in a special manner. We canter with the off-fore leading; we change to the near-fore leading, do three strides exactly, change back to the off-fore leading, and walk. We repeat several times, always in the same sequence, so that the horse changes back each time to the off-fore after three strides on the near-fore. In that way we practise one particular change only, from near-fore to off-fore. We do not attempt to correlate two subsequent changes. It is simpler, and our progress, and that of the horse, will be quicker and safer; there is less risk of excitement and muddle. We practise this one type of change for a couple of days, until it is well under control. We then reverse the proceedings, changing to the near-fore after three strides on the off-fore; again we practise this change for a couple of days.

Subsequently, we correlate, doing three strides on the off-fore, change to three strides on the near-fore, change back to off-fore, followed by walk. Next we do the exercise in reverse, beginning with three strides on the near-fore, change to three strides on the off-fore, change back to near-fore, and walk.

Having mastered the change at every three strides, we next see to it that the horse does not change by routine. So we alternate, at our fancy, changes at three strides, with those at four and at five.

The changes at every two strides is approached in the same manner. It is only right to state that these changes at very short intervals are difficult to master; they require very finely timed aids, and a very high degree of understanding between horse and rider and much experience and judgment on the part of the latter. The experts of the Spanish Riding School of Vienna do not go beyond changes at every two strides.

The change at every stride is, however, a requirement of the Olympic Dressage. It is a most spectacular movement, very effective and most elegant. It is recognized as one of the most difficult achievements in riding. It is obviously quite impossible to attempt it unless all other types of change, at four, at three and at two strides have been mastered completely. And even then it introduces considerable new difficulties. There is but a minimum of time to apply constantly changing aids which have to be at one and the same time absolutely precise and exceedingly light. Loss of impulsion and interference through the mouth are both fatal.

However, assuming that both horse and rider are expert in changing at every two strides, we proceed as follows.

We canter on the near-fore leading. We change to off-fore leading; at the very moment that we feel the change coming we reverse the aid to obtain the next change; accordingly the horse does one stride only on the off-fore and changes back to the near-fore. We walk. We repeat a few times. We study this one movement for several days, always the same: change from near-fore, one stride on off-fore, back to near-fore. When fully mastered, we reverse, changing from off-fore, one stride on near-fore, back to off-fore. Finally, we again correlate the two movements.

The Olympic competition calls for fifteen consecutive changes; that is to say fifteen precisely, not fourteen, nor sixteen. This accurate control is of great difficulty.

Considerable tact is needed to avoid any trace of excitement whilst teaching this work. It is a most interesting and rewarding study when successful. But it is not without its dangers. It is all too easy to confuse the horse, which may lead to grave misunderstandings.

THE CANTER ON TWO TRACKS

The canter on two tracks presents no special difficulties. All exercises described in Chapter XIV, with the exception of the pirouette, to be discussed separately, are comprised in this statement.

The changes of hand across the school, done at a half pass, normally require a change of leg upon reaching the opposite side. Again, this presents no great difficulty to the horse who can do his changes. It is, however, advisable not to ask the horse for this change until he has ceased to be on two tracks and is straight. To change and straighten at the same time requires considerable experience on the part of the horse, which can only come in course of time.

Also, it is never wise to study more than one problem at the same time; it is always better, more effective and quicker to divide the problems first and to co-ordinate afterwards.

Thus we begin by studying these half passes at the canter only, without change of leg; on arriving at the opposite side of the school, we put our horse at a walk. We do not introduce the change before the half passes themselves have become easy and fluent.

In Chapter XVII (p. 206) we have discussed the counter-changes of hand on two tracks at the trot, and in particular the difficult repeated counter-changes of hand, also called "zig-zag", at every few strides. Everything that has been said about this work at the trot applies to the canter equally. We proceed precisely in the same manner.

Only, at the canter we introduce the further complication of the repeated changes of leg. This will make it obvious that this exercise is beyond the reach of any horse until complete fluency has been achieved at the canter on two tracks as well as at the changes. In the latter respect in particular, horse and rider should have reached the expert stage.

It should be obvious also that the repeated changes of bend and of direction, combined with the repeated changes of leg at the same moment, make it still more difficult for the horse to solve the problems involved for himself, than was the case at the trot. The search for progress should be accordingly careful.

THE PIROUETTE

The pirouette, as we know, is a full turn on the haunches, a turn of 360°. This movement at the canter presents great difficulties. It is required that the horse shall pivot round the haunches whilst the hindlegs keep cantering on the spot. Taking the requirement "on the spot" literally, I believe that to be almost impossible, at any rate in combination with the pivot. I have certainly never seen it done perfectly in that way. But I have seen many attempts at it, resulting in a "swing round", admittedly with the hindlegs on the spot, but never with the hindlegs cantering. Such a swing round is of little value.

When I have seen perfection, or at any rate near-perfection, with the hindlegs cantering, I have always seen these hindlegs describe a very small circle; small enough to appear "on the spot", but large enough to retain forward impulsion and with it the cantering movement of the hindlegs. Since that retention of forward impulsion constitutes the supreme difficulty of this movement, it is my opinion that the exercise should be studied with that in view.

In Grand Prix competitions this movement is demanded in the centre of a diagonal change of hand, at point X of the arena. The horse follows the diagonal line at a school canter and, arrived at X, must make a transition into a canter on the spot and commence the turn on the haunches, cantering, simultaneously.

The transition is the first difficulty. If the horse be simply checked in his progress, as is so often seen, he can do no other than stop cantering; under these conditions the rider can do no other than swing the horse round; he is no longer in a position to ride him round. It is therefore essential to teach the horse transitions from the school canter into a very slow canter indeed, almost on the spot yet, in my opinion, not quite on the spot. This requires tremendous impulsion. In order to maintain and to stimulate that impulsion, we bring the horse back to a few strides of very slow canter and make sure that he is ready to stride freely forward at any moment, immediately on demand. This readiness to move freely forward is our only remedy against the horse's tendency to stop cantering through extinction of impulsion.

In addition to being able to canter almost on the spot, the horse must be expert at cantering on two tracks. He must be able, in particular, to do a full pass at the canter at an angle approaching 90°. And he must learn to do that quite slowly and deliberately. This demands an exceedingly supple horse, with great power in hocks and loins; some horses are unable to reach this stage. We can only attempt to get there by gradual progress.

The normally very well-schooled horse will sidestep at the canter, doing a diagonal change of hands, at an angle from 45° to 50° with his line of progress. We will now increase that angle, very gradually, to 60°, to 70° and finally, after weeks of careful work, to as near 90° as we can. We will realize, of course, that this work is very strenuous, and that it is quite sufficient to maintain these acute angles for a matter of fifteen to twenty yards at the most.

Simultaneously, we continue to canter on two tracks on the circle, in the position head to the wall, at an ordinary angle of about 45°. And we do not make these circles too small! I do not think it advisable to try and approach the pirouette at the canter by decreasing the diameter of the circles. To do so makes too great a demand on the horse's powers and ends almost invariably in loss of impulsion and extinction of the canter.

The following is my method, to be put into practice after the very slow canter with accelerations, and the full pass at the canter, have been mastered completely.

I canter along the side of my school. I reduce to a very slow canter for a few strides. Whilst at this very slow canter, I bring my horse's forehand round towards the inside of the track, maintaining the quarters on the track. My principal object is to keep my horse cantering; so I limit the turning movement of the forehand to one or two strides at the most; I then accelerate immediately into the speed of a normal school canter. It is through that acceleration each time, after a stride or two on the turn, that my horse will realize that he is to keep on cantering! It is, as always, a matter of explaining to the horse, leaving it to him to work out the answer. Naturally, I do this exercise on both reins.

Gradually, I increase from two strides on the turn to three, or to four. Always, I accelerate, as described. Presently, my horse will do one quarter turn of 90° easily. I keep at these for quite a while; they are fundamental. After that it is merely a matter of gradual, very carefully considered progress, to increase the turning movement from 90° to 120°, 140°, 180° and, finally, to 360°.

The Extended Canter

The extended canter presents few problems. The horse's range of speed at canter and gallop is almost unlimited and nature puts no difficulties in his way. It is very much easier to obtain a good extended canter than a good extended trot.

Yet, the performances seen in the dressage arena are frequently disappointing. Presumably riders become so engrossed in the vastly greater difficulties of the collected exercises, that they overlook the need to keep their horses reasonably trained in natural extension as well.

The extended canter is required in practically every dressage competition and the judges will attach considerable importance to it. They will observe the transitions with particular attention.

The transition from a collected into an extended canter, and vice versa, is not merely a matter of speed. It is a matter also of length of stride and in particular of the horse's outward form, which must conform to his action and speed. During the transition of a collected into an extended canter the horse comes out of the fairly upright form on a comparatively short base, of the former pace into the longer and more horizontal form, on a markedly longer base, of the extended pace.

The horse's neck is lengthened and carried lower, and accordingly the strides lengthen considerably also and the speed increases markedly.

In order to extend the horse, the rein is lengthened accompanied by leg pressure (see page 135, *descente de main*).

What difficulties there are derive from the transitions. These should be rapid, take no more than a stride or two, yet be completely free from any semblance of abruptness. They should be fluent, meaning that the horse should appear to flow from one pace and from one form into the other without causing a ripple.

Again, it is a matter where horse and rider have to seek for growing mutual understanding by increasing these variations of pace and of form gradually. Riders are rather easily inclined to change their aids too abruptly. Both the increased leg pressure and the longer rein have to take shape together in such a way that the horse is given the necessary time for fluency of execution. As the leg pressure comes on gradually to create increased impulsion, so the rein lengthens gradually to translate this increase of impulsion into extension; as the desired extension is achieved, so the leg pressure ceases; the leg comes to rest, remaining just sufficiently vigilant to maintain the horse in the required form.

To succeed in this transition to extension, it is imperative to maintain the horse on the aids all the time; the horse can only be expected to extend fluently if the aids extend fluently with him. If the rider fails in this respect, the horse may lose the regular rhythm of his canter; quite possibly he may change legs.

The transition from extension to collection requires equal care; again, any suddenness of execution will surprise the horse, will disturb his rhythm and may once more cause him to change legs.

The difference between the horse's collected and extended canter ought to be marked as clearly as is commensurate with the size of the arena, the abilities of the horse and the requirement that the presentation shall look polished, fluent and easy. Good transitions should be and should look effortless, and the horse remain balanced throughout.

CHAPTER XIX

DRESSAGE COMPETITIONS

---

*Appeal of dressage competitio⌐s – Degrees of difficulty –
Basic requirements – Purpose of competitions – Composition
of tests – Arenas – System of marking – Preparing for a competition – Taking part in a competition – Judging – Practical
hints for the novice rider and the novice judge – Role of the
judge*

APPEAL OF DRESSAGE COMPETITIONS

I N Chapter I of this book I have defined dressage as "the art
of improving one's horse beyond the stage of plain usefulness,
of making him more amenable, easier to control, pleasanter to
ride, more graceful in his bearing and better to look upon".

I have also said that the "the pursuit of the ideal is a passionate quest in itself, full of reward in the constant discovery of
newer and ever more subtle harmony between horse and rider",
and that the practice of dressage "provides the guidance whereof
every horseman stands in need who wishes to raise his horsemanship, and with it the performance of his horses, just that much
above the standard of mediocrity as will make all the difference
to his enjoyment and success".

It follows that dressage riding will appeal to the type of rider
who has the ideal, referred to in the first quotation, truly at heart
and who is prepared to seek, by concentrated and intelligent
study—with his horse—for the guidance whereof he stands in
need.

Working by oneself, it is not always easy to be certain that
one is following the right road. It is in that respect that competitions can be so helpful. There is the adjudication by competent judges, whose remarks can often be revealing, even if at

times disappointing. There are, in particular, the competitors! There just is no better school—no matter for what type of horsemanship—than competitive riding. To see others do better, to try and emulate them, endeavour to surpass them is the best tonic, the best fillip to sustained work and progress. It raises one's interest and so adds to one's pleasure. Apart from the pleasure there always is in becoming one of a circle of friends with whom to discuss the same interests and attempt to help solving one another's difficulties.

It is undoubtedly these, and similar considerations, which have made dressage riding so increasingly popular and have attracted so many talented riders to its practice.

DEGREES OF DIFFICULTY

Competitions vary widely in difficulty, to suit the stage of schooling of the horses and the ability of the riders.

There will be very simple tests, intended mainly for young horses, and suitable also for less experienced riders. In England these are known as novice tests and comprise none but basically simple movements. The so-called elementary tests are only slightly more difficult, calling for a few exercises which need a somewhat higher degree of control.

Basically, there will—or should—be nothing in either of these tests which any normally suitable riding horse, broken and prepared with normal care and ridden with understanding and reasonable ability, cannot perform adequately.

Tests of medium difficulty will call for distinct refinements of control, balance and lightness not usually seen in ordinary riding. They demand a polished display of riding of the low school; this cannot well be achieved without some degree of specialization in dressage on the part of both rider and horse. But that degree does not, in my opinion, exceed what any educated rider would quite normally require from any horse worth keeping, be he charger, hack, jumper or show jumper. Anyway, I can state quite truthfully that I have never kept a horse on for any such purpose without bringing him up to at least that standard. I might add that I have never yet kept any horse for dressage exclusively. All my horses, without exception, have always been well and fairly hunted and they have all been better all-round performers, and infinitely more agreeable and less tiring rides, as a result of their dressage schooling.

The well known Prix St. Georges of the International Federation calls undoubtedly for considerable specialization in dressage. The movements demanded, their sequence and their accuracy, are already of considerable difficulty. To do this test well requires a horse in the *rassembler*, with cadence and strictly regular gaits and a rider of considerable finesse. The Prix St. Georges is the foundation for the high school of riding.

Finally, the international Grand Prix is high school. It calls for all the refinements discussed in this volume. The number of riders able to bring a horse up to this standard will always be small.

Basic Requirements

Whilst the degree of difficulty between the easiest and the most difficult tests vary enormously, it is of the utmost importance to realize that the basic requirements vary not at all!

The essentials for which the good judge is looking and for which the good rider will strive are the following.

The horse shall be light; light, airy and free in all his movements and light and easy to control with delicate aids. To be that he must be on the aids, with a good mouth and the quarters well engaged, full of impulsion. If he be that, he will have balance and rhythm. Rhythm, of course, demands pure, regular and even gaits. He shall be straight.

His bearing and carriage will be of a high-couraged, generous horse, energetic, confident, calm, obedient to, and trusting his rider.

The rider shall have a good seat, good hands, good legs, unobtrusive aids. He will show that he understands his horse, is in sympathy with him, feels him.

Together, they will present a picture of ease and elegance as will delight the heart of every true horseman and as will, in a competition, awake and retain the interest of the judges.

PURPOSE OF COMPETITIONS

It is then the purpose of a dressage competition to examine horse and rider in these essentials, in conformity with the degree of training reached by the horse and the ability and experience of its rider.

In order to do so within a reasonable time limit, and in order also to compare like with like, riders and horses are required to ride a specific test. Such tests comprise a sequence of movements and exercises to be performed before the judges in an arena, which resolves itself to a certain extent into the riding of a number of figures.

Now it is true that such figures must be ridden with considerable accuracy, because the various changes of direction or gait, the transitions and halts, or whatever else may be demanded, assist the judges in determining the degree of suppleness of the horse, his obedience, his paces and likewise the ability of his rider, his seat, the application of the aids. But it is also true—and all too often not understood—that the figures demanded are only a means to an end! The means to see how near horse and rider come to the basic requirements set out in the preceding sub-chapter. It is perfectly obvious that novice competitors sometimes believe that there is merit in performing the required figures in accurate sequence. There is in that, by itself, no merit whatever and the judges will not be impressed by it. They expect to see " dressage " riding, showing that rider and horse are seeking to produce " the picture " referred to and have gained insight into the principles which alone can bring that about.

COMPOSITION OF TESTS

It follows from what has been said that the composition of any test should be so planned that horse and rider, who are up to the particular standard demanded, shall be able to give a free going and pleasant performance in it, which is interesting to watch.

The picture required will have to be seen at every gait and in such forms of every gait, ordinary, collected, extended and so on, as are commensurate with the degree of a particular test. It

Left: COUNTERLEAD
" BASCAR "

Right: CHANGE OF LEG TO NEAR-FORE
LEADING. " BASCAR "

Above: EXTENDED CANTER. "BASCAR"

Left: CANTER ON TWO TRACKS (HALF-PAST *Appuyer*). "BASCAR"

is the harmonious development of these gaits, and the skill of the rider in producing them, that matters uppermost. It is this that will bring out whether rider and horse are proceeding along the right lines.

Naturally, every test will comprise certain special difficulties, halts, rein-backs or whatever it be, whereby specific details of correct schooling are brought out. It is my opinion that these details shall be incorporated in such manner as to fit logically into the programme, and not to upset a smooth and elegant performance.

It will be understood that the composition of a good test is far from easy. It is definitely an expert's job. An expert, that is, who, from experience and feel, has a thorough understanding of when and where special difficulties may reasonably be interpolated without risk to the smoothness and elegance of the test as a whole.

This requirement applies to the easiest of tests as much as to the most difficult ones, but is more difficult of fulfilment as the tests become more advanced. It is particularly difficult in a Grand Prix and some of the compositions prepared for that type of contest in recent years have failed rather lamentably in that respect. This was most apparent in the test laid down for the Olympic Games at Stockholm in 1956.

ARENAS

The only official dimensions, recognized internationally, are those of the full-size arena, which measures 20 metres × 60 metres, or approximately 22 × 66 yards. The layout and lettering are shown in Diagram 19.

This is undoubtedly the correct size to permit the development of the horse's gaits to their fullest expression.

In Britain, in Germany, and possibly in other countries, a smaller arena is often used for the novice, elementary and similar tests of a simple character. The dimensions of this small arena are 20 × 40 metres, or approximately 22 × 44 yards. Layout and lettering are shown in Diagram 20.

The disadvantage of the smaller arena is that it makes extended gaits rather difficult, particularly so for the novice type of horse for whom it is intended. The advantages are that the

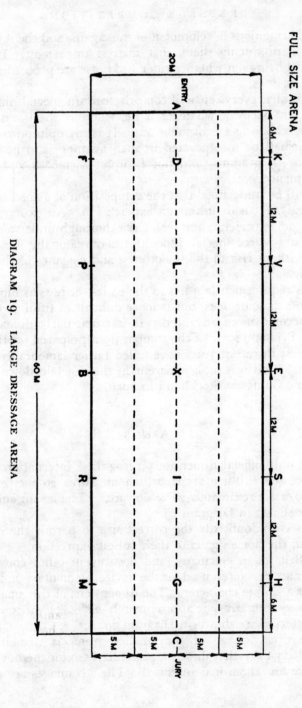

FULL SIZE ARENA

DIAGRAM 19. LARGE DRESSAGE ARENA

novice horse meets corners more frequently, which is good for his schooling and balance.   Also that an examination in this arena takes less time, which is important because the number of entries for the simpler type of tests tends to be large.   Finally this kind of competition is liable to be held in places where it

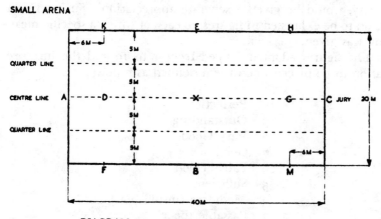

SMALL ARENA

DIAGRAM 20.   SMALL DRESSAGE ARENA

may be difficult to lay out a full size arena.   The preparation of the smaller piece of ground is also easier and cheaper.   All in all it appears reasonable to conclude that the advantages outweigh the disadvantages.

It is the rule that the public shall be kept at a distance of 20 metres (22 yards) from the arena.

SYSTEM OF MARKING

The first and the second international dressage competitions were held at the Olympic Games at Stockholm in 1912 and at Antwerp in 1920.   It is the experience there gained which led to the formation of the International Equestrian Federation in 1921, and the first set of rules then drawn up came into force on the 1st January, 1922.   It would be ungracious here not to mention the name of Commandment G. Hector, of the French Cavalry, as that of the true originator of this Federation.   He remained its moving spirit and Secretary-General until November, 1951, when advanced age and ill health obliged him to lay down this function. He was then elected Honorary President-Founder and died three months later.

Since every dressage test comprises a sequence of movements and exercises, or of groups of movements, it was decided that each movement, or group of movements, considered to form an entity, would be given a separate appreciation. Such appreciation to be expressed in figures, to each of which a specific meaning was given.

The figures adopted ranged from 1 to 10 and the interpretation to be placed upon them defined as follows:

10	Perfection
9	Outstanding
8	Very Good
7	Good
6	Fairly Good
5	Sufficient
4	Mediocre (insufficient)
3	Passable (poor)
2	Bad
1	Very Bad
0	Unmarkable

Subject to some reservations I shall make under the sub-heading on judging, this proved itself in practice as about the best system anyone could devise. It does give the judge ample latitude, which he assuredly needs, to grade individual performances with considerable accuracy and finesse. For reasons which need not here be gone into, the verdict of judges will sometimes vary to a considerable extent. This has been particularly noticeable in important international contests and has frequently given rise to unfavourable comment—to such extent that the responsible committee of the F.E.I. have felt considerable concern. The only remedy so far thought of has been to reduce the available markings from 0-10 to 0-6. This, not going to the heart of the matter, proved no remedy at all. But it did prove itself unsatisfactory to the vast majority of international judges. The alteration was introduced in 1953 and tried out for the first time at the International Three Days Event of that year, at Badminton, where I was one of the judges.

At the time of writing this, 1957, the rule for international competitions remains o-6. I relate these circumstances so that it may be appreciated that particular rules referred to may be subject to change from time to time. Essentials are not affected by such detail.

PREPARING FOR A COMPETITION

The first thing an intending competitor has to do is to make a careful study of the schedule of his test. He will consider each movement carefully, the sequence of the movements and the transitions from each movement into another. He will consider in particular whether any of these movements are likely to cause him or his horse any special difficulty; and if so, which method of riding may be at his disposal to lighten such difficulties.

He will pay particular attention to the markers at which certain movements begin or end; he will decide on the precise distance from such marker at which he must begin to prepare his horse in order to ensure smooth execution of the movement or transition at such marker exactly.

Next he will have to learn the whole test by heart; so thoroughly that the entire arena, the entrance, the place of the judges, the white lines and the precise place of each letter and of their inter-relation become photographed on his mind; he must now make himself so thoroughly acquainted with every movement, and with the sequence of movements that he can see those also in his mind's eye, in full detail, in connection with each other and in relation to the situation of the arena; in addition, he should be able to view any likely difficulties in precise connection with the particular movement liable to bring them about; a difficulty foreseen is probably more than half prevented!

Finally, he must see two movements simultaneously, the one which he imagines to be doing, and the one to follow next.

This perfect memorizing of the test is of primary importance. Failing that, he will, once in the arena, have to pay attention to his horse, and to himself, and to memorizing the test at the same time. It is impossible to do both really well simultaneously. Either the riding, or the memorizing, or in general both, will suffer. His nerves and those of his horse will be affected, and his presentation will decline in consequence.

It is most inadvisable, for reasons about to be stated, to attempt this business of memorizing from the saddle. The most effective way is with the help of a piece of paper and a pencil. One draws out one's arena, complete with all letters and white lines. One sketches all movements, one by one and in their sequence, and begins to learn them by heart as one goes along. One repeats several times a day for several days; for just as long as is necessary to see and to perform the entire test, with all its implications, perfectly clearly and easily in imagination.

We are then ready to concentrate on our horse. To make quite certain that we have discovered each and every difficulty to be encountered in the test, we try out its movements and transitions one by one. But not in the order of the test! I consider that most important. Whilst it is necessary that we know the test by heart, it is almost equally essential that the horse shall not. He, in fact, is much quicker at memorizing than we are ourselves. If we allow him to go by memory, he will go by routine; he is certain to anticipate and to give the show away in that and other ways; his behaviour will not escape observant judges, who will mark him lower accordingly.

So, whilst it may be useful from the rider's point of view to ride a complete test a few times, well in advance of a competition, great moderation is recommended. It is perfectly legitimate, and in general essential, to work one's horse and oneself in preparation for a forthcoming competition. But again, it is essential to use moderation and it is recommended in particular to ease up on any schooling during the last week or so preceding the great day. It is so easy to make a horse stale, to say nothing of oneself, by an excess of cramming. At any rate, it is quite useless to try to teach the horse anything which he does not know already during the very last week.

But there is one very simple precaution that should never be neglected. All arenas have white lines and white dots. Horses have to walk, trot or canter straight along such white lines and probably they will have to halt on top of a large white dot. Most horses will be determined to avoid such lines and dots without some little preliminary repetition. It is quite easy to draw a few such markings on a stretch of grass and so to avoid any such contretemps.

Hints and guidance offered by a knowledgeable friend or instructor can be very helpful; but it is most unwise to attempt any radical change of style or method of riding shortly before a competition.

TAKING PART IN A COMPETITION

Horses are inclined to be sensitive to strange surroundings. The journey to the showground itself is enough to set them wondering about the excitement that may be in store for them.

It is advisable then to have our horses on the ground as long as possible before the commencement of the day's contest. The horse is more than likely to express keen interest, some surprise and a measure of excitement in the place and at the sight of a number of strange horses.

It is essential to get him over this feeling. Generally, this is best done by giving him plenty of time to look around quietly and to let the strange sights sink in. It is usually best to ride the animal around at an ordinary walk on an easy rein for an hour or so. In that way he is most likely to settle down. Strenuous exercise is not to be recommended as a general rule; it tends to keep the horse on his toes and to keep the state of excitement up; it may even increase it.

However, horses vary so much in temperament that it is impossible to generalize. Riders will have to discover the precise methods best suited to their own charges.

Before entering the ring all horses will require some little suppling up; precisely how much it is difficult to say; but, again in general, just enough is better than too much.

Everyone knows that one's horses always go better at home, usually very much better, than in a competition. So the nearer we can keep to home conditions, the more likely we are to reproduce home form. If it takes us fifteen minutes at home, walk and rhythmic trot, to supple our horse up nicely, it is advisable to use precisely the same method before we are called into the ring. It is certainly unwise to use the last fifteen minutes for the purpose of compressing a lot of difficult exercises into that short space of time. To do so can have no other result than to get our horse on edge. The horse must be kept calm.

It is, of course, very nice to watch friends and other competitors perform in the ring; but it is a pleasure which the serious rider would do well to forgo until he has finished his own turn; pending that he had better keep quiet and concentrate on his own problems.

Once in the ring, and in front of the judges, the rider's paramount problem is the control of nerves: his own and his horse's. There are several factors affecting nerves.

In the first place, there is often the anxiety of memorizing the test properly, very serious, because interfering with our unruffled control of the horse; if it does so interfere, the uncertainty is bound to be reflected in the animal's performance. This anxiety, as we have seen, can be completely avoided. The rider should act in the arena in exactly the same manner as previously practised in his imagination. Before coming in, he knows how to come in, where to halt and how to salute. As he comes in he reviews in his mind, which takes no more than a fraction of a second, the next movement to follow upon the halt. As he rides along, he is free to devote full attention to his horse; with plenty of opportunity to cast an eye round the arena so as to feel at home. As he moves off from the salute into the first movement of the test, he at once reviews the next movement that is to follow; he keeps a small part of his mind's eye fixed on the particular letter or marker at which the second movement is to begin; he remembers to prepare his horse for that second movement before that particular marker is actually reached. And so on until the end, always prepared for the movement to follow whilst doing the previous one.

Another factor affecting nerves is the anxiety of so many riders to show their horse at the very top of his form. That, though understandable enough in itself, is better avoided. It leads so easily to demanding just a shade more than the horse can really do, which will always cause disappointment. At any rate, concentration on maximum performance is usually accompanied by some tightening of control; this will surprise the horse; he, already somewhat under the impression of the unusual surroundings, will begin to wonder what to expect next from these tightened controls; they will make him nervous, he will tighten up and the very relaxation which is the basis of a good performance will be destroyed.

The rider should make every endeavour to ride his horse

just as he does at home, just as if there were nothing unusual in the air. The horse will take his cue from that, settle down, and perform smoothly. Many more marks will be lost by a horse which tightens up under pressure than by one who goes smoothly, even though perhaps a shade below his best.

Lastly, there remains stage fright and examination fever.

The former is rather a personal affliction, which it may take some time to conquer through experience and increased confidence. At any rate, the rider who has prepared himself carefully, and who endeavours to ride his horse quietly, in accordance with the advice given him, will go a long way in mitigating its effects. There is nothing better calculated to instil confidence than the feel of a smooth-going, responsive horse.

Examination fever the rider should try to forget. Once having given the salute, he may well ignore the presence of the judges. There is now nothing whatever he can do about it anyway, excepting to ride his horse nicely and enjoy the experience.

He should be quite determined in his mind not to get upset at all through any faults committed by himself or his horse. He should feel quite certain beforehand that he is bound to make some. And that he will not be the only one. For nobody has ever seen anyone, including the top-ranking international experts, who did not commit some slip or other during the execution of a dressage test.

It will help competitors to know what the judges are looking for and the methods whereby they arrive at their conclusions. This will be discussed in the pages that follow.

JUDGING

It should be obvious that a judge has to know the particular test on which he is to adjudicate as well as the competitors. In fact he has to know it a great deal better. He must not only study and know all individual movements, or groups of movements, and their sequence, he must also know precisely which movements are marked separately and which are marked in groups; and, in the case of groups of movements, he must have a clear idea in his mind of the relative value which he will allocate to each individual movement coming within the group.

Once the judge is in his place, with a competitor in front of him, his attention will be concentrated on that competitor alone. He has no time to look at any particulars of the test; he should have no need to. He knows the precise marker at which he must decide on the appreciation to be awarded to the movement which will finish at that marker. He follows the horse's every step and the rider's every gesture; if he be following a group of movements his final appreciation will be in the balance until all the movements in the group have been completed; but he will be shaping, and maybe reshaping, his opinion all the while; and he will announce his final verdict at the precise moment when the final movement of the group has been completed; and not a moment later, for his attention must then be concentrated exclusively and at once on the next movement.

The object of the marks allotted by the judge is no other than to arrive at a fair and accurate comparison of the respective merits of individual competitors.

This "comparative idea" has its dangers.

There is a method or system of judging which is based on it specifically; it is known as the "comparative" or also "relative" method of judging. This method is employed by almost every inexperienced judge and, much more rarely, by some more experienced judges as well.

It is natural enough that the wish to be strictly fair and impartial is so uppermost in the mind of many judges that they find it difficult to relegate that idea to the background. As a result, they work on the comparative system.

Accordingly, in allocating their markings to individual performances, they are always endeavouring to compare such performances with others that have preceded them; they endeavour to remember their previous markings, and then adjudicate accordingly.

The system is based on creditable motives.

And in small competitions, with few competitors, it may well work out in the manner desired.

But it has serious inconveniences. The attempt at making continuous comparisons and at remembering lots of preceding markings must detract from the judge's concentration on what is in front of him. It is also doubtful whether the comparison of one individual with another by memory, which may well be somewhat uncertain, will not lead to subconscious influences of sympathies and preconceived ideas. At any rate, it is bound to lead to inaccuracies.

In modern competitions, judges may be at it the whole day long, dealing with perhaps thirty or forty horses and adjudicating on some twenty or more movements, or groups of movements, of each individual horse.

It ought surely to be crystal clear that no judge can possibly remember the detail of from six to eight hundred individual movements!

In serious dressage competitions, the comparative method of judging is bound to defeat its own objects and to result, more often than not, in quite unexpected results.

The alternative method of judging which disdains any attempt at comparison and which concentrates solely, without fear or favour, on the individual who happens to be in front of the judges, is known as the "absolute method". By this method the judge gives his verdict on the quality of the particular movement in front of him, in accordance with a clear-cut standard of values which he carries in his mind. He makes no comparison with any other horse or rider; he merely compares with his own standard of values.

That standard of values is absolute in so far as the competition in front of him is concerned. But in a general way it is only relatively absolute; obviously the judge cannot apply identical standards to a Grand Prix and to a novice test. He will be able to adjust his values in accordance with the class of horses in front of him. To do so will cause no difficulty to the judge who possesses a sound knowledge of the niceties of dressage and experience of the particular difficulties involved.

It has been stated that the judge has to carry this standard of values in his mind; quite, for there is no other way. It is not a lesson that can be specified in writing and learned by heart; even if that could be done, it would be of small value; the value of a judge's opinion rests on his experience, understanding and insight, and, of course, on the absolute impartiality of his verdict.

Finally, then, the judging of dressage is a matter of opinion. There must always be some differences in that respect between

one judge and another; it could hardly be otherwise. Yet I
have always found, in discussing these matters with prominent
judges, and in officiating with them, that such differences as do
arise are surprisingly small.

Whilst the above exposition of the absolute method of judging
is *grosso modo* correct, it is yet necessary to call attention to some
specific difficulties with which the conscientious judge is faced,
and which will occasionally affect his satisfaction with the end-
result of his score. If we return for a moment to the basic
requirements described on a preceding page, and if we then
take into consideration also the many purely technical requirements of each individual movement or exercise, it will be
realized that quite a complexity of factors must be considered—
and decided on quickly—for each individual marking. In
general such markings will apply to groups of movements, followed by the judge's eye and observed in every detail. If the
execution were perfect, the judge's task would indeed be easy.
But perfection is rarely met with, so it is in reality the judge's
task to deduct from his perfection mark in accordance with the
imperfections observed. These may be slight but can be
immensely varied in character and degree. For a moment or so
the horse may overbend, if ever so slightly; or show a trace of
resistance, as might escape any but the most observant: a very
slight momentary loss of impulsion, a momentary loss of straightness, possibly one uneven stride, a swish of the tail, an ear laid
back, an opening of the mouth. The rider may show a trace of
backward action of the hands, be seen to try and lift his horse's
head by the bridle, a visible aid, a momentary stiffness and so
on, a host of little things to be taken into consideration all at
once.

It is obviously impossible to lay down any absolute or other
scale for the innumerable little influences of this type as occur
in every performance. The judge can only act in accordance
with his impression of the moment. He may be a good judge,
possibly a very good one, but certainly not perfect. Perfect
judges do not exist, any more than perfect horses or perfect
riders. At times he may hesitate, say between a 7 and an 8. In
that, there may lie an element of luck, or bad luck, as between
one horse and another.

This element of luck is accentuated by two psychological

influences from which very few judges are absolutely immune. It has already been said that the judge must, to a certain extent, adjust his standard in accordance with the class of horses to appear before him. That standard may be new to him. If that be the case, he may well want to feel his way to start with, and be, in other words, a little severe on the first two or three horses to appear before him. That, admittedly, is a weakness on the part of the judge, but it is not uncommon.

If all performances were of a reasonably level standard, the judge's task would be considerably lightened. Unfortunately for him, the standard is never level. Normally it varies from very good to distinctly poor. That brings us to the second psychological influence. The very good performer who follows an indifferent or poor one, or perhaps a succession of indifferent ones, will generally profit a little. Conversely, the average, reasonably good performer who follows upon the heels of an outstanding one, will generally be unlucky.

Now it follows from these considerations that final scores are to some extent influenced by luck. The better the judges, the less the influence, but some there will always be. Possibly amounting to only one or two or at any rate a very few marks.

Every good judge knows this to be the case, for every good judge retains a quite distinct impression in his mind as to the respective merits of the two or three best performances to have appeared before him. Under rules at present existing, scores are sacrosanct and the judge can do nothing about it, should he feel the apparent result to be wrong.

In my opinion the judges should be given the power to require a ride-off between competitors whose marks are so little apart as to make no matter; that power to be used at the discretion of the judges in cases where they did not feel fully satisfied that the placings as determined by the score were right. Such ride-off not be marked again, but to be judged on general impression.

Bearing the above in mind, I will now endeavour to explain the main considerations that are uppermost in my mind when called upon to judge a dressage competition.

Every test demands the execution of a number of movements, in prescribed order, at certain predestined places of the arena. It is often considerably easier to do certain movements a little too early, or a little too late, than to do them at the exact place indicated. In fact, the precise merit of a given movement is sometimes entirely dependent on its execution at the right place. That applies, to give but one instance, to the execution of a two-track movement from any stated beginning to any required destination exactly.

Accordingly, accuracy of execution is of the essence of the performance. Very slight errors, which do not otherwise affect the merit of the movement required, I will treat leniently. But substantial inaccuracies, by which some of the difficulty is avoided, whether on purpose or not, I will treat severely; I may even go so far as to qualify the movement in which they occur as "unmarkable".

Movements are required to begin or to end at certain markers; they do so begin or end when the rider's shoulder is level with such marker.

I make a principle of announcing every award I make in plain words first, giving the corresponding figure afterwards. I will say: "good—7", or "insufficient—4"; in that way I am always certain that the figure on the marking-sheet corresponds exactly to my appreciation; in so doing, I run no risk of ever forgetting the precise implication of each figure; there will be nothing haphazard about the use of my figures.

As long as horse and rider are in front of me in the arena, I look first and foremost and all the time at the picture which they represent. I want to know whether that picture does or does not come up to the requirements of a well-trained horse, well ridden. I expect to see a horse which accepts his bridle, flexes and is light in hand. If the horse fails in that respect, his performance can never be "good"; accordingly, he can never earn as much as a "7". Similarly, I expect the horse to be energetic, to go freely forward and to look happy and pleased in his work; again, if he fails in that, he cannot be "good". I expect the rider to sit comfortably, to have good hands, good legs and quiet, unobtrusive aids. A rider with strong hands, or rough, or who is constantly kicking his horse, will never book a "7" at my hands.

In brief, what I want to see first and foremost is a horse that goes and looks in the way a good dressage horse should go and look, and I expect the same of the rider. For what would be the use of all the work involved in this dressage if it failed to produce a pleasing picture? It is only having seen that picture that I become interested in the degree of merit of individual movements. And it is only movements well and accurately done by such a picture that will gain really high marks of 7 and upwards.

For that, to me, is the essence of good dressage!

If that sparkle be there, that touch of brilliance, and the performance be generally good, which it can hardly fail to be, I am fully prepared to treat certain little lapses leniently, even very leniently; I refer to such things as maybe a sign of over-keenness of a high-couraged horse; perhaps a little bound or possibly a change of leg out of place; naturally, I can only be lenient if the rider shows by prompt corrective action, applied smoothly, that he and his horse know their job!

I like to see a picture full of life, elegant and gay. I am not in the least impressed by mere correction in utter dullness; and I see no reason why that type of performance, in which there is but little difficulty and scant merit, should impress me. The exercises of a dressage test are devised to give me a comprehensive picture of horse and rider, as they can be at their best, in a short time; these exercises are a means to an end, not an end in themselves.

It is remarkable how little time it usually takes for this "picture" to register in the experienced judge's mind; perhaps during the first or second movement round the ring; sometimes the entrance alone suffices.

The picture may say: "I am a 7 horse, good, yes, but I lack a bit of sparkle"; or I am 8, very good, and a picture for sore eyes; more often, I am going to be fairly good, a 6 horse, or, well, a 5, possibly just sufficient.

And it is still more remarkable how the form works out almost invariably in accordance with that first impression.

Some flights of fancy of the 8 horse will surprise no one, a 9 or two, perhaps a 10; quite as likely some unexpected technical lapse, suddenly down to a 5; what does it matter, the picture is still "very good".

The 7 horse is different; no flights of fancy for him, but, more than likely, no lapses either!

And the 6 horse, well, mostly sixes, perhaps a 7, certainly several fives.

And just so, quite often, right along the line.

The above, then, describes my general attitude of mind.

PRACTICAL HINTS FOR THE NOVICE RIDER AND FOR THE NOVICE JUDGE

Novice competitors, as every experienced judge knows, sometimes show that the basic requirements expected of them are little understood. Such performances are likely to lead to disappointment, even though kind-hearted judges are generally inclined to deal somewhat generously with the weaker brothers and sisters. In a sense, this tends to make the judging of such presentations rather more than less difficult. Novice judges, who are liable to be invited for just this grade of competition, are at times puzzled by such problems.

Hence it may be helpful to resume, very briefly, a few of the basic elements involved.

Entrance, halt, salute.

The entrance shall be straight, on the white line. Yes, but the merit of being on the white line is of no great value unless the horse be active and on the aids, goes bridled, with a good mouth. With regard to the requirement that the horse be straight, attention is drawn to the fact that many riders are in the habit of riding with one rein slightly shorter than the other. The horse then has to carry his head slightly to one side, which is a distinct failing.

In the halt, the horse shall remain on the aids, standing straight and square, to attention, calm and immobile. If these conditions are fulfilled, the salute will cause no difficulty.

The first impression created by these essential movements may be of great significance.

Going round corners.

In every test, a considerable number of corners have to be taken. Each corner is a quarter circle and the horse shall be bent to such circle, that bend being particularly noticeable in the position of head and neck. There is, in this requirement, no real difficulty, yet it is much sinned against. It is a grave fault. This observation applies to all circular types of tracks. Horses

THE END. SALUTE! "BASCAR"

are liable to show loss of balance in the corners, due to insufficient impulsion.

Following the track.

It is elementary that the horse, going round the arena, should follow the track reasonably accurately. A horse failing to do so is not under proper control.

Variations of pace.

It is equally elementary that horses should be able to vary their pace, at each gait, in a balanced manner. Horses which fail to show their ability to do so lack merit. Some competitors rush through their programme at a hurried pace throughout. To do so lacks all polish and is but a poor performance. Those who are slow and lifeless throughout are, of course, no better.

Transitions.

Variations of pace and changing from one gait to another, and coming to a halt, demand transitions. These should be smooth. That implies that there must be no hint of abruptness. If there is, the horse will always notify the fact by a resistance—a sign of discomfort—in the mouth. It is remarkable how often the transition from an extended into an ordinary walk is spoilt in that way. Due to lack of smoothness and feel, on the part of the rider, when shortening or picking up his reins. Before marking an extended walk, the judge should watch this transition.

Rein-back.

A horse which cannot halt well, as described above, will never do a good rein-back. To rein-back well, the horse has to be light, answer the action of the legs combined with a retaining action of the hand. Being thus "in impulsion", he will back in two-time, straight, with his head in the normal correct riding position, neither behind nor above the vertical. Resistance against the bridle is a very grave fault.

Turn on the forehand.

This movement is generally required in novice competitions and should, in my opinion, be judged accordingly. As explained in Chapter XIV, the pirouette on the forehand, done perfectly, is the smallest circle at the shoulder-in. The horse will then cross with one hind leg across and before the other. It would appear illogical to expect this form of execution from the novice horse not yet trained at this kind of work.

I am satisfied if the horse pivots round his front legs, under adequate control, with evenly sustained steps. I do not require to see the legs cross.

Turn on the haunches.

This is a considerably more difficult exercise. It is not always well done. Frequently the horse turns on the centre, steps back or does both. It should be remembered that the *pirouette sur les hanches* is the smallest circle in the position of quarters-in. It is in essence a forward movement, which requires forward drive by the rider's legs.

Simple change of leg.

This movement consists of three phases. Firstly the transition from canter into walk; this may be done through the trot, but the horse must walk a couple of steps. Secondly the transition from the walk into the strike-off on the alternative leg. Again, this transition may, but need not, be done through the trot. The judge will consider the two transitions and the strike-off and the movement cannot be considered good unless the transitions are smooth.

ROLE OF THE JUDGE

Dressage, like every other art, is based upon certain principles and techniques. It follows, then, that the judge must possess command of the technical foundation of the art of riding. His role may be compared to that of the art or literary critic, who must both possess a sound appreciation of the technique of their subjects; the laws of perspective, of grammar and of style, for instance. But perspective alone creates no masterpieces, any more than mere style and grammar. The technique is only the basis on which art can be created. So the judge needs, like the critic, a true artistic feel for the beauty of horsemanship.

He also needs understanding and sympathy; he has to appreciate the efforts of those who appear in front of him at their true value, rather than to criticize them. In that respect he will wish to be generous within the limits of strict justice to all.

CHAPTER XX

THE HORSE FOR DRESSAGE

---

*" We can never presume to improve upon nature and we
can never, under any circumstances, create in the horse any
qualities wherewith he has not by nature been blessed."*
(p 49/50, Chapter III)

EVERY type and kind of horse can be improved by dressage
training within the limits of his physical and mental limitations. If these limitations be severe, the ultimate results will not
be very spectacular, even in the hands of the most capable of
trainers. Some horses are more suitable than others. Whilst
it is true that the student can often learn a great deal from his
attempts at schooling animals of the less suitable type, it is yet
equally certain that the use of such animals for competitive purposes will lead to disappointment.

The informed trainer, interested in show jumping, will obviously begin by selecting an animal with a natural aptitude for
jumping; if he did otherwise, he would be wasting his time.

Similarly, the rider interested in competitive dressage should
select the sort of horse most likely to reward him in due course
for his efforts.

Whilst the perfect horse does not exist and need not be looked
for, there are yet a number of well defined characteristics, both
good qualities and defects, by which the suitability or otherwise
for the purpose of specialized dressage can be assessed.

Let us first examine the physical points and begin by taking a
look at our horse standing still, not posed, but naturally.

The horse shall stand square on all four legs, the legs acting
as pillars, in the way pillars should, as near vertical as possible.
A horse which stands under in front will always tend to go on the

forehand. A horse which stands stretched in front will be difficult to collect and is not likely to be a good mover. A horse which stands stretched behind will not be able to get his hocks under him. Hind legs to be well shaped, with a good second thigh and good hocks. Sickle hooks are not an advantage. Pasterns to be free from defects. They must not be short and thick, which leads to stumpy gaits. A little more length than one would look for in a hunter is no detriment. Long pasterns make for soft movement. Legs should be looked at from in front and from behind. Deviations from the vertical tend to spoil the gaits. Toes turned in or out and cowhocks or hocks standing wide are to be avoided for that reason. Short cannon bones are liked in a hunter. For a dressage horse a somewhat longer cannon bone is no detriment, rather the contrary. Feet to be well shaped, open, with a good frog. Boxy feet condemn the horse. So do big and clumsy feet.

As to the body itself, we like great depth and short legs in a hunter. In a dressage horse a lighter build is to be preferred. A nice fine sloping shoulder, well defined, with excellent withers, is of the first importance. The forearm (humerus), connecting the joint of the shoulder blade with the elbow, should not be at too acute an angle. If it is, it will tend to make the forelegs stand under and will impede their free movement. The formation of the elbow joint deserves particular attention. If this joint be too close to the body, the horse being elbow-tied, free and straight movement are out of the question. One likes to see good hindquarters of adequate length. If quarters are short, the angle between the hip-bone (ilium) and thigh (femur) will be too small and the angle at the stifle joint between thigh and tibia is likely to be similarly affected. By that formation the development of a good swinging gallop stride is impeded.

The topline of the horse, head, neck and back is of the greatest consequence. The appearance should be balanced. This implies in the first place that the topline shall rise towards the withers. A horse which is overbuilt, with the quarters higher than the withers, or tending to be so, will never make a dressage horse. His forehand will always be overloaded, preventing all possibility of developing lightness. The back well formed and preferably of average length. Too short a back is a disadvantage, because it makes it even more difficult than it always is to obtain lateral flexibility of the spinal column. For a dressage horse one would rather see the back a trifle on the long side. A back which is slightly hollow, as one would call slack over the loins, is no great disadvantage. It will supple up more easily. A roach-backed horse should be rejected; it is a misery to try and train them. The tail should carry well. A tail which fails to carry often indicates weakness and lack of courage, and anyway spoils the picture. On the other hand too high a carriage, except in the Arab, may denote stiffness over the loins.

However good the horse may be in the details so far examined, his future as a dressage horse may be made or marred by the conformation of neck and head. The neck should be long and fine and its natural elevation at an angle of about 45°. If the angle be notably less, it will always be difficult and sometimes impossible to obtain the carriage without which elevation of the forehand, and with it lightness, cannot be obtained. If the neck rises too steeply, is carried too high, it may be difficult for the horse to arrive at the correct bridled position; this conformation tends to lead to a ewe neck. The neck should emerge from the trunk at the right place. Sometimes, though not very frequently, the point of emergence of the neck is set too low. That con-formation, again, tends to overload the forehand and will cause great difficulty in obtaining a good carriage.

A well formed small head is always desirable, even if for no other reason than that it is pretty. It has a technical advantage, however, in that it is light to carry. All the same, the size of the head matters far less than the manner in which it is set on to the neck! It is only the well-set-on head that can really flex from the top of the poll, and without that type of flexion precisely, the true *rassembler*, or collection of the third degree, and the general lightness derived from it, cannot be achieved. The horse must be, as the French call it, *bien cravaté*. A horse with a heavy jaw and thick through the throat cannot produce that type of flexion and will always be disappointing. An enforced flexion will result in pressure on the underside of the neck, on the Mastoido-Humeralis, the principal group of muscles respon-sible for the action of the forehand. It will be understood that horses with short, heavy, thick necks will never go far in dressage.

Having thus reviewed the most important points of detail which may be helpful or otherwise for our intended purpose we shall now take a good look at our horse as a whole. The overall impression should be one of balance, quality and lightness. Provided balance be there, lightness is of the utmost moment. The essence of dressage is the search for light and elegant movement. It cannot be expected from the heavily built broad-chested horse, however good he might be as a weight-carrying hunter.

The best type for dressage is undoubtedly the thorough-bred type of riding horse with show hack characteristics but not necessarily of show hack size. The height of the horse should be proportionate, within reason, to the height of the rider. Too small a horse lacks presence and stands to lose something on that account. Too tall a horse finds increased difficulty in the more intricate *manège* figures. Depending upon the size of the rider, a height of from 15h. 2″ to 16h. 1″ appears about ideal.

Having satisfied ourselves about the horse's conformation, we shall now wish to see him move, in hand and under saddle. Where possible, it is an excellent idea to see the horse turned out loose in a suitable paddock or similar place. If the horse be fresh, so much the better. We shall then see what he makes of himself, at the trot and canter, his carriage, the play of his legs, the amplitude of his stride, his handiness and his lightness. This sort of exhibition can teach us a great deal, in particular about his aptitude at the canter. Cantering free, the horse changes leg very easily—and quite perfectly—at the slightest change of direction. If he does not do so, but shows a marked preference for the canter on one particular leg, to the point of false cantering on it, we should be wary; his education at the canter—and the changes on command—may cause grave difficulties. If the horse shows any sign of cantering disunited, he should be rejected without further ado.

We shall then see him led at the walk and trot and ridden at all gaits. We shall watch every gait from the side, from the front and from behind. From the side we shall concentrate first on the absolute symmetry between all four limbs and between each pair of limbs; all strides shall be perfectly level and of the same length. At the trot in particular, any defect in that direction will show up distinctly. At the trot, too, we shall watch the comparative elevation of hind and front legs. The front legs being lifted slightly higher is no detriment in a dressage horse; but if the hind legs be lifted higher than the front, the animal is unlikely to give satisfaction. At the canter the length and type of stride shall be the same with either leg leading; if that be not the case it will prove difficult in due course to obtain good changes, and those at every stride may well prove impossible of achievement. Once satisfied about the symmetry of movement, we will, of course, attach due importance to its amplitude. Brilliant movement is a gift of the gods!

Watching the horse from in front and from behind, we shall make quite certain that there be no irregularity, or deviation from perfectly straight and parallel movement. Slight defects in that direction, which may be barely visible at ordinary gaits, will show up distinctly—and possibly very distinctly—in advanced movements, in the fully extended trot, and particularly in the passage and piaffe. Since purity of gait is one of the basic elements which the judge must take into consideration, any faulty form of gait constitutes a severe handicap.

Seeing the horse ridden, we will, of course, pay attention to his behaviour and deportment. Normally, we should be buying a young horse, with a view to undertaking his dressage schooling ourselves. So, we would naturally not expect to see a schooled animal. But we ought to look for an animal which, however green and inexperienced he may be, has not been spoiled! Spoilt gaits, a hurried walk, jogging, uneven trot, canter in four-time are all difficult to cure. Spoilt head-carriage, star-gazing, boring, a spoilt mouth, fighting the bit, head throwing, open mouth, tongue over bit and—not to forget—grinding teeth—all lead to endless misery. One should refrain from buying misery!

Last but not least, the horse's temperament has to be taken into consideration. It can make all the difference between satisfaction and disappointment. The horse that is generous gives of his best easily, has the will to go forward, has courage, is teachable, comes to hand more quickly and—above all—co-operates. He will answer to light aids, disdain evasions, be a pleasure to ride and a joy to watch. Generosity and courage are characteristics of a hot temperament. Such horses require a sympathetic and understanding rider, for whom they will go like a lamb.

Hot, in the context in which it is here used, does not mean gassy, scatter-brained or temperamental; horses so affected are always liable to let one down at the slightest provocation; they are never reliable and should be avoided. I would similarly reject any horse given to habitual shying, a defect frequently due to poor sight. I do not fancy a cold or lazy horse, who offers little himself and has to be driven hard to make any show. It is difficult to ride such horses without constant strong leg aids, which will be seen by the judge and which will also affect the rider's easy and quiet seat.

Generally, it is again in the really well-bred horse, thoroughbred or nearly so, or Anglo-Arab, that the desirable temperament can best be found.

Geldings are frequently preferred to mares. The latter can be troublesome at certain times of the year, though this condition affects some mares much more than others. On the other hand there are mares with near perfect temperaments that make excellent dressage horses. Stallions are not so frequently seen in the dressage arena, even though their temperament and courage are frequently of the best.

The final examination of the horse we propose to buy, provided he be broken and rideable, takes place from the saddle, of course. It is there that we can get the feel of him and decide whether or not we are likely to suit each other. If the horse be unbroken, we cannot put him to that final test, which will make the risk just that little bit greater. But risk there always will be, for even the greatest expert can never tell for certain whether the young horse, however promising he may appear, will finally turn up tops in dressage.

But the rider who begins with the right type of horse, of the right temperament, has at least taken out the best, and the only insurance there is, against ultimate disappointment. Well above the average will be his chance of success!

BOOKS OF REFERENCE

COMTE D'AURE: *Traité d'Équitation*.

BARROIL: *Art Équestre*.

F. BAUCHER: *Œuvres complètes*.

BRITISH HORSE SOCIETY: *Notes on Dressage*.

GÉNÉRAL DECARPENTRY: *Équitation Académique*.

CAPITAINE J. B. DUMAS: *L'Équitation Diagonale dans le mouvement en avant*.

GÉNÉRAL FAVEROT DE KERBRECH: *Derniers Enseignements receuillis par un de ses élèves* (de F. Baucher).

FÉDÉRATION ÉQUESTRE INTERNATIONALE: *Statutes and General Regulations, 1939 and 1950*.

JAMES FILLIS: *Principes de Dressage et d'Équitation*.

LIEUT.-COLONEL DE LA GARENNE: *A la Française*.

DE LA GUÉRINIÈRE: *École de Cavalerie*.

GÉNÉRAL L'HOTTE: *Questions Équestres*.

HUNDERSDORF: *Equitation Allemande*.

W. MÜSELER: *Die Reitlehre*.

LE NOBLE DU TEIL: *Cours d'Équitation*.

DU PATY DE CLAM: *La Science et l'Art de l'Équitation*.

CAPITAINE RAABE: *Traité de Haute École*.

L. RUL: *Le Bauchérisme réduit à sa plus simple expression*.

DR. G. C. SIMPSON: *Horses*.

STEINBRECHT: *Das Gymnasium des Pferdes*.

HENRY WYNMALEN: *Equitation*.

HENRY WYNMALEN: *The Horse in Action*.

INDEX

IN a book of this type numerous terms, such as the word "horse" for instance, are bound to recur over and over again in a variety of contexts.

It has been thought that a complete index of such terms would be confusing rather than helpful, since the reader using this index will wish to find subjects and not words. He will be able to do that more easily by consulting the table of contents which gives the division of the entire subject matter of this book into carefully grouped Chapters and Sub-Chapters.

The index that follows then is limited to references, titles, names, expressions and terms which the reader might wish to turn up without being able to remember in which context he had seen them.

A

Acceptance of the bridle, 80
Advanced training, the key to, 51
Aids, by association, 98, 226
   diagonal, 224, 225
   lateral, 225
   the, 109
Airs, 26, 207
Amble, 182
Arabia, Deserts of, 100
Art of jumping, 54
Art of riding, 89
Aubert, 129
Aure, Comte d', 24, 25

B

Badly broken horses; 66
Ballotade, 210
Barroil, 25
Baucher, 24, 25, 118, 129, 136, 142
Beau pli, le, 26, 171
Best natural paces, 50

Bouche, la bouche murmure, 60
Bracing the back, 96
Bridle, acceptance of, 80
British Horse Society, 22

C

Cadence, 190
Cadre Noir, 21
Calm, forward, straight, 109
Calme, en avant, droit, 109
Capriole, 210
Carriage, the best, 50
Cavalry School, Hanover, 21
   Saumur, 21
   Sweden, 21
   Switzerland, 21
Cavesson, 57
Central Europe, 210
Cercle, le cheval se couche dans son, 147
Change, disunited, 243
   flying, 240
Cheval, le—fuit le vent de la botte, 184
Cheval, le—se traverse, 110

Classical riding, 25
  school, 27
Collection, perfect, 242
Columbia University, 153
Combined effect of mouth and body, 115
Comte d'Aure, 24, 25
Contact, lightness of, 52
Counterchange, 207
Courbette, 210
Croupade, 210

D

Dans le beau pli, 171
Débourrage, 20
Decarpentry, 118, 136, 171, 210
Détroyat, Général, 136
Diagonal aids, 224, 225
Diagonalize, 212
Disunited changes, 243
Disunited gaits, 223, 239
Dressage, Olympic, 246
Dumas, Capitaine J. B., 210
Du Paty de Clam, 25

E

École de Cavalerie, 25
École de Versailles, 25
Education from the ground, 210
Energy, 51
Épaule en dedans, 157
Éperon, leçon de l', 129
" Equitation ", 103
  Academique, 171, 210
  Diagonale, 210
  savante, 21, 22

F

Faverot de Kerbrech, 25
Fédération Équestre Internationale,
  F. E. I., 21, 23, 170, 171, 173, 200, 204, 255, 259
Fillis, 25, 118, 142
Flexions in hand, 118
Fliegender galoppwechsel, 240
Flying change, 240
France, 210
French literature, 204

G

Gaits, disunited, 233, 239
  united, 233
Général Decarpentry, 118, 136, 171, 210
Général Détroyat, 136
Général l'Hotte, 25, 109, 110, 171
Gerhardt, 210
German cavalry, 99
German School, 96, 157, 204
Germany, 64, 210
Glove, iron, 53
  velvet, 53
Good trot, 51
Grand Prix Competitions, 249, 255, 267
Ground, education from the, 210
  work from, 67, 210
Guérin, 210
Guérinière, de la, 25, 136, 149, 157, 190
Gymnasium des Pferdes, 99

H

Hector, Commandant G, 259
High School Horse, 111
High School of Riding, 21, 177, 207, 260
Hotte, Général l', 25, 109, 110, 171
Horse, " The — in Action ", 107, 223, 233
Hundersdorf, 25
Hungarian Puszta, 100
Hunting, 104
Hurry, 51

I

Imperial Riding School of Vienna, 21
Improve upon nature, 50
Influences, 211
Iron glove, 53
Italian School of the Renaissance, 209

J

Jump, changing leg during, 57
Jumpers, above the ground, 210
  training and schooling, 57
Jumping, art of, 54

K

Key to advanced training, 51
Key to every horse's mouth, 61
Kreuz, das — anziehen, 96

L

Lateral aids, 225
Leçon de l'Éperon, 129
Le Noble du Teil, 25
Lesson of the spur, 129
L'Hotte, Général, 25, 109, 110, 171
Lightness, 49
  of contact, 52
  of control, 50
Lippizaner Horses, 67
Lumbago, 139
Lyne, Michael, 107

M

Magpie jump, 218
Martingale, 77
Modern School, 26
Mongolia, 100
Montigny, 210
Mouth, a good mouth whispers, 65
Müseler, W., 95, 97, 98

N

Necessity of the trot, 190
Notes on dressage, 22

O

Obedience, 48
Olympic dressage, 246
On parole, 244
  a prisoner, 136

P

Paleontology, 153
Parole, on, 244
Passage, doux, 214
  soft, 214
Piaffe, 26
Pillars, 209
Pirouette sur les épaules, 138
Pli, dans le beau, 171
Prairies, 100
Prisoner on parole, 136
Prix St. Georges, 255
Puszta, 100

Q

Questions Équestres, 109, 171

R

Raabe, 25
Rarey, 35
Rassembler, 26, 72, 111, 171, 199, 201, 233, 242, 256
Regulations of the F.E.I., 1939, 173
Regulation seat of German cavalry, 99
Reitlehre, Die, 95
Rhythm, 191
Riding logic, 95
Rough-riding, 20
Routine, 229
Rul, 25
Running Martingale, 77

S

Saumur, 210
Saut de pie, 218
Sauteurs, 210
School, above the ground, 210
  canter, 227
  classical, 27
Schoolmaster, 103
School, modern, 27
School of the Italian Renaissance, 209
Schulter-vor, 157
Simpson, Dr. G. C., 153
Spanish Riding School of Vienna, 25, 64, 67, 210, 246
Spoilt horses, 66
Spur, lesson of the, 129
Steinbrecht, 25, 99, 157
Swedish gymnastics, 190

T

Terre à terre, 26
Theory of modern dressage, 25
Third hand, 35
Tirer dessus et taper dedans, 228
Transitions, 251
Trot, a good, 51
  à l'Anglaise, 193
  à la Française, 193
  cadencé, 209
  passagé, 209, 217, 219, 220

U

Uberstreichen, 136
United gaits, 223
University of Riding, 21
Utility of the walk, 190

V

Velvet glove, 53

Vienna, 210
Virgil, 100

W

Work from the ground, 67, 210

Z

Zigzag, 248

MELVIN POWERS SELF-IMPROVEMENT LIBRARY

ASTROLOGY

____ASTROLOGY: HOW TO CHART YOUR HOROSCOPE *Max Heindel* — 3.00
____ASTROLOGY: YOUR PERSONAL SUN-SIGN GUIDE *Beatrice Ryder* — 3.00
____ASTROLOGY FOR EVERYDAY LIVING *Janet Harris* — 2.00
____ASTROLOGY MADE EASY *Astarte* — 3.00
____ASTROLOGY MADE PRACTICAL *Alexandra Kayhle* — 3.00
____ASTROLOGY, ROMANCE, YOU AND THE STARS *Anthony Norvell* — 4.00
____MY WORLD OF ASTROLOGY *Sydney Omarr* — 5.00
____THOUGHT DIAL *Sydney Omarr* — 4.00
____WHAT THE STARS REVEAL ABOUT THE MEN IN YOUR LIFE *Thelma White* — 3.00

BRIDGE

____BRIDGE BIDDING MADE EASY *Edwin B. Kantar* — 7.00
____BRIDGE CONVENTIONS *Edwin B. Kantar* — 5.00
____BRIDGE HUMOR *Edwin B. Kantar* — 5.00
____COMPETITIVE BIDDING IN MODERN BRIDGE *Edgar Kaplan* — 4.00
____DEFENSIVE BRIDGE PLAY COMPLETE *Edwin B. Kantar* — 10.00
____GAMESMAN BRIDGE—Play Better with Kantar *Edwin B. Kantar* — 5.00
____HOW TO IMPROVE YOUR BRIDGE *Alfred Sheinwold* — 3.00
____IMPROVING YOUR BIDDING SKILLS *Edwin B. Kantar* — 4.00
____INTRODUCTION TO DEFENDER'S PLAY *Edwin B. Kantar* — 3.00
____SHORT CUT TO WINNING BRIDGE *Alfred Sheinwold* — 3.00
____TEST YOUR BRIDGE PLAY *Edwin B. Kantar* — 3.00
____VOLUME 2—TEST YOUR BRIDGE PLAY *Edwin B. Kantar* — 5.00
____WINNING DECLARER PLAY *Dorothy Hayden Truscott* — 4.00

BUSINESS, STUDY & REFERENCE

____CONVERSATION MADE EASY *Elliot Russell* — 3.00
____EXAM SECRET *Dennis B. Jackson* — 3.00
____FIX-IT BOOK *Arthur Symons* — 2.00
____HOW TO DEVELOP A BETTER SPEAKING VOICE *M. Hellier* — 3.00
____HOW TO MAKE A FORTUNE IN REAL ESTATE *Albert Winnikoff* — 4.00
____INCREASE YOUR LEARNING POWER *Geoffrey A. Dudley* — 3.00
____MAGIC OF NUMBERS *Robert Tocquet* — 2.00
____PRACTICAL GUIDE TO BETTER CONCENTRATION *Melvin Powers* — 3.00
____PRACTICAL GUIDE TO PUBLIC SPEAKING *Maurice Forley* — 3.00
____7 DAYS TO FASTER READING *William S. Schaill* — 3.00
____SONGWRITERS RHYMING DICTIONARY *Jane Shaw Whitfield* — 5.00
____SPELLING MADE EASY *Lester D. Basch & Dr. Milton Finkelstein* — 2.00
____STUDENT'S GUIDE TO BETTER GRADES *J. A. Rickard* — 3.00
____TEST YOURSELF—Find Your Hidden Talent *Jack Shafer* — 3.00
____YOUR WILL & WHAT TO DO ABOUT IT *Attorney Samuel G. Kling* — 3.00

CALLIGRAPHY

____ADVANCED CALLIGRAPHY *Katherine Jeffares* — 7.00
____CALLIGRAPHER'S REFERENCE BOOK *Anne Leptich & Jacque Evans* — 7.00
____CALLIGRAPHY—The Art of Beautiful Writing *Katherine Jeffares* — 7.00
____CALLIGRAPHY FOR FUN & PROFIT *Anne Leptich & Jacque Evans* — 7.00
____CALLIGRAPHY MADE EASY *Tina Serafini* — 7.00

CHESS & CHECKERS

____BEGINNER'S GUIDE TO WINNING CHESS *Fred Reinfeld* — 3.00
____CHECKERS MADE EASY *Tom Wiswell* — 2.00
____CHESS IN TEN EASY LESSONS *Larry Evans* — 3.00
____CHESS MADE EASY *Milton L. Hanauer* — 3.00
____CHESS PROBLEMS FOR BEGINNERS *edited by Fred Reinfeld* — 2.00
____CHESS SECRETS REVEALED *Fred Reinfeld* — 2.00
____CHESS STRATEGY—An Expert's Guide *Fred Reinfeld* — 2.00
____CHESS TACTICS FOR BEGINNERS *edited by Fred Reinfeld* — 3.00
____CHESS THEORY & PRACTICE *Morry & Mitchell* — 2.00
____HOW TO WIN AT CHECKERS *Fred Reinfeld* — 3.00
____1001 BRILLIANT WAYS TO CHECKMATE *Fred Reinfeld* — 4.00
____1001 WINNING CHESS SACRIFICES & COMBINATIONS *Fred Reinfeld* — 4.00
____SOVIET CHESS *Edited by R. G. Wade* — 3.00

COOKERY & HERBS

____CULPEPER'S HERBAL REMEDIES *Dr. Nicholas Culpeper*	3.00
____FAST GOURMET COOKBOOK *Poppy Cannon*	2.50
____GINSENG The Myth & The Truth *Joseph P. Hou*	3.00
____HEALING POWER OF HERBS *May Bethel*	3.00
____HEALING POWER OF NATURAL FOODS *May Bethel*	3.00
____HERB HANDBOOK *Dawn MacLeod*	3.00
____HERBS FOR COOKING AND HEALING *Dr. Donald Law*	2.00
____HERBS FOR HEALTH—How to Grow & Use Them *Louise Evans Doole*	3.00
____HOME GARDEN COOKBOOK—Delicious Natural Food Recipes *Ken Kraft*	3.00
____MEDICAL HERBALIST *edited by Dr. J. R. Yemm*	3.00
____NATURAL FOOD COOKBOOK *Dr. Harry C. Bond*	3.00
____NATURE'S MEDICINES *Richard Lucas*	3.00
____VEGETABLE GARDENING FOR BEGINNERS *Hugh Wiberg*	2.00
____VEGETABLES FOR TODAY'S GARDENS *R. Milton Carleton*	2.00
____VEGETARIAN COOKERY *Janet Walker*	4.00
____VEGETARIAN COOKING MADE EASY & DELECTABLE *Veronica Vezza*	3.00
____VEGETARIAN DELIGHTS—A Happy Cookbook for Health *K. R. Mehta*	2.00
____VEGETARIAN GOURMET COOKBOOK *Joyce McKinnel*	3.00

GAMBLING & POKER

____ADVANCED POKER STRATEGY & WINNING PLAY *A. D. Livingston*	3.00
____HOW NOT TO LOSE AT POKER *Jeffrey Lloyd Castle*	3.00
____HOW TO WIN AT DICE GAMES *Skip Frey*	3.00
____HOW TO WIN AT POKER *Terence Reese & Anthony T. Watkins*	3.00
____SECRETS OF WINNING POKER *George S. Coffin*	3.00
____WINNING AT CRAPS *Dr. Lloyd T. Commins*	3.00
____WINNING AT GIN *Chester Wander & Cy Rice*	3.00
____WINNING AT POKER—An Expert's Guide *John Archer*	3.00
____WINNING AT 21—An Expert's Guide *John Archer*	4.00
____WINNING POKER SYSTEMS *Norman Zadeh*	3.00

HEALTH

____BEE POLLEN *Lynda Lyngheim & Jack Scagnetti*	3.00
____DR. LINDNER'S SPECIAL WEIGHT CONTROL METHOD *P. G. Lindner, M.D.*	1.50
____HELP YOURSELF TO BETTER SIGHT *Margaret Darst Corbett*	3.00
____HOW TO IMPROVE YOUR VISION *Dr. Robert A. Kraskin*	3.00
____HOW YOU CAN STOP SMOKING PERMANENTLY *Ernest Caldwell*	3.00
____MIND OVER PLATTER *Peter G. Lindner, M.D.*	3.00
____NATURE'S WAY TO NUTRITION & VIBRANT HEALTH *Robert J. Scrutton*	3.00
____NEW CARBOHYDRATE DIET COUNTER *Patti Lopez-Pereira*	1.50
____QUICK & EASY EXERCISES FOR FACIAL BEAUTY *Judy Smith-deal*	2.00
____QUICK & EASY EXERCISES FOR FIGURE BEAUTY *Judy Smith-deal*	2.00
____REFLEXOLOGY *Dr. Maybelle Segal*	3.00
____REFLEXOLOGY FOR GOOD HEALTH *Anna Kaye & Don C. Matchan*	3.00
____YOU CAN LEARN TO RELAX *Dr. Samuel Gutwirth*	3.00
____YOUR ALLERGY—What To Do About It *Allan Knight, M.D.*	3.00

HOBBIES

____BEACHCOMBING FOR BEGINNERS *Norman Hickin*	2.00
____BLACKSTONE'S MODERN CARD TRICKS *Harry Blackstone*	3.00
____BLACKSTONE'S SECRETS OF MAGIC *Harry Blackstone*	3.00
____COIN COLLECTING FOR BEGINNERS *Burton Hobson & Fred Reinfeld*	3.00
____ENTERTAINING WITH ESP *Tony 'Doc' Shiels*	2.00
____400 FASCINATING MAGIC TRICKS YOU CAN DO *Howard Thurston*	3.00
____HOW I TURN JUNK INTO FUN AND PROFIT *Sari*	3.00
____HOW TO WRITE A HIT SONG & SELL IT *Tommy Boyce*	7.00
____JUGGLING MADE EASY *Rudolf Dittrich*	2.00
____MAGIC FOR ALL AGES *Walter Gibson*	4.00
____MAGIC MADE EASY *Byron Wels*	2.00
____STAMP COLLECTING FOR BEGINNERS *Burton Hobson*	2.00

HORSE PLAYERS' WINNING GUIDES

____BETTING HORSES TO WIN *Les Conklin*	3.00
____ELIMINATE THE LOSERS *Bob McKnight*	3.00
____HOW TO PICK WINNING HORSES *Bob McKnight*	3.00

_____HOW TO WIN AT THE RACES *Sam (The Genius) Lewin*		3.00
_____HOW YOU CAN BEAT THE RACES *Jack Kavanagh*		3.00
_____MAKING MONEY AT THE RACES *David Barr*		3.00
_____PAYDAY AT THE RACES *Les Conklin*		3.00
_____SMART HANDICAPPING MADE EASY *William Bauman*		3.00
_____SUCCESS AT THE HARNESS RACES *Barry Meadow*		3.00
_____WINNING AT THE HARNESS RACES—An Expert's Guide *Nick Cammarano*		3.00

HUMOR

_____HOW TO BE A COMEDIAN FOR FUN & PROFIT *King & Laufer*		2.00
_____HOW TO FLATTEN YOUR TUSH *Coach Marge Reardon*		2.00
_____JOKE TELLER'S HANDBOOK *Bob Orben*		3.00
_____JOKES FOR ALL OCCASIONS *Al Schock*		3.00
_____2000 NEW LAUGHS FOR SPEAKERS *Bob Orben*		3.00
_____2,500 JOKES TO START 'EM LAUGHING *Bob Orben*		3.00

HYPNOTISM

_____ADVANCED TECHNIQUES OF HYPNOSIS *Melvin Powers*		2.00
_____BRAINWASHING AND THE CULTS *Paul A. Verdier, Ph.D.*		3.00
_____CHILDBIRTH WITH HYPNOSIS *William S. Kroger, M.D.*		3.00
_____HOW TO SOLVE Your Sex Problems with Self-Hypnosis *Frank S. Caprio, M.D.*		5.00
_____HOW TO STOP SMOKING THRU SELF-HYPNOSIS *Leslie M. LeCron*		3.00
_____HOW TO USE AUTO-SUGGESTION EFFECTIVELY *John Duckworth*		3.00
_____HOW YOU CAN BOWL BETTER USING SELF-HYPNOSIS *Jack Heise*		3.00
_____HOW YOU CAN PLAY BETTER GOLF USING SELF-HYPNOSIS *Jack Heise*		3.00
_____HYPNOSIS AND SELF-HYPNOSIS *Bernard Hollander, M.D.*		3.00
_____HYPNOTISM *(Originally published in 1893) Carl Sextus*		5.00
_____HYPNOTISM & PSYCHIC PHENOMENA *Simeon Edmunds*		4.00
_____HYPNOTISM MADE EASY *Dr. Ralph Winn*		3.00
_____HYPNOTISM MADE PRACTICAL *Louis Orton*		3.00
_____HYPNOTISM REVEALED *Melvin Powers*		2.00
_____HYPNOTISM TODAY *Leslie LeCron and Jean Bordeaux, Ph.D.*		5.00
_____MODERN HYPNOSIS *Lesley Kuhn & Salvatore Russo, Ph.D.*		5.00
_____NEW CONCEPTS OF HYPNOSIS *Bernard C. Gindes, M.D.*		5.00
_____NEW SELF-HYPNOSIS *Paul Adams*		4.00
_____POST-HYPNOTIC INSTRUCTIONS—Suggestions for Therapy *Arnold Furst*		3.00
_____PRACTICAL GUIDE TO SELF-HYPNOSIS *Melvin Powers*		3.00
_____PRACTICAL HYPNOTISM *Philip Magonet, M.D.*		3.00
_____SECRETS OF HYPNOTISM *S. J. Van Pelt, M.D.*		3.00
_____SELF-HYPNOSIS A Conditioned-Response Technique *Laurance Sparks*		5.00
_____SELF-HYPNOSIS Its Theory, Technique & Application *Melvin Powers*		3.00
_____THERAPY THROUGH HYPNOSIS *edited by Raphael H. Rhodes*		4.00

JUDAICA

_____HOW TO LIVE A RICHER & FULLER LIFE *Rabbi Edgar F. Magnin*		2.00
_____MODERN ISRAEL *Lily Edelman*		2.00
_____SERVICE OF THE HEART *Evelyn Garfiel, Ph.D.*		4.00
_____STORY OF ISRAEL IN COINS *Jean & Maurice Gould*		2.00
_____STORY OF ISRAEL IN STAMPS *Maxim & Gabriel Shamir*		1.00
_____TONGUE OF THE PROPHETS *Robert St.John*		5.00

JUST FOR WOMEN

_____COSMOPOLITAN'S GUIDE TO MARVELOUS MEN Fwd. by *Helen Gurley Brown*		3.00
_____COSMOPOLITAN'S HANG-UP HANDBOOK Foreword by *Helen Gurley Brown*		4.00
_____COSMOPOLITAN'S LOVE BOOK—A Guide to Ecstasy in Bed		4.00
_____COSMOPOLITAN'S NEW ETIQUETTE GUIDE Fwd. by *Helen Gurley Brown*		4.00
_____I AM A COMPLEAT WOMAN *Doris Hagopian & Karen O'Connor Sweeney*		3.00
_____JUST FOR WOMEN—A Guide to the Female Body *Richard E. Sand, M.D.*		5.00
_____NEW APPROACHES TO SEX IN MARRIAGE *John E. Eichenlaub, M.D.*		3.00
_____SEXUALLY ADEQUATE FEMALE *Frank S. Caprio, M.D.*		3.00
_____YOUR FIRST YEAR OF MARRIAGE *Dr. Tom McGinnis*		3.00

MARRIAGE, SEX & PARENTHOOD

_____ABILITY TO LOVE *Dr. Allan Fromme*		5.00
_____ENCYCLOPEDIA OF MODERN SEX & LOVE TECHNIQUES *Macandrew*		5.00
_____GUIDE TO SUCCESSFUL MARRIAGE *Drs. Albert Ellis & Robert Harper*		5.00

_____HOW TO RAISE AN EMOTIONALLY HEALTHY, HAPPY CHILD *A. Ellis* 3.00
_____IMPOTENCE & FRIGIDITY *Edwin W. Hirsch, M.D.* 3.00
_____SEX WITHOUT GUILT *Albert Ellis, Ph.D.* 3.00
_____SEXUALLY ADEQUATE MALE *Frank S. Caprio, M.D.* 3.00

MELVIN POWERS' MAIL ORDER LIBRARY
_____HOW TO GET RICH IN MAIL ORDER *Melvin Powers* 10.00
_____HOW TO WRITE A GOOD ADVERTISEMENT *Victor O. Schwab* 15.00
_____U.S. MAIL ORDER SHOPPER'S GUIDE *Susan Spitzer* 10.00

METAPHYSICS & OCCULT
_____BOOK OF TALISMANS, AMULETS & ZODIACAL GEMS *William Pavitt* 4.00
_____CONCENTRATION—A Guide to Mental Mastery *Mouni Sadhu* 3.00
_____CRITIQUES OF GOD *Edited by Peter Angeles* 7.00
_____DREAMS & OMENS REVEALED *Fred Gettings* 3.00
_____EXTRA-TERRESTRIAL INTELLIGENCE—The First Encounter 6.00
_____FORTUNE TELLING WITH CARDS *P. Foli* 3.00
_____HANDWRITING ANALYSIS MADE EASY *John Marley* 3.00
_____HANDWRITING TELLS *Nadya Olyanova* 5.00
_____HOW TO UNDERSTAND YOUR DREAMS *Geoffrey A. Dudley* 3.00
_____ILLUSTRATED YOGA *William Zorn* 3.00
_____IN DAYS OF GREAT PEACE *Mouni Sadhu* 3.00
_____KING SOLOMON'S TEMPLE IN THE MASONIC TRADITION *Alex Horne* 5.00
_____LSD—THE AGE OF MIND *Bernard Roseman* 2.00
_____MAGICIAN—His training and work *W. E. Butler* 3.00
_____MEDITATION *Mouni Sadhu* 5.00
_____MODERN NUMEROLOGY *Morris C. Goodman* 3.00
_____NUMEROLOGY—ITS FACTS AND SECRETS *Ariel Yvon Taylor* 3.00
_____NUMEROLOGY MADE EASY *W. Mykian* 3.00
_____PALMISTRY MADE EASY *Fred Gettings* 3.00
_____PALMISTRY MADE PRACTICAL *Elizabeth Daniels Squire* 3.00
_____PALMISTRY SECRETS REVEALED *Henry Frith* 3.00
_____PROPHECY IN OUR TIME *Martin Ebon* 2.50
_____PSYCHOLOGY OF HANDWRITING *Nadya Olyanova* 3.00
_____SUPERSTITION—Are you superstitious? *Eric Maple* 2.00
_____TAROT *Mouni Sadhu* 6.00
_____TAROT OF THE BOHEMIANS *Papus* 5.00
_____WAYS TO SELF-REALIZATION *Mouni Sadhu* 3.00
_____WHAT YOUR HANDWRITING REVEALS *Albert E. Hughes* 2.00
_____WITCHCRAFT, MAGIC & OCCULTISM—A Fascinating History *W. B. Crow* 5.00
_____WITCHCRAFT—THE SIXTH SENSE *Justine Glass* 4.00
_____WORLD OF PSYCHIC RESEARCH *Hereward Carrington* 2.00

SELF-HELP & INSPIRATIONAL
_____DAILY POWER FOR JOYFUL LIVING *Dr. Donald Curtis* 3.00
_____DYNAMIC THINKING *Melvin Powers* 2.00
_____EXUBERANCE—Your Guide to Happiness & Fulfillment *Dr. Paul Kurtz* 3.00
_____GREATEST POWER IN THE UNIVERSE *U. S. Andersen* 5.00
_____GROW RICH WHILE YOU SLEEP *Ben Sweetland* 3.00
_____GROWTH THROUGH REASON *Albert Ellis, Ph.D.* 4.00
_____GUIDE TO DEVELOPING YOUR POTENTIAL *Herbert A. Otto, Ph.D.* 3.00
_____GUIDE TO LIVING IN BALANCE *Frank S. Caprio, M.D.* 2.00
_____HELPING YOURSELF WITH APPLIED PSYCHOLOGY *R. Henderson* 2.00
_____HELPING YOURSELF WITH PSYCHIATRY *Frank S. Caprio, M.D.* 2.00
_____HOW TO ATTRACT GOOD LUCK *A. H. Z. Carr* 4.00
_____HOW TO CONTROL YOUR DESTINY *Norvell* 3.00
_____HOW TO DEVELOP A WINNING PERSONALITY *Martin Panzer* 3.00
_____HOW TO DEVELOP AN EXCEPTIONAL MEMORY *Young & Gibson* 4.00
_____HOW TO OVERCOME YOUR FEARS *M. P. Leahy, M.D.* 3.00
_____HOW YOU CAN HAVE CONFIDENCE AND POWER *Les Giblin* 3.00
_____HUMAN PROBLEMS & HOW TO SOLVE THEM *Dr. Donald Curtis* 4.00
_____I CAN *Ben Sweetland* 4.00
_____I WILL *Ben Sweetland* 3.00

___LEFT-HANDED PEOPLE *Michael Barsley*		4.00
___MAGIC IN YOUR MIND *U. S. Andersen*		5.00
___MAGIC OF THINKING BIG *Dr. David J. Schwartz*		3.00
___MAGIC POWER OF YOUR MIND *Walter M. Germain*		4.00
___MENTAL POWER THROUGH SLEEP SUGGESTION *Melvin Powers*		3.00
___NEW GUIDE TO RATIONAL LIVING *Albert Ellis, Ph.D. & R. Harper, Ph.D.*		3.00
___OUR TROUBLED SELVES *Dr. Allan Fromme*		3.00
___PSYCHO-CYBERNETICS *Maxwell Maltz, M.D.*		3.00
___SCIENCE OF MIND IN DAILY LIVING *Dr. Donald Curtis*		3.00
___SECRET OF SECRETS *U. S. Andersen*		5.00
___SECRET POWER OF THE PYRAMIDS *U. S. Andersen*		5.00
___STUTTERING AND WHAT YOU CAN DO ABOUT IT *W. Johnson, Ph.D.*		2.50
___SUCCESS-CYBERNETICS *U. S. Andersen*		4.00
___10 DAYS TO A GREAT NEW LIFE *William E. Edwards*		3.00
___THINK AND GROW RICH *Napoleon Hill*		3.00
___THREE MAGIC WORDS *U. S. Andersen*		5.00
___TREASURY OF COMFORT *edited by Rabbi Sidney Greenberg*		5.00
___TREASURY OF THE ART OF LIVING *Sidney S. Greenberg*		5.00
___YOU ARE NOT THE TARGET *Laura Huxley*		4.00
___YOUR SUBCONSCIOUS POWER *Charles M. Simmons*		4.00
___YOUR THOUGHTS CAN CHANGE YOUR LIFE *Dr. Donald Curtis*		4.00

SPORTS

___BICYCLING FOR FUN AND GOOD HEALTH *Kenneth E. Luther*		2.00
___BILLIARDS—Pocket • Carom • Three Cushion *Clive Cottingham, Jr.*		3.00
___CAMPING-OUT 101 Ideas & Activities *Bruno Knobel*		2.00
___COMPLETE GUIDE TO FISHING *Vlad Evanoff*		2.00
___HOW TO IMPROVE YOUR RACQUETBALL *Lubarsky, Kaufman, & Scagnetti*		3.00
___HOW TO WIN AT POCKET BILLIARDS *Edward D. Knuchell*		4.00
___JOY OF WALKING *Jack Scagnetti*		3.00
___LEARNING & TEACHING SOCCER SKILLS *Eric Worthington*		3.00
___MOTORCYCLING FOR BEGINNERS *I. G. Edmonds*		3.00
___RACQUETBALL FOR WOMEN *Toni Hudson, Jack Scagnetti & Vince Rondone*		3.00
___RACQUETBALL MADE EASY *Steve Lubarsky, Rod Delson & Jack Scagnetti*		3.00
___SECRET OF BOWLING STRIKES *Dawson Taylor*		3.00
___SECRET OF PERFECT PUTTING *Horton Smith & Dawson Taylor*		3.00
___SOCCER—The game & how to play it *Gary Rosenthal*		3.00
___STARTING SOCCER *Edward F. Dolan, Jr.*		3.00
___TABLE TENNIS MADE EASY *Johnny Leach*		2.00

TENNIS LOVERS' LIBRARY

___BEGINNER'S GUIDE TO WINNING TENNIS *Helen Hull Jacobs*		2.00
___HOW TO BEAT BETTER TENNIS PLAYERS *Loring Fiske*		4.00
___HOW TO IMPROVE YOUR TENNIS—Style, Strategy & Analysis *C. Wilson*		2.00
___INSIDE TENNIS—Techniques of Winning *Jim Leighton*		3.00
___PLAY TENNIS WITH ROSEWALL *Ken Rosewall*		2.00
___PSYCH YOURSELF TO BETTER TENNIS *Dr. Walter A. Luszki*		2.00
___SUCCESSFUL TENNIS *Neale Fraser*		2.00
___TENNIS FOR BEGINNERS *Dr. H. A. Murray*		2.00
___TENNIS MADE EASY *Joel Brecheen*		2.00
___WEEKEND TENNIS—How to have fun & win at the same time *Bill Talbert*		3.00
___WINNING WITH PERCENTAGE TENNIS—Smart Strategy *Jack Lowe*		2.00

WILSHIRE PET LIBRARY

___DOG OBEDIENCE TRAINING *Gust Kessopulos*		4.00
___DOG TRAINING MADE EASY & FUN *John W. Kellogg*		3.00
___HOW TO BRING UP YOUR PET DOG *Kurt Unkelbach*		2.00
___HOW TO RAISE & TRAIN YOUR PUPPY *Jeff Griffen*		2.00
___PIGEONS: HOW TO RAISE & TRAIN THEM *William H. Allen, Jr.*		2.00

*The books listed above can be obtained from your book dealer or directly from
Melvin Powers. When ordering, please remit 50¢ per book postage & handling.
Send for our free illustrated catalog of self-improvement books.*

Melvin Powers

12015 Sherman Road, No. Hollywood, California 91605

Melvin Powers' Favorite Books

HOW TO GET RICH IN MAIL ORDER
by Melvin Powers

Contents:
1. How to Develop Your Mail Order Expertise 2. How to Find a Unique Product or Service to Sell 3. How to Make Money with Classified Ads 4. How to Make Money with Display Ads 5. The Unlimited Potential for Making Money with Direct Mail 6. How to Copycat Successful Mail Order Operations 7. How I Created A Best Seller Using the Copycat Technique 8. How to Start and Run a Profitable Mail Order, Special Interest Book or Record Business 9. I Enjoy Selling Books by Mail—Some of My Successful and Not-So-Successful Ads and Direct Mail Circulars 10. Five of My Most Successful Direct Mail Pieces That Sold and Are Still Selling Millions of Dollars Worth of Books 11. Melvin Powers' Mail Order Success Strategy—Follow It and You'll Become a Millionaire 12. How to Sell Your Products to Mail Order Companies, Retail Outlets, Jobbers, and Fund Raisers for Maximum Distribution and Profits 13. How to Get Free Display Ads and Publicity That Can Put You on the Road to Riches 14. How to Make Your Advertising Copy Sizzle to Make You Wealthy 15. Questions and Answers to Help You Get Started Making Money in Your Own Mail Order Business 16. A Personal Word from Melvin Powers

8½"x 11"—336 Pages . . . $11 postpaid

HOW YOU CAN HAVE CONFIDENCE & POWER
by Les Giblin

Contents:
1. Your Key to Success and Happiness 2. How to Use the Basic Secret for Influencing Others 3. How to Cash in on Your Hidden Assets 4. How to Control the Actions & Attitudes of Others 5. How You Can Create a Good Impression on Other People 6. Techniques for Making & Keeping Friends 7. How to Use Three Big Secrets for Attracting People 8. How to Make the Other Person Feel Friendly—Instantly

192 Pages . . . $3.50 postpaid

A NEW GUIDE TO RATIONAL LIVING
by Albert Ellis, Ph.D. & Robert A. Harper, Ph.D.

Contents:
1. How Far Can You Go With Self-Analysis? 2. You Feel the Way You Think 3. Feeling Well by Thinking Straight 4. How You Create Your Feelings 5. Thinking Yourself Out of Emotional Disturbances 6. Recognizing and Attacking Neurotic Behavior 7. Overcoming the Influences of the Past 8. Does Reason Always Prove Reasonable? 9. Refusing to Feel Desperately Unhappy 10. Tackling Dire Needs for Approval 11. Eradicating Dire Fears of Failure 12. How to Stop Blaming and Start Living 13. How to Feel Undepressed though Frustrated 14. Controlling Your Own Destiny 15. Conquering Anxiety

256 Pages . . . $3.50 postpaid

PSYCHO-CYBERNETICS
A New Technique for Using Your Subconscious Power
by Maxwell Maltz, M.D., F.I.C.S.

Contents:
1. The Self Image: Your Key to a Better Life 2. Discovering the Success Mechanism Within You 3. Imagination—The First Key to Your Success Mechanism 4. Dehypnotize Yourself from False Beliefs 5. How to Utilize the Power of Rational Thinking 6. Relax and Let Your Success Mechanism Work for You 7. You Can Acquire the Habit of Happiness 8. Ingredients of the Success-Type Personality and How to Acquire Them 9. The Failure Mechanism: How to Make It Work For You Instead of Against You 10. How to Remove Emotional Scars, or How to Give Yourself an Emotional Face Lift 11. How to Unlock Your Real Personality 12. Do-It-Yourself Tranquilizers

288 Pages . . . $3.50 postpaid

A PRACTICAL GUIDE TO SELF-HYPNOSIS
by Melvin Powers

Contents:
1. What You Should Know About Self-Hypnosis 2. What About the Dangers of Hypnosis? 3. Is Hypnosis the Answer? 4. How Does Self-Hypnosis Work? 5. How to Arouse Yourself from the Self-Hypnotic State 6. How to Attain Self-Hypnosis 7. Deepening the Self-Hypnotic State 8. What You Should Know About Becoming an Excellent Subject 9. Techniques for Reaching the Somnambulistic State 10. A New Approach to Self-Hypnosis When All Else Fails 11. Psychological Aids and Their Function 12. The Nature of Hypnosis 13. Practical Applications of Self-Hypnosis.

128 Pages . . . $3.50 postpaid

The books listed above can be obtained from your book dealer or directly from Melvin Powers.

Melvin Powers
12015 Sherman Road, No. Hollywood, California 91605